Shades of Difference

A History of Ethnicity in America

RICHARD W. REES

ROWMAN & LITTLEFIELD PUBLISHERS, INC.
Lanham • Boulder • New York • Toronto • Plymouth, UK

ROWMAN & LITTLEFIELD PUBLISHERS, INC.

Published in the United States of America
by Rowman & Littlefield Publishers, Inc.
A wholly owned subsidiary of The Rowman & Littlefield Publishing Group, Inc.
4501 Forbes Boulevard, Suite 200, Lanham, Maryland 20706
www.rowmanlittlefield.com

Estover Road
Plymouth PL6 7PY
United Kingdom

British Library Cataloguing in Publication Information Available

Library of Congress Cataloging-in-Publication Data

Rees, Richard W., 1962–
    Shades of difference : a history of ethnicity in America / Richard W. Rees.
        p. cm. — (Perspectives on a multiracial America series)
    Includes bibliographical references and index.
    ISBN-13: 978-0-7425-4316-4 (cloth : alk. paper)
    ISBN-10: 0-7425-4316-1 (cloth : alk. paper)
    ISBN-13: 978-0-7425-4317-1 (pbk. : alk. paper)
    ISBN-10: 0-7425-4317-X (pbk. : alk. paper)
    1. Ethnicity—United States—History. 2. United States—Ethnic relations—History.
3. United States—Race relations—History. I. Title. II. Series.
E184.A1R426 2007
305.800973—dc22

                                                                            2005028005

Printed in the United States of America

♾™ The paper used in this publication meets the minimum requirements of
American National Standard for Information Sciences—Permanence of Paper
for Printed Library Materials, ANSI/NISO Z39.48-1992.

Shades of Difference

Perspectives on a Multiracial America series

Joe R. Feagin, Texas A&M University, series editor

The racial composition of the United States is rapidly changing. Books in the series will explore various aspects of the coming multiracial society, one in which European Americans are no longer the majority and where issues of white-on-black racism have been joined by many other challenges to white dominance.

Titles:

Melanie Bush, *Breaking the Code of Good Intentions*

Amir Mavasti and Karyn McKinney, *Unwelcome Immigrants: Middle Eastern Lives in America*

Richard W. Rees, *Shades of Difference: A History of Ethnicity in America*

Katheryn Russell-Brown, *Protecting Our Own: Race, Crime, and African Americans*

Forthcoming titles include:

Erica Chito Childs, *Fade to Black and White*

Elizabeth M. Aranda, *Puerto Rican Hearts and Minds*

For Tiffany and Sky

Contents

Acknowledgments

There have been many people without whose help and support this book would never have been possible. I would like to thank Nelda Cambron-McCabe and the Department of Educational Leadership at Miami University for the opportunity of a postdoctoral fellowship. I also want to thank Kathleen Knight Abowitz. She offered comments on some early drafts and has always been supportive and thoughtful. Rich and Lydia Hofmann have been extremely helpful and generous in many ways. I try to thank them frequently, but it feels too small in comparison to their many kindnesses.

I want to thank Joe Feagin for recommending this work to Rowman & Littlefield for the Perspectives on a Multiracial America series. Thanks to the staff at Rowman & Littlefield, especially Sheila-Katherine Zwiebel, for their patience and help in preparing the manuscript.

I owe a huge debt of gratitude to Chris Wellin for his hard work and many considerations. He read several drafts and wrote extensive feedback. I value the discussions we had about the project and his many words of wisdom and encouragement. Regardless of his own deadlines, Chris always dropped everything when I needed his help. Whatever mistakes or errors of judgment remain here are most likely the result of my failure to follow his advice. Chris demonstrates for me the highest ideals of collegiality and friendship.

Thanks to my parents, Bill and Marilyn Rees, who have always helped in every way they could. They provided the foundation.

Thanks to Tiffany and Sky who are my home and happiness. Tiffany made sacrifices that bought me windows of time that I used to devote to this book. She is as pleased as I am to see it through. Sky is always teaching me how to live in the here and now and how much joy can be found there.

Introduction: The Invention of (the Concept of) Ethnicity

FROM *HUNKY* TO *HONKY*

In 1990, sculptor Luis Jimenez exhibited his contribution to Pittsburgh's Three Rivers Arts Festival—a fifteen-foot fiberglass figure titled *Steelworker*. The towering figure, in heavy work clothes holding a long-handled testing spoon in his upraised hand, reminiscent of the Statue of Liberty, honors the sturdy strength of its working-class subject. However, Jimenez's inscription "Hunky 'Steelworker'" near the base became the target of attack soon after the statue's unveiling. The City Controller called a press conference condemning the work as an ethnic slur. In short order, a dozen different ethnic groups and state agencies joined in, protesting the use of the word.[1] The degree of hostility the inscription fueled might be gauged by the comment of a United Steelworkers' spokesman who said, "They don't have enough guards to keep that [statue] from being floated down the river" ("A Festival"). Despite objections of censorship from Arts Festival officials and others, Jimenez eventually agreed to grind off the offending word (Schur).

It is interesting that it did not occur to Jimenez that a public use of the word *hunky* in Pittsburgh in 1990 would arouse a certain amount of indignation. A similar furor had erupted six years earlier when an architectural historian used the term to describe one of Pittsburgh's landmarks as "a pleasant hunky church" ("The Festival's"). Jimenez even claimed he had researched the word at the Carnegie Library before adding it to his sculpture. And it is not just that the artist assumed time had blunted the word's sting. Jimenez had not forgotten when "Chicano" had a "negative connotation" (Barnes, "Sculptor"). However, the sculptor claimed that he did not think it was ever an ethnic slur but merely a shortened version of the nonthreatening "millhunk" and

1

"a way that steel workers referred to themselves" (Barnes, "Sculptor"). "The last thing I mean to do is insult anybody," Jimenez said in response to the uproar. "I'm trying to glorify these guys . . . to portray working-class heroes, so to speak" ("The Fesitival's"). The term was meant, in other words, as a tribute to the class and ethnicity of the artist's subject.

Nor was Jimenez alone in overlooking the hurtful history of the term. As is played out in letters to the *Pittsburgh Post-Gazette,* the ensuing controversy over the meaning of the word reveals an interesting generational divide between those who found the term abusive and those for whom it recalled intimate family relations. Those protesting the public display of an epithet, like Michael L. Vezilich, acting president of the Croation-American Professional and Business Association, argued that "the term still perpetuates a prejudice and stereotype that organizations [such as the one he represents] are trying to tear down" (Vezilich). He allows that there are those in Pittsburgh's ethnic community, to whom the term applies, who "no longer perceive themselves socially or otherwise threatened, and therefore, can accept 'hunky' in a non-insulting manner." Vezilich disagrees, however, that this is the "prevailing attitude," a claim borne out in approximately half of the fourteen letters on the issue, and he implies that the term remains threatening to many because the anti-ethnic threat persists "socially" (though he does not specify the particularities of that threat). Vezilich mounts his protest on behalf of his forebears and "the pride we take in the heritage of our fathers and grandfathers that endured such ethnic intolerance and social injustices to help build America."

On the other hand, some of the letters and the editorial position of the *Post-Gazette* supported the statue's title. The paper's position was that this was a matter of free expression versus censorship and that the City Controller had initially raised the controversy for the purposes of self-promotion and as a diversion from recent negative publicity.[2] Those letters of support that identified with the term asserted that it evoked warm family memories in which it was used as a term of endearment. Charlene Lindsey, for example, wrote the editor in support of the title because "as a small child growing up in a Slovak neighborhood in Youngstown, Ohio, my grandmother (who came to the United States at sixteen as an immigrant) affectionately referred to me as a her 'little hunky' because I delighted in everything from the 'old country.'" And for Audrey Ruth Caspero, "'hunky' expresses love." She recalls that before her mother's recent death, she told her, "You are a beautiful 'hunky,' Mom, and I'm a beautiful hunky's daughter." In both cases, *hunky* functions to confirm intergenerational ethnic identity. Part of the discussion made the distinction, with reference to other racial or ethnic labels, like *nigger,* between in-group usage, which expresses solidarity, and historically oppressive out-group usage. But support of the statue's title indicates that for many the term had ceased to function as the social threat Vezilich suggests and rather served as nostalgic memento. Charles Dee Mitchell notes that locals afterward reverently rubbed the place where the controversial inscription had been effaced, bestowing on the piece the status of religious icon.

As Jimenez noted, etymologies indicate that *hunky* is a derivative of *Hungarian*, *millhunk*, or *Bohunk*, and Vezilich is also correct that the word derives from the late-nineteenth-century urban Northeast among native Anglo-Americans as a term of contempt for their social inferiors, the newly arrived central and eastern European immigrants.[3] A "hunky town," for instance, was the row where the poor and the foreigners lived (Cassidy 1,078). I would suggest that today, however, only a minority of mostly older Americans in Rust Belt regions still remember the term. More familiar is its more recent derivation in *honky*.[4] The one-letter alteration is an instance of what Irving Lewis Allen calls blowback, where derisive terms for others return to name the originators (62). In this case, *hunky*, a term used by some European Americans for other European Americans with less status, apparently transforms into the word *honky*, a black American word of contempt for all whites. The *Dictionary of American Regional English* indicates that *honky*, as a reference to all whites, comes to predominate in the late 1960s over *hunky*, which had meant only some whites (Cassidy 1,078). Ken Johnson, in his study of black terminology, suggests that the pronunciation change, indicated by a changed spelling that allows for greater emphasis on the first syllable, "indicates the intensity of the hate black people have for white people" (143). Clarence Major suggests that *honkey* (or *honky* or *honkie*) dates from the 1650s and derives from the Wolof *honq* meaning pink man (239). If this is the case, the word seems not to have entered common usage until very recently. In fact, Johnson asserts that *honky* is "not exactly a black word," but nevertheless became one "when it was first used by Stokely Carmichael to refer to whites" (143). Regardless of the apocryphal nature of such precise origins, it does appear from the histories of both words that *hunky* begins to lose much of its earlier force among whites at roughly the same time in the 1960s that *honky* gained currency among blacks. The shifting ownership, meaning, and pronunciation of the terms in the 1960s would help to account for the striking generation gap in the understandings of *hunky* brought to light by the *Steelworker*'s title.

The shift from *hunky* to *honky*, as well as the *Steelworker* controversy, point to broader changes in the nature of racial and ethnic identity in the United States in the nineteenth and twentieth centuries. First, the origins of *hunky* tell us about a time in the late 1800s when settled Americans regarded the new arrivals from the periphery of Europe as their inferiors. As we shall see, even their whiteness was dubious. Such racial ambiguity would be bad enough in a racially divided and hierarchical society. But the fact that American citizenship hung on one's claims to white identity doubly threatened the survival of the new immigrants. Michael Vezilich draws on the memories of this precarious situation in his opposition to *Steelworker*. His outrage comes not necessarily from his own experience but on the basis of "the pride we take in the heritage of our fathers and grandfathers that endured such ethnic intolerance and social injustices to help build America" (Vezilich).

Second, the fading of the word *hunky*, as well as its hurt (indicated by more recent generations who remember the term with fondness), point to the erasure of divisions between European Americans and their relegation to childhood memories. The upward mobility of the new immigrants' children, the expansion of the white middle class, and the creation of exclusive white suburbs were a few of the factors converging in the twentieth century to consolidate the white race as an undifferentiated European American formation. The appearance of *honky* also points to a historical moment, like the withdrawal of *hunky* from the popular vernacular, when old divisions between whites cease to be relevant. *Honky* makes no such distinctions and applies to all whites, regardless of which European nation their families left behind, which boat brought them, and when it docked. But much more than that, the transformation of *hunky* into *honky* depends on the rise of black consciousness in the post–World War II period. Or rather, the appropriation of *hunky* in the creation of *honky* signals in the American lexicon a jump from white to black consciousness. *Hunky* is spoken from a dominant white perspective; *honky* objectifies the domination of whiteness from a black vantage point. In other words, the appearance of the word testifies to the power of a black perspective, backed by the transformative power of the Civil Rights Movement, when whites were forced to look at themselves as oppressors (whether or not they agreed). Racial identities are relational and mutually defining. But those relations and those definitions are always changing. White identity has always been a function of black identity (not to mention red, yellow, and brown) and vice versa; we must consider then that another factor in the consolidation of the white race in America after World War II has been the rise of black consciousness as a major social force. As Stokely Carmichael and Charles Hamilton put it in 1967, "American pluralism quickly becomes a monolithic structure on issues of race. When faced with the demands from black people, the multi-faction whites unite and present a common front" (7).

THE ARGUMENT

This book fleshes out the narrative that is encapsulated in the appearance of *hunky* and its transition to *honky* by looking closely at the history of *ethnicity*. Underlying such specific semantic shifts as *hunky* to *honky*, the history of the concept of ethnicity is itself a major tributary in the wider currents of

American racial categories in the nineteenth and twentieth centuries. But, one might ask, does *ethnicity* really have a history? The idea is so common it would hardly seem to need much explanation. It is used alternatively to refer to a group or individual's race, nationality, physical characteristics, or cultural habits. And despite such elasticity, the term seems sufficiently self-evident. *Ethnicity* is now so frequently used in both popular and scholarly discourse, and is so indispensable and fundamental to descriptions of human society, that the idea the term has a history or that it could ever have not existed sounds contrary to common sense. Yet *ethnicity* is surprisingly new. While it was coined in the 1940s, the concept did not come into popular usage until the 1960s and 1970s. Indeed, few if any dictionaries of common American English include the word before the 1970s, and it is not included in the *Oxford English Dictionary* until the 1972 supplement. As recently as 1975, Nathan Glazer, a recognized authority on the subject, could say that "ethnicity seems to be a new term" ("Introduction" 1). "Something new has appeared," Glazer remarks and, almost apologetically ill at ease, continues, "The phenomenon is too new and, doubtless, our range too limited" ("Introduction" 2). Despite the unfamiliarity of the term, there have been no systematic attempts to account for its origins then or since. Why did the term appear just when it did? Can we assume that the condition of ethnicity existed before the word? Did the way it was previously named affect the way it was lived? Does the term's history have implications for its present and future use?

This book is an attempt to answer these questions through a cultural and political history of the word *ethnicity* in America. Because the concept bears a strong, and often contrasting, relation with the idea of race, we must begin in the eighteenth century with the emergence of biological theories of racial difference. Our aim is to detail the conditions that, later, made such a concept as ethnicity both possible and necessary. We shall then develop a kind of prehistory of *ethnicity* through the nineteenth and early twentieth centuries. Here, we examine the social currents that opened an intellectual space for the concept. From there, we focus on its first uses in the 1940s, and, finally, its most significant transformations in the 1960s. While the concept has largely been the product of academic debate, its formulation responds as well to broader social forces. So while I concentrate on the texts of scholars whose readership was often quite specialized, there is an attempt throughout to identify the larger historical forces shaping the needs to which the concept responded and the purposes to which it was applied. My central thesis is that *ethnicity* emerges in the early 1940s as a means of resolving contradictions and ambiguities in the racial status of European immigrants. Scholars have identified the first use of the term from that period and have noted its restricted use for specific groups of European Americans. But little attention has been given to the question of why it was only then, in the 1940s, that the term both could have been and needed to be conceived. Recent scholarship on the history of white racial identity in America has revealed that the racial discourse of the nineteenth century had placed the "darker" immigrants in an ambiguous racial position that undermined the whiteness that might otherwise have been granted to them by virtue of their European origins. They were rendered racially different by their "Nordic" hosts, jeopardizing their equal participation in American citizenship. This is the time from which the slur *hunky* hails. My argument is that it is only with the development of new human science discourses in the early twentieth century that a foundation for the concept of ethnicity could be constructed that would transform and resolve the problem of the outcast immigrants. I argue that the new discourses provided a language in which the newcomers' racial differences could be reconceived to more benign cultural ones, a transformation which allowed the new immigrants to be theoretically incorporated into the white race. Ethnicity, in other words, allowed for a change in the status of difference.

Ethnicity emerges, I argue, as a way to explain difference within whiteness. My point here, however, is the opposite of what is generally implied by writers who argue that "white ethnics" have always had the advantage of their whiteness relative to people of color. European American groups never faced the level of exclusion and systematic oppression that characterize the experience of their nonwhite counterparts. They were never identified as a slave class and there was nothing comparable to Black Laws legislated to allow legal discrimination against them. But it is not, I believe, accurate to assume that ethnicity was seen as an inherent characteristic of European immigrants because they were white. Instead, I argue, ethnicity is constructed and conferred on the southern and eastern European immigrants because they were *not* white, or only suspiciously so. Ethnicity, in the sense of cultural difference, brings them theoretically into the white fold and was originally constructed for this purpose. I further argue that it is only with this understanding of the political and cultural purposes of ethnicity that we can understand the significance of the concept's transformation during the Black Revolution of the post–World War II period. Only with a more detailed account of its original meaning and purpose can we appreciate the concept's revaluation when it is appropriated by the discourse of black nationalism in the 1960s and 1970s. Because of ethnicity's history of replacing a racial with a cultural basis of group definition, a racialized group's determination to "ethnicize" itself constituted a political strategy to escape dominant biological schemas. Such frameworks were, after all, beyond their control and typically defined groups of color beneath and beyond the realm of normalcy, citizenship, and humanity. But while hoping to transform racial schemas and their place in them, African Americans' adoption of the concept involved a reciprocal transformation of the concept. Ethnicity has since become available to virtually all national and racial groups in America but with meanings that are the result of this recent history to create a black cultural identity. In short, ethnicity has shifted from a precursor of assimilation to an identity distinct and "unmeltable."

DEFINING ETHNICITY

One of the most surprising features of ethnicity's history is its recent origin. Its antecedent, *ethnic*, is quite old, of course, and derives from the Greek word *ethnos* whose two competing meanings, "heathen" and "nation," have alternatively been foregrounded and suppressed in the history of its English variant. The earliest use of *ethnic* in print in English, in the fifteenth century, carried the sense of "heathen" to indicate, within a theological framework, an absolute kind of difference. Ethnic were those foreigners whose difference from Judeo-Christian reference points rendered them utterly alien. Though in print as early as 1772, according to the *Oxford English Dictionary*, *ethnicity* is defined as "heathendom" but was rarely used. Race science, the now largely discredited study of human classification based on physiological variation, appeared in the nineteenth century; it redefined the way that human difference could be thought. In so doing, *race* subsumed *ethnic*, perhaps because "nation," the other connotation of the original Greek *ethnos*, became quite close to, if not synonymous with, "race." Dictionary entries for *ethnic* from this period reveal this shift by displacing "heathen" for "race" as its first definition. Entries for *ethnicity*, meanwhile, are absent throughout the eighteenth, nineteenth, and most of the twentieth centuries.

As we shall see, *ethnic* began to break away from *race* in the early twentieth century as theories of cultural identity adopted it for their own purposes. *Ethnicity* was shortly to follow. As Manning Marable has noted, the concept "surfaced as an important social science category of analysis in the writings of sociologists during the Great Depression, as a means to describe the diverse immigrant populations largely from southern and eastern Europe" ("Problematics" 245). Yet, in its new nominative form, the term becomes more than an analytical category and indicates more than a grammatical variation on *ethnic*. As it evolved, *ethnicity* would connote a new kind of experience and mode of being. Its original sense still explicitly carried the sense of otherness and divergence from the norm. But in the space between white, which was fully human, and the dark-skinned racial subhuman Other, there emerged the possibility for a new conception of human identity.[5] Here was a modern, secular, socially based mode of existence born of the emergent human sciences and divorced from the nineteenth-century idea that groups were the function of unique biological traits. It is as if its creation as an objective, sociological category opened up the possibility of its gradual formulation as a subjective and communal experience. In time, scholars would identify it with Tönnies' concept of *Gemeinschaft*[6] and with the subjective "we-feeling" of a social group's members who shared a common bond of national origin, heritage, and worldview. In this sense, to recognize a group's ethnicity is to recognize the subjectivity and, by extension, the humanity of those thought to possess it.

The concept also indicated a new way to understand the nature of human difference. Accounting for physical variation in the eighteenth century required consideration of climatic and geographical conditions within a universal human family descended alike from Adam. When the early-nineteenth-century scientific racism discredited the Old Testament–based narrative of monogenesis, it banished the only terms available to denote human variety as the function of "environmental" variation. Perhaps no less hierarchical (as cultural superiority merely replaced racial superiority), ethnicity nevertheless reintroduced, in the early to mid-twentieth century, the concept of human difference as the result of nurture over nature. But rather than the product of natural surroundings, ethnicity implied variation resulting from the social context and, more specifically, human action. Its initial appearance accommodated the deepest racial tenets of race science and debuted with the assurance that it would be soon absorbed into a more monolithic racial order. At the same time, the introduction of ethnicity was nevertheless part of the first steps away from biological determinism and toward the notion of human difference as a result of social practice. But it was not until the term was appropriated by the discourse of black nationalism in the 1960s that it would be extricated from its ties to racialist conceptions of human difference. Today, the understanding of ethnicity as an irreducible and unique group characteristic, manifest in the groups' traditions and cultural practices, is the result of this semantic struggle.

Despite its recent origins, *ethnicity* is now mapped selectively over virtually every discussion of European American group differences of any period without a consideration that the concept actually existed in few of those times. As Manning Marable points out, "There are no references to ethnicity per se in the social science literature of the nineteenth and early twentieth centuries" ("Problematics" 245). *Ethnicity* is almost always used as if it was a transparent term meaning, generally, cultural as opposed to racial identity, as if it did not need further problematizing. Debates about ethnicity revolve around the nature of its object, whether it is an instinctual essence (the so-called "primordialist" position) or is better understood as a historical construction (the "constructivist" position). Undoubtedly, differences that are functions of specific historical developments and cultural practices have been a part of the nature of all human groups, but it is crucial to recognize that those differences have not always been attributed to history and culture. The devastating era of scientific racism in America, which we can mark off roughly from the 1830s to the 1940s, minimized or ruled out altogether any other consideration than biology as the basis of human identity or group difference.

Thus one of the considerations this work is intended to raise for relevant scholarship is that the concept of ethnicity may not always be a part of the world being studied. Our language must be more careful in examinations of such cases. More likely is the fact that group differences before the twentieth century were perceived and lived through the lens of race, a concept which itself must be understood within the historical context in which it appears. That is, ethnicity certainly existed before the concept, in the sense that group identities were probably always the function of their cultural practice and social history rather than some biological essence. But prior to the concept, it makes no sense to distinguish, as is quite common in the scholarly literature, groups that were ethnic from those that were not. We must be more finely attuned to the historicity of the discursive frame we bring to bear on the objects of our analysis. It is hoped that this work will provide a greater sense not only of the historical distance that divides us from our objects but also of the history that connects us to them.

THE SCHOLARLY RECORD

The tendency to look for ethnicity, or the cultural distinctiveness of specific groups, during periods in which those characteristics would have been seen as functions of race, has no doubt contributed heavily to current confusions about the difference between ethnicity and race. Scholars routinely remark on the bewildering inconsistency in the ways that ethnicity is applied and in the ways it is distinguished from race. Werner Sollors, perhaps the best known theorist of literary ethnicity, has listed some of the questions that have arisen in the scholarly debates around the relation between the two terms:

> Is "race'" an aspect of "ethnicity"? Or does "race" conceptually differ from "ethnicity"? And if so, is it a difference in degree or in kind? For scholarly practice, should "race" and "ethnicity" be understood as aspects of the same set of phenomenon, in relation to each other, or individually? Do they deserve to be discussed together, comparatively, or as separate issues? What is to be gained, what lost, if one adopts one of these positions? (*Theories* xxix)

In common usage, the terms are often paired as if they were synonyms or two parts of the same dimension. Robert Blauner found this to be typical in discussions with his students: "Confounding race and ethnicity is not just limited to the young. The general public, including journalists and other opinion makers, does this regularly, with serious consequences for the clarity of public dialogue and sociological analysis" (*Big News* 202). And indeed, no less a figure than Glazer lends this tendency to blur the distinctions authoritative scholarly backing. Glazer claims that among the positions on the issue, "the one I hold" has it that the two concepts, race and ethnicity, "form part of a single family of social identities—a family which, in addition to races and ethnic groups, includes religions (as in Holland), language groups (as in Belgium), and all of which can be included in the most general term, ethnic groups, groups defined by descent, real or mythical, and sharing a common history and experience" ("Blacks" 447). In everyday conversation it seems that "ethnicity" functions as a polite euphemism for the more awkward, discomforting "race." Even in the social science literature there is a strong tendency to blend the terms and to use them as if they were interchangeable. The dominant influence of the "melting-pot" myth for most of this century has had the effect of subsuming "race" under "ethnicity" as simply one special characteristic that would eventually fade into the ever-emerging American amalgam. Michael Omi and Howard Winant call this tendency the "ethnicity paradigm" and argue that it has been the dominant ideological framework in the United States since the 1930s (12). For example, the monumental *Harvard Encyclopedia of American Ethnic Groups*, published in 1980, subsumes race under ethnicity by designating the former as one of fourteen possible bases of ethnic group identity (Thernstrom et al. vi; Smith, "Ethnicity" 8).

However, another thread of critical historiography and "race relations" sociology sheds more light on the race-ethnicity confusion. This body of work challenges the "ethnicity paradigm" and brings greater clarity to the question of the difference between race and ethnicity. This approach criticizes the "ethnicity paradigm" perspective for, among other problems, failing to recognize the social and political implications of the race-ethnicity distinction. Noted among these is Pierre van den Berghe's *Race and Racism* (1967), which begins with a critique of the theoretical shortcomings of the "new orthodoxy" that came to prominence in the 1930s. Despite its advances over the nineteenth-century pseudoscientific racism that it was reacting against, the dominant approach nevertheless involved confusion between the various senses of the word *race*. Further, van den Berghe recommends that the connotation of *race* as a group based on shared cultural criteria should be replaced by *ethnicity* while saving *race* exclusively for group identity based on inherited physical traits. He insists that both are, to the same degree, socially defined since even physical differences are meaningful as racial only to those societies that recognize them as such. Though comparative studies show that the terms are sufficiently malleable from one national context to another in overlapping connotations, many American writers after van den Berghe have employed the term *ethnicity* to designate the specific cultural, historical character of a group. *Race*, on the other hand, has carried the sense of a more absolute difference, as in that between different species. With an unwarranted scientific authority, *race* designates an immutable genetic or biological essence of a group's identity impervious to time or human practice.[7] *Ethnicity* for many scholars, however, often indicates relative difference between peoples as the result of human accident, produced through the influences of history, region, and custom. Looking at race and ethnicity as discursive, David Theo Goldberg distinguishes them this way: "Ethnicity . . . tends to emphasize a rhetoric of cultural content, whereas race tends to resort to rhetoric of descent" (qtd. in Sollors, *Theories* xxxiii).

The significance of the connotative differences between the terms is due to the political differences that obtain when groups are designated as one or the other, as van den Berghe further explains:

> When cultural criteria of group differentiation are exclusively or predominantly resorted to, there results a more flexible system of stratification than one based on race, for culture can be learned and movement from one ethnic group to another is thus possible. Racial stratification, on the other hand, results in a nearly impermeable caste system more easily than ethnic stratification; race thus represents an extreme case of ascribed status and lack of social mobility. There are even instances of ethnic segmentation without any clear-cut hierarchy of groups, whereas it would be difficult to find an analogous situation in which the criterion is racial. (*Race* 22)

The crucial political difference between race and ethnicity is the inevitable and rigid hierarchy that attends the former compared to its more "flexible" rival term. Thus, in social formations like the United States, it is a significant advantage, in terms of access to material benefits and opportunities, for a group's differentiating characteristics to be classified as ethnic rather than racial. Those who follow van den Berghe's lead have pointed out that race is "the ultimate boundary between 'us' and 'them'" and that "designating a group of people as a distinct race has been sufficient in the United States to mark them off as more profoundly and distinctively 'other'—more radically different from 'us'—than those ethnic groups who have not had to carry the burden of racial distinction" (Cornell and Hartman 25–26). In other words, the ultimate significance of the difference is political; relative to the subjection that race historically imposes on its victims, ethnicity confers autonomous subjectivity and self-determination.[8] To be defined by what one does historically, rather than by what one is biologically, is to possess a measure of self-determination excluded when one is defined racially.[9] This is why the issues of race and ethnicity are intrinsically bound up, as we shall see, with questions of social participation and which groups are and are not fit for inclusion in the American Republic.

In the United States, this abstract relation of power that distinguishes groups marked as ethnic from those marked as racial corresponds to the concrete history of European immigrants and African Americans. Taking up this history and the political basis for the race-ethnicity distinction, Ronald Takaki has shown the problems that arise when the two terms are used interchangeably or when the crucial differences between the two are not carefully discerned. That is, the substance of his argument is a historically specific account of the differences between groups that fall under the ethnic category and those that have been racialized. His point of attack is Glazer's "basic American ethnic pattern," a variant of the dominant melting-pot theory that attempts to describe the process of assimilation common to all minority groups in America. In his critique, Takaki shows that the pattern works well for European immigrants but immediately breaks down when applied to groups across the color line, such as African Americans, Asian Americans, and Native Americans. Glazer's theory is based on three historical "decisions" that have shaped the American "consensus" on ethnic difference ("Emergence" 11). The first decision, though not initially agreed upon, is that America will accept all the world's peoples and grant them equal rights. Second, no group would be treated as a separate polity or allowed to establish an independent collectivity. Third, no groups would be required to abandon their group identity as the price of admission to American society. Takaki's response is to reveal the limitation of these principles in practice by testing them against the history of racial minorities and European immigrants. Predictably, he finds that Glazer's high-minded standards apply almost exclusively only to the latter. For example, Takaki points out that the Naturalization Law of 1790, which reserved the right of naturalized citizenship to "free white" immigrants, was not repealed until the Walter-McCarran Act of 1952. Thus for 162 years "what actually developed historically in American society was a pattern of citizenship and suffrage which drew a very sharp distinction between 'ethnicity' and 'race'" (Takaki 27).

Takaki argues forcefully that racialized groups have fared far less well than "ethnic," that is, European, groups. W.E.B. DuBois made a similar point in 1920, that "against this surging forward of Irish and German, of Russian Jew, Slav and 'dago' [America's] social bars have not availed, but against Negroes she can and does take her unflinching and immovable stand" ("Souls of White Folks" 51). More recent scholars, along with Takaki, have argued convincingly against applying the narrative of European American mobility to communities of color,[10] but the highly politicized nature of the debate undermines the possibility of a consensus. Extending the model of European immigrants to racialized groups supports the conclusion that inequality results from the inherent inability of certain peoples to assimilate. Alexander Saxton's critique of the "pathological black family" thesis, for example, demonstrates that its function is to explain group stratification without admitting white dominance: "Here once again the problem is defined as being all their *own* problem, and effectively of their own making, since it is clearly implied that other minorities have thrived in America despite comparably onerous historical experiences" (149). Frequently, the immigrant analogy is used to discipline racial minorities and to blame the victims of systematic racial oppression. Omi and Winant's critique of the "Bootstraps Model" (21) is that it assumes the success of an immigrant or minority group is relative to how well their values match up with the values of American society's majority, with no consideration of independently operating sociopolitical dynamics (such as structural racism).

Though he does not explore the implications, Takaki's distinction between ethnicity and race suggests that ethnicity has primarily been a special feature of whiteness. That is, "ethnicity" has been a qualifier whose benefits have historically been the exclusive possession of white skin. "Ethnic" and "white" are almost redundant in his argument that, while Glazer's egalitarian version of America's diversity policies "may have been true for white 'ethnic' groups like the Irish and Germans, they certainly do not accurately describe the historical experiences of 'racial' groups" (Takaki 27). Thus, as Saxton asserts, race may be discussed as an aspect of ethnicity in other contexts, "but in the United States—because of the importance of white racism as a causal factor—the two have moved on separate tracks and demand separate treatment" (146). Yet despite the importance of understanding the distinctions between them, at the same time it must be allowed that ethnicity and race have been closely bound up with one another. Moreover, the conceptions of "ethnic" and "ethnicity" implied here are fairly recent. Equally problematic in this context is the fact that the European immigrants could not always take their whiteness for granted. For example, David Roediger has argued that the use of the word *white* in the Naturalization Law of 1790 only raised the difficulty for the courts thereafter of determining where to draw the line. Robert T. Devlin, United States Attorney at San Francisco, observed in 1907 that "there is considerable uncertainty as to just what nationalities come within the term 'white person'" (qtd. in Roediger, *Towards* 181).

The questions then become, first, by what process has the distinction between race and ethnicity developed such that *ethnicity* carries the sense of a cultural variation compared to the more absolute, biological difference implied by race? And, second, how is it that ethnicity has been predominantly relevant only to the white side of the color line, implying comparative social advantages not (or only recently) available to groups categorized as racially other or nonwhite? This set of associations is now so ingrained that "ethnic groups" in the scholarship almost always means European immigrants.[11] At the same time, there is no term corresponding to "white ethnic" such as "black ethnic." Yet, it is only with the relatively recent appearance of ethnicity that white Americans, or anyone else, could think their group affinity in terms other than racial. The histories of how this reconception of identity from race to ethnic has occurred, and of the circumstances under which ethnicity took shape as a means of identification and classification, have yet to be written. There are several excellent histories of the concept of race in America, many of which have provided models for my own study.[12] The concept of ethnicity is occasionally discussed as part of those projects and such scholarship has been invaluable to my own. But the history and evolution of the concept itself has scarcely ever been considered. For example, Werner Sollors, generally regarded as an authority on ethnicity in American literature, in his entry for "Ethnicity" in *Critical Terms for Literary Study* offers no history of the development of the concept but invokes it throughout as if its meaning were self-evident and unchanging. Despite the complex historical relation between *ethnic* and *race*, he elides the two or presents the latter as an extreme degree of the former: "What is often called 'race' in the modern United States is perhaps the country's most virulent ethnic factor" (289). By defining race as a special case of ethnicity and otherwise using them interchangeably, he omits an important historical aspect of ethnicity's difference from race. Sollors observes that "the construction of the ethnic boundary is a *general* procedure and centers in attempts to override the basic fact that all human beings—though far from being alike—are similar at least insofar as they are human. Boundary-supporting verbal strategies may distance other human beings so far from the speaker that they seem closer to the other species" (299). Sollors refers here more precisely to the *racial* boundary, historically a division between species. Lost is the idea that ethnicity is part of the recent history of race, invented to mollify the dehumanizing impulse behind race's absolute distinction.[13]

In another article in which one might reasonably expect to find self-reflection on terminology, Conzen et al.'s 1992 essay, "The Invention of Ethnicity: A Perspective from the USA," its absence is revealing. The essay rehearses the history of the debates over the nature of its object (the primordialists versus the constructivists) and argues for a conception of ethnicity as "a process of construction or invention which incorporates, adapts, and amplifies preexisting communal solidarities, cultural attributes, and historical memories" (4–5). While such a theoretically promising approach might be employed to understand the development of virtually any group, the authors never suggest they mean it to apply to African Americans or any other communities of color. Their three case studies all involve European American groups. That ethnicity, as a complex and overdetermined process of group formation, is strictly a white matter never seems to need addressing. Despite emphasizing the importance of historicizing, they locate the emergence of "ethnic" differentiation in the nineteenth century with the arrival of European populations even though the concept in the way they mean it did not yet exist. Speaking of the mid-nineteenth-century view of the Irish, they remark that "it was not only the obvious presence of culturally alien immigrants that provoked a new ethnic way of categorizing people" (9). Yet the historical record indicates that this new way of categorizing was racial, so that what the authors mean here is rather something like intra-European racial difference.[14] Conzen et al. are on more reliable ground when they are discussing the thing itself—the shifting cultural modalities of group self-perceptions. But where the concept of ethnicity comes from, why it has been applied only to European immigrant groups, and why it exists at all is not addressed. In his response to Conzen et al., Herbert J. Gans notes provocatively that "ethnicity has become so much a part of the general discourse that it is easy to forget that the term was coined less than half a century ago and that it was first used by sociologists and anthropologists to describe the people they studied" ("Comment" 50–51). He warns that we cannot assume the people studied use the same concepts as researchers to describe their experience and that "those of us who write about ethnicity should begin to think about the role *we* play in contemporary ethnicity" ("Comment" 51). Such gestures of self-reflection have been rare in discussions about the concept and application of ethnicity. The history of the discursive construction of the concept of ethnicity has received scant scholarly attention. Perhaps, as Glazer suggests, the "phenomenon is too new" ("Introduction" 2). At the same time, the speed with which the concept has installed itself in common sense in the time since Glazer made his observation has perhaps made it seem too transparent and obvious to warrant any such special attention. This work is an attempt to contribute to such a project and to offer the kind of meta-commentary for which Gans was calling.[15]

Moreover, the seemingly unproblematic obviousness of ethnicity and its easy attribution to those groups assumed to be white has also forestalled any pressing need to look at the changing content and qualities of the concept. Apart from the debates between primordialists and constructivists, its simple connotation as cultural identity has generally been taken as sufficient for the various uses to which it has been put. But in the chapters that follow, I look at the context of the concept's first articulations in order to better understand the functions it was created to perform. I also offer a theory about why the concept was constructed exclusively for European immigrants and what prevented its application to differences across the color line.

Many new hypotheses about race and identity have resulted from the work of Roediger and others in critical whiteness studies. They have shown that whiteness is, like all socially constructed racial identities, not fixed, even for Europeans, but is dynamic and historically contingent. But the unquestioned link between whiteness and ethnicity retroactively obviates the need to explain why that connection came to be. By rights, the concept of cultural identity, which needed, for its own legitimacy, to challenge and discredit the older race science, should logically have challenged all racial identities. The same discourse that helped southern and eastern European differences transform from racial to cultural might have worked its alchemy on any racialized group. One of the contradictions of the new theoretical approaches to human difference is that it did not. Such work was left to the racialized groups themselves. In that effort, the concept of ethnicity was transformed again, when pressed into the service of the Black Revolution of the 1960s and 1970s. But because the historical function of ethnicity has not been fully recognized to begin with, neither has the significance of this more recent transvaluation.

THE CHAPTERS

The argument of this book is divided into four chapters, each covering (in roughly chronological order) the phases in the development of the concept of ethnicity. The period in which the first chapter is situated spans the nineteenth century to the first decades of the twentieth century. This period is approximately that of the rise and fall of the paradigm of race science as the arbiter of all discussions of human difference. In this period, the boundaries were more permeable than in the twentieth century between different sites where this discussion took place, such as within scholarly and scientific journals and books, on the floor of Congress, on the street corner, and in popular culture. However, throughout the work, my focus is primarily on the scholarly debates that formulated the conceptual groundwork and the concept of ethnicity. Prevailing popular notions of race and the political expediency of the moment placed real barriers around what scholars were able and willing to think, and so I also try to note where those forces were influential.

Such influences on nineteenth-century conceptions are multiple, as I note in chapter 1. My argument is that, while no concept of ethnicity seems to have existed during the period, creating the concept later would not have been necessary, nor taken the shape it did, without the nineteenth-century creation of biological race. That discourse, as it evolved, articulated new categorical divisions between the varieties of humankind. Lines were drawn not only between the big divisions of humanity, between the now-awkward and embarrassing categories of Caucasoid, Mongoloid, and Negroid, but even within the category of Caucasoid itself. The mid-century Irish were effectively the test case, and race science demonstrated that it was capable of conceptualizing even a European group as a race apart from the core of Anglo-Saxon Americans. This process was repeated again at the end of the nineteenth century in the case of the new immigrants from eastern and southern Europe, racializing them into a strange, ambiguous category between black and white that would earn them historians' designation as the "inbetween people." I argue that the nineteenth century presents a pre-history of the concept of ethnicity. As the new immigrants became, over the course of the early twentieth century, de facto white (through assimilation, intermarriage, class mobility, and new definitions of whiteness), a need arises for a new theory to explain who they are. This new theory would help rationalize how they could be both white and, at the same time, different from other whites.

Chapter 2 focuses on the new academic discourses that emerged in the early decades of the twentieth century, which form another phase in the prehistory of the invention of ethnicity. Specifically, the work of Robert Park and other early practitioners of "race relations" sociology, and Franz Boas's influence over the development of cultural anthropology, helped to create the basis for modern theories of race and human difference as social constructions. They were the most influential forces in the campaign to sweep away the dark ages of nineteenth-century race science. Together the two disciplines created the foundations for culturally based theories of human group identity in the twentieth century. As such, they are indispensable in understanding the theoretical basis for the formulation of a concept like ethnicity. On the face of it, the theory of human identity and difference based on innate biological determinations is simply incompatible with a theory that explains such phenomena in terms of historically specific cultural practices. With the rise of the latter to largely displace and discredit the former within the human sciences, it would seem inevitable that all racialized identities might be swept away or, at least, subject to new ways of thinking. The work of black scholars of the period, chiefly that of Alain Locke, in fact proves that the critique for all racial identities was possible.

Ironically, however, the academic institutionalization of the new discourses of difference proved able to accommodate the older racial convictions about the fundamental physical differences between black and white. Crucial to the question of ethnicity, I argue in chapter 2, is that the innovative cultural theories of identity were selectively applied to the question of European difference and left intact was the rationale of black subordination based on biology. Thus the potential challenge that cultural theories presented to the ideological justification of racial hierarchies was contained. More perversely, as we will see, the new discourse of ethnicity served the maintenance of the racial formation by providing the means of reconceiving and stabilizing the white race. That is, ethnicity reunifies the previously divided white race but leaves the color line and white supremacy untouched. This chapter thus answers the question that is rarely asked: why does "ethnic," in the new sense of cultural identity, become, against its own potential to transform all positions, the exclusive property of whiteness?

Chapter 3 is a close look at how the word *ethnicity* actually enters the language. The first appearance of the word, as far as I or other commentators can detect, was in 1942 in volume 2 of W. Lloyd Warner's *Yankee City* devoted to group dynamics in a small American city. No explanations have yet been offered about why it was then that such an auspicious event occurred. Nor have the implications been fully examined concerning the fact that it first appears in the context of Warner's elaboration of the caste model of race relations. This chapter shows how the word *ethnic* is drawn out of relative obscurity in the sociological repertoire. We trace how the word is revamped for the new purpose of filling the theoretical gap that had been opened by the ambiguous racial and social situation of the new immigrants. As the sociological discourse develops, *race* and *ethnic* are paired and, for the first time, distinguished from one another. *Ethnic*, once a synonym for *race*, is recast in the light of the emerging discourse of cultural identity and installed, along with *race* in its older sense, into the mainstream sociological lexicon. It is here that current debates, rehearsed above, originate over the differences between the two words. I also argue that the pairing of the now incommensurate terms *ethnic* and *race* and the caste model provide the means for sociology to formalize the contradictions (outlined in chapter 2) between its simultaneous attack on, and retention of, race science. I contend that the concept of ethnicity is invented expressly to confer a new form of whiteness on the formerly outcast European immigrants. Insofar as it was then limited to European Americans and employed for the purposes of whiteness, it therefore helps to limit the newer cultural theories of identity from delegitimating racial hierarchies based on color. For the southern and eastern Europeans, it meant an important promotion, a resolution of their theoretically ambiguous position, and greater possibility to advance. On the other hand, insofar as their Anglo-American betters did not have "ethnicity," the designation also confirms and institutionalizes, at least temporarily, the subordinate status of the newly white. Yet as a transitory state, unlike race, if ethnicity betokens subordination, it also authorizes the mobility and assimilation that were already well under way by the 1940s and heading toward an undifferentiated, pan-European white race in America. The discourse of ethnicity legitimated, I argue, both the emerging de facto whiteness of southern and eastern European Americans as well the fundamental racial division of black and white.

The upheavals of the 1960s, and especially the Black Revolution, transformed racial concepts and caught most white scholars of race relations off-guard. Little in their assumptions about people of color had prepared them for the way African Americans would lay hold of historical agency and rearrange the practices of racial power. The prevailing institutions of legal segregation that had stood for a century were dismantled within a decade. On the basis of this powerful, popular mass mobilization, ethnicity too would be transformed. The final chapter looks at the way the earlier, 1940s version of ethnicity is redefined when it is seized by the discourse of black cultural nationalism and pressed into the service of the discourse of revolutionary anticolonialism. I look primarily at the work of Robert Blauner and reason that, in taking up the concept of ethnicity, his work refunctions it for new purposes. I argue that his conception of the historically complex black experience recodes ethnicity in terms of black cultural identity. If his work cannot take sole credit for the sea change made possible by broader social forces, his work contributes significantly to transforming the term *ethnicity*, making it available to identities beyond those for which it was originally created. A trained sociologist, speaking within the discourse of his discipline, Blauner's formulation of black ethnicity is in itself revolutionary within a tradition that had rarely considered the existence of a distinct African American cultural identity. Black culture was, according to the sociological consensus, merely a "pathologically" distorted version of the dominant white American culture. Black ethnicity in Blauner's work, instead of a transitional and temporary identity in the process of assimilation, is an identity defined by its distinctness and independence from the dominant and other cultural positions. And, instead of the concept's initial function in the maintenance of dominant and oppressive racial hierarchies, I argue that Blauner's conception of black identity renders ethnicity a revolutionary weapon defined by its opposition to the racial status quo.

HEGEMONY AND RACIAL FORMATION

Among the various schools of thought on the issue of race, the perspective brought to bear here relies on a structural conception of race.[16] Racism is more than a derogatory attitude toward people of color held by some whites. The privileging of whites is part of the routine, daily functioning of the entire social system on virtually every level. As Joe Feagin suggests, the "American house of racism" is a "total racist society" in the sense that "every major aspect of life is shaped to some degree by the core racist realities" (16). Racial ideology, of which the concept of ethnicity is part, is one element of the racist social structure whose primary function is to rationalize white supremacy and resource inequalities along racial lines.

Within the structuralist or institutional racism framework, Michael Omi and Howard Winant's neo-Gramscian approach has been the most satisfactory to me in explaining the relation of racial ideologies and identities to the racist social structure. Their project begins with a critique of past paradigms for situating the social and political nature of race. Briefly, these have been the ethnic-, class-, and nation-based frameworks, each of which, they argue, reduces the particular nature of race to its ruling analogy. Omi and Winant argue that the "ethnicity paradigm," whose foundations they locate in the work of Robert Park (the subject of chapter 2), reduces the specificity of race through an analogy with European immigrants, emphasizing the conflicts between the needs for assimilation and group cohesion. As such, they argue, the paradigm blurs the historically distinct roles that ethnic and racial differences, respectively, have played.[17]

Omi and Winant further contend that Park's pioneering work became the basis for the dominant approach to race in the United States, one that measures all groups by the experience of European immigrants in the early twentieth century. As a result, the model assumes the process of assimilation and provides insufficient attention to the power of the color line in differentiating the experience of the new immigrants from blacks and other racialized minorities. As discussed in chapter 4, the discipline of the sociology of race relations was thrown into crisis in the 1960s since, having adopted the "ethnicity paradigm," it was unable to account for the emergence of the Civil Rights Movement. Mainstream sociology had assumed that white prejudice would determine whether black Americans would assimilate or remain isolated. There was little in the dominant sociological model to account for massive, coordinated resistance against racial oppression. One result of the failure of "ethnicity theory" was the emergence of competing frameworks, namely the class- and nation-based perspectives. Yet these theoretical frameworks similarly address the issue of race through analogies that only partially capture the irreducible specificity of race. Omi and Winant argue that the class-based paradigm explains race with reference to the processes of class antagonism and exploitation and fails to account for the effects of race that fall outside the sphere of production. The nation-based paradigm casts the nature of racial difference within the terms of an analogy with colonialism which, Omi and Winant argue, assumes falsely a structural division between the two "nations." As I argue in chapter 4, however, despite its analytical limitations, the colonial framework provided the basis for an important revision of the concept of ethnicity.

Despite the limitations of the immigrant-, class-, and nation-based approaches, Omi and Winant argue that each has grasped an important aspect of the problem of race. They attempt to gather the three paradigms under a new Gramscian conception of the social reality of racial differences they call "the racial formation." Adopting anti-economistic critiques of Marxism, they define racial formation as the dialectical process by which economic, political, and cultural forces both determine and are determined by racial categories. The concept of racial formation takes race as the fundamental reference point for an analysis of the workings of hegemony, which, for Omi and Winant, is a war of position between racially based movements and "the racial state." In this case, the racial state is the set of state institutions that, despite disunity and disorganization, nevertheless function to maintain the "unstable equilibrium" of the racial order and to "organize and enforce the racial politics of everyday life" (Omi and Winant 83).

In order to apply the theory of racial formation, Omi and Winant briefly recount the history of the post–World War II black movement in the United States, one of the few examples in American history in which the equilibrium of the racial order is disrupted (and the most significant since Reconstruction). "The great transformation" in American racial politics is the phrase

Omi and Winant use to characterize the "epochal" paradigm shift brought on by the black movement in general and the *"rearticulation of black collective subjectivity"* (98) in particular. They argue that the transformation of black identity is also the movement's greatest contribution to the present framework of racial politics despite rollbacks in the 1970s and 1980s of many of the movement's political gains. One of the repercussions of the revolutionary transformation in black identity is reflected here in chapter 4, which looks at the way the reconceptualization of blackness fundamentally changed the concept of ethnicity.

Racial formation, however, remains at a relatively general level of abstraction and suggests little about how any nonracial forces might effect the terms of hegemony (such as gender or economic class).[18] But Omi and Winant's concept of racial formation supplies the theoretical foundation for claims in the present study about the relation between the discursive formulations of race and ethnicity, on the one hand, and the social structure, on the other. The fundamental place Omi and Winant theorize for the category of race at all levels of social practice and the significance they place on the cultural issue of racial identity have made their work of central importance to my project. I rely on the concept of racial formation to ground my analysis of the ways in which political forces shape and are shaped by discourse. Racial formation theory, in other words, provides much of the basis from which I critique the political implications of the various contributions to race relations theory discussed here. As I argue, especially in chapters 2 and 3, the discourse on race that comes out of the disciplines of sociology and anthropology, while often contradictory and never monolithic, predominantly functions to provide "scientific" discursive support and justification for the prevailing, white supremacist racial order. At the same time, new theories maintain racial hegemony by negotiating emergent and potentially disruptive threats, incorporating and containing them through concessions and compromises.

As such, within the hegemonic negotiations taking place across the institutions of civil society, academic race theory has largely worked in tandem with and as an extension of the interests of the racial state. Racial formation theory exposes the discourse of ethnicity, in its premier appearance, as a model of hegemonic discourse. The initially contradictory discourse of ethnicity offers a degree of concession in the face of emerging forces challenging the post-Reconstruction biological justifications for existing racial hierarchies. The early twentieth-century development of an organized black intelligentsia and African American resistance movements in such organizations as Marcus Garvey's Universal Negro Improvement Association (UNIA) and the National Association for the Advancement of Colored People (NAACP) required a more sophisticated formulation of dominant racial ideology. Thus ethnicity incorporates the newer conceptions about the sociocultural, rather than natural, basis of group character. But by tying it exclusively to variations of whiteness, ethnicity functions hegemonically by ultimately channeling the subversive power of the new discourse back into the maintenance of white racial supremacy.

The example of Oliver Cox, however, discussed in chapter 3, suggests that the arena of academic discourse on race is often a contested terrain. Scholarly work on race does not always or everywhere serve the maintenance of racial hegemony, despite the preponderance of its application in such a manner. The consideration of the work of Robert Blauner in chapter 4 provides another example of a counter-hegemonic intervention into racial discourse with transformative results. The added force of Blauner's project derives from the confluence of broader historical currents and new social movements of the 1960s (that Cox lacked in the 1940s), which Omi and Winant refer to as constitutive elements of "the great transformation."

RACIAL IDENTITY

While Omi and Winant offer ways to theorize the relation between ideologies of race and racial identities, on the one hand, and the historical social structure, on the other, they do not offer detailed theorization of the relation between discourse and identities. My assumptions regarding the issues of discourse and identity are based largely on the structural Marxism of Louis Althusser and his followers. Althusser was part of a general shift in French thought in the 1950s and 1960s away from subject-centered theory, such as phenomenology and existentialism, that began rather to "de-center" and rethink the nature of human subjectivity as less of a foundation than an effect of the social structures in which it is embedded. Such a shift is promising to the degree that it offers the means for historicizing thought and, because of its attention to the subject, the formation of specific identities. As Althusser famously puts it, ideology "represents the imaginary relationship of individuals to their real conditions of existence" (162). This line of thought is generally regarded as an important and useful contribution to the conception of ideology because it avoids the problems inherent in theories of ideology as a fog of false consciousness. Instead, an ideological framework is constitutive of human subjectivity and therefore a necessary element of human consciousness rather than something to be dispensed with by the clear light of scientific truth. The function of ideology is the "[constitution of] *concrete individuals as subjects*" (Althusser 171). While still distinguished from science and scientific knowledge in Althusser, ideology remains an irreducible aspect of human consciousness and textuality.

And while often criticized for a less-than-careful borrowing of Lacan, Althusser's further notion of interpellation has been, for me, an indispensable guide to theorizing the process by which discourse, as the concrete vehicle for ideology, constructs or "sutures" identities through the process in which it "hails" its reader. Though perhaps not always as successful as Althusser allows, the process of interpellation provides a theory for the way individuals become historical subjects through their interactions with the concrete signifying systems of their social environment. As Althusser states, "All ideology hails or interpellates concrete individuals as concrete subjects" (173). Discourse is not reducible to a mere vehicle for ideology and the production of subjects, for it does offer verifiable truth claims about the world. But estimating the political ramifications of discourse must take its interpellative dimension into account. Indeed, race and racial identity are entirely the products of discourse, which function in human history only to the degree that they successfully hail (and in so doing, construct) human subjects. Key to much of the success of the discourse on race to hail subjects has been its scientific truth claims. Further, one of the primary interpellative, ideological effects in the tradition of the sociological discourse on race is, ironically, the production of disinterested "scientific" subjects. The subject of such discourse is an objective observer of the social order, rather than an agent in the maintenance of its relations of power through the production of that discourse. The initial discursive production of the ethnic identity is presented, and often accepted, as mere observation rather than, as I argue, a production whose effect is the naturalization of power relations based on racial categories. Writers whose work comes from outside the academic mainstream, such as Cox and Blauner, critique the "scientific" pretensions of dominant sociology and expose its political interests. Their work thus interpellates a more critical, antagonistic subject than the dominant discourse allows.

IDEOLOGICAL COMPROMISE FORMATION

Althusserian Marxism has also provided a more specific theoretical direction to this study. That is, I am indebted in my formulations of the concept of ethnicity to Étienne Balibar and Pierre Macherey's propositions, which are strongly influenced by Althusserian theory, about a Marxist theory of literature. They argue that the first principle of a materialist literary analysis must reject the assumption about the unity of a work of art and instead work to locate its structuring contradictions. Unity and the reconciliation of conflict within the work is always a displaced attempt to stage an imaginary solution to real material contradictions that originate outside the work in the contradictions of class struggle. Balibar and Macherey argue that "literature 'begins' with the imaginary solution of the implacable ideological contradictions, with the representation of that solution" (88). By reading the texts in the present study in terms of Balibar and Macherey's analysis, I argue that the concept of ethnicity provides the kind of imaginary solution, or ideological compromise formation, characteristic of bourgeois literary production. As I explain in more detail in chapter 3, "ethnicity" provides the appearance, behind the presumed unity of a concept, of a resolution to the contradiction between irreconcilable theories of human difference, namely race science's biological framework and the new culturally based theories of sociology and anthropology. That is, ethnicity, in its original formulation, incorporates the notion of cultural difference, supplied by new twentieth-century discourses, within a racial hierarchy based on biological difference, inherited from the nineteenth century.

The ideological compromise formation of "ethnicity" has at least two major effects. First, by directing the discourse of cultural difference toward a specific minority group (the new immigrants) rather than all of them, the formulation of ethnicity leaves the authority of racial hierarchies founded on permanent biological differences essentially intact. The concept of ethnicity borrows from, but at the same time contains, the potentially counter-hegemonic ideological effects of the new discourses of cultural identity. (And "contains" here should be read in both the sense of "including" but also "limiting" and "constraining.") Second, the concept of ethnicity provides both a rationale to redefine the racial status of the eastern and southern European immigrants and a theory to clarify their ambiguous classification. The formulation applies the new cultural theories toward a potentially destabilizing problem of the off-white immigrants' racial position. Ethnicity renders the new immigrants unambiguously white and therefore theoretically incorporates them, as members and defenders, into the racial order of white supremacy. While the material contradiction that is displaced and conceptually "resolved" derives from structural racism rather than economic class, the conceptualization of ethnicity resonates with Balibar and Macherey's idea that literary language "finds a language of 'compromise' which presents the conciliation as 'natural' and so both necessary and inevitable" (88).

CRITICAL WHITENESS STUDIES

My project also occurs within the context of the current scholarship on whiteness that analyzes the cultural construction, political effects, and historical conditions of white racial identity. Despite the differences between various theoretical and scholarly projects devoted to the topic, they share the assumption that white racial identity, rather than a natural or biological category, emerges as a product of the complex socioeconomic conditions of North America in order to serve specific social functions. Critiques of whiteness assume that "the white race" is a cultural construct and thus seek to uncover the complex social conditions that create, sustain, and change it. Studies in whiteness share the strategy, similar to the deconstruction of masculinity within feminism or heterosexuality within queer studies, of trying to denaturalize the dominant position in asymmetrical power relations otherwise granted as the standard against which the subaltern is measured. Its implications are frequently taken to the point of dissolving the dominant position altogether, as is suggested by Roediger's title *Towards the Abolition of the Whiteness*. The collective responsible for the publication of the journal *Race Traitor* also promotes a variety of practices and strategies designed to expose and abolish the white race as a viable collective or imagined community with which an individual might identify. At the very least, the critique of whiteness and white-skin privilege signifies an acknowledgment of the complaint, long made by people of color, that the burden of race and racism is left up to persons of color. White studies accepts that the problem of racism is "the white problem" (rather than the black or "Negro problem"). Whiteness scholars argue that the critique of white racial identity and the denaturalizing of white privilege provide concrete ways to make political use of the understanding that, rather than a biological reality, race is a social construction. As Roediger argues, "The central political implication arising from the insight that race is socially constructed is the specific need to attack *whiteness* as a destructive ideology rather than to attack the concept [of race] abstractly" (*Towards the Abolition* 3).

My own study in American whiteness takes as models the recent scholarly treatments that seek to isolate whiteness as an object of knowledge. Theodore Allen, in his *Invention of the White Race*, for example, examines the case of English racial oppression against the Irish, comparing those circumstances to American racism based on skin color. Because of the small number of slaveholders relative to the population as a whole, the maintenance of slavery required the support of an "intermediate social control stratum." In many slave societies, this function was supplied by the "mulatto class" who are conceded sufficient privileges to ally their interests to the slaveholders. The absence of a sufficiently proportionate mulatto class in North American settlement required the creation of some other comparable group to serve the purpose of protecting a social order that benefited the ruling elite. Allen argues that this problem is solved with the invention of the white race. I have largely adopted Allen's (and others') understanding that the creation of a white identity stemmed largely from the need for a common interest that would ally the landless working classes of early North America with the vulnerable elite minority of propertied slaveholders. In this context, whiteness was, and remains, a kind of hegemonic deal with the devil, in which the majority of European Americans accept permanent subordination and a commitment to the status quo in exchange for the "privileges" of being spared the more intense forms of social and economic degradation or superexploitation meted out to their counterparts of color.

In *The Wages of Whiteness*, David Roediger identifies whiteness in North America from the Revolution to Reconstruction as a key component in the formation of the industrial working class. Whiteness historically functioned as a means to limit the scope of the labor movement by splitting the working class along racial lines, but it also provided European immigrants with social and psychological benefits necessary for their survival under the emerging industrial regime. Regardless of the depths of their hardship and oppression, the worker identified as white could take refuge in the notion that he or she would never occupy the bottom of the social hierarchy reserved for people of color. Whiteness thus becomes a possession of chief importance in America and thus a structuring element in everything from the life of new immigrants to the discourse of race-relations sociology. It should not be assumed, however, that the ideology of white identity is false consciousness cleverly disseminated by the ruling classes in order to maintain the political, economic status quo. Roediger emphasizes that the whitened workers themselves repeatedly, deliberately, and ruthlessly chose whiteness and participated in its construction and therefore their own unwitting disempowerment. This is, I believe, part of what W.E.B. DuBois meant when he wrote of the development of late nineteenth-century industrial white labor, that "democracy died save in the hearts of black folk" (*Black Reconstruction* 30). Though seldom acknowledged, the initial production of the concept of ethnicity is one small part of this history. However, it is frequently assumed in whiteness studies that such histories might reveal that whiteness is not inevitable and that what was once created might later be dissolved. Thus I would hope that my own work here would contribute to that aspect of whiteness studies that seeks to denaturalize whiteness in preparation for new and more democratic forms of identity and social relations other than those structured by and structuring whiteness. I have also tried to highlight that chapter in *ethnicity's* history in which, for a brief period when it was radicalized by the language of black nationalism, it took on liberatory, revolutionary hues (see chapter 4).

Consequently, one of the values of whiteness studies for this work is its capacity to demonstrate the complex ways that whiteness, like all other racial identities, has been constructed and reconstructed. That rapidly growing body of work has not only discovered significant new perspectives on America's racial history but has also, in a sense, recovered something of which previous generations were well aware: that European Americans could not always count on the relative security of whiteness. It is possible that the creation of ethnicity, and its corollary consolidation and stabilization of whiteness, have contributed some measure to a historical amnesia that has allowed us to forget that time before whites were all white. Similar to whiteness studies, I believe that my own work does, in part, restore a portion of the "forgotten" history of the concept of ethnicity so that it can be used not only with greater awareness of the initial purposes of its creation and those it has served since, but also with a heightened self-consciousness by those who have no alternatives but to use it still. I do not claim that the fashioners of ethnicity knew they were doing anything but objectively advancing the knowledge of their disciplines. Indeed, the development of the concept of ethnicity merely legitimated and named a social process already under way—the whitening of the new immigrants. But once conceived, the concept closed a door, making it possible for writers to talk about groups rendered "ethnic" independently from those not deemed so, while all still remained in the trap of race to one degree or another. It is not at all uncommon to see discussions of the ethnicity of European Americans without reference to race or the presence of African Americans. A history of the concept of ethnicity, however, reveals how intimately entwined it has always been with race, just as it continues to be so. This work attempts to provide a better sense of the racial struggles from which the term derives. From such study, we might better assess the concept's benefits and hidden costs, not only to those for whom the term is a tool and to those for whom it has been extended, but also to those from whom it has been withheld. We should not lose sight that in America, it is humanity that is at stake for those groups who struggle to transform a racial designation into an ethnicity.

NOTES

1. The groups that finally joined the two-week offensive included state agencies, labor organizations, and ethnic groups: the Croatian Fraternal Union of America, Pennsylvania Heritage Affairs Commission, the State Department of Environmental Resources, United Steelworkers, Central Council of Polish Organizations, the National Black Political Caucus, the National Fraternal Congress of America, the William Penn Association, the Pittsburgh Fraternal Society, and the Polish Falcons of America (Schur).

2. Though he denied that his public objections to the statue were diversionary or self-promotional, Flaherty was embroiled in a controversy at the time involving accusations that he was prohibiting some of his employees from joining the United Steelworkers Union (Barnes, "'Hunky'").

3. There appears to be a general consensus on the origins of *hunky*. See Irving Lewis Allen, Cassidy, Ken Johnson, and Smitherman. The *Oxford English Dictionary* likewise suggests the links *bohunk* (Bohemian + Hungarian) to *hunky* and *honky*.

4. Recently at Miami University in Oxford, Ohio, I asked a racially mixed class of about thirty students in their late teens and early twenties if they had ever heard the words *hunky* or *honky*. Not one had heard the former except as an adjective for an attractive male. One student was familiar with the latter. An older black male in the audience, Dr. Rodney Coates, informed me that *honky* is still occasionally heard in the black community as an invective.

5. The concept of identity is perhaps just as new to the lexicon of the social sciences as *ethnicity* and, as Philip Gleason argues, their almost simultaneous emergence suggests they may be mutually bound up. As we shall see, ethnicity begins as an objective sociological category but seems gradually in the 1950s and 1960s to mean a condition of a group or individual's identity and consciousness.

6. In 1947, E. K. Francis theorized the concept of "ethnic group" as a version of Ferdinand Tönnies' idea of *Gemeinschaft*, or, roughly, an organic, communal association. Members of such communities are characterized by a shared consciousness of their group identity or "we-feeling." Francis also argued that the designation "'ethnic group' is not limited to ethnic fragments and minorities within a larger culture" (395) but can be applied to national or cultural communities regardless of their minority, majority, or even racial status. James McKee suggests Francis's theorization might have been a turning point in the sociology of race relations, leading to more fruitful considerations of the specificity of black American culture. However, "sociologists in the 1940s were not ready to seize upon such a conceptual opening and move into new territory" (McKee 276).

7. Chapter 1 provides further detail on the history of race and the ways it has been defined in America.

8. In its first appearance in the 1940s in Lloyd Warner's *Yankee City* series, ethnicity is a label of subordination since it refers to those European immigrant stock whose place in the social stratification lies above groups of color but below native white Americans. On the other hand, it rescues its possessors from racial Otherness, and, in recognizing their whiteness, endorses their potential for full citizenship and class mobility. This point is more fully documented in chapter 3.

9. The subjection of race versus the agency of ethnicity in America is very clear in the comparison between people of color and European immigrants. However, a special case arises, as we shall see in chapter 1, when native white Americans racialize themselves in the nineteenth century as Anglo-Saxons. Interestingly, their most distinctive self-described racial characteristic is that they are, and have always been, the agents of human history.

10. See Blauner, *Racial Oppression*; Cornacchia and Nelson; and Lieberson.

11. Specifically, I am thinking of historical work in the nineteenth and early twentieth centuries, though *ethnic* has more recently been applied to Asian and Hispanic groups in America. *Ethnic* is also occasionally used with reference to black Caribbean immigrants, especially in distinction with "native" African Americans.

12. Among the most helpful broad overviews of race theory have been Michael Banton's *The Idea of Race* (1977) and James McKee's *Sociology and the Race Problem: The Failure of a Perspective* (1993). However, it has been the extensive, landmark history of racial discourse by Thomas Gossett, *Race: The History of an Idea in America* (1963), that stands out for me in this field.

13. Sollors reads Twain's *A Connecticut Yankee in King Arthur's Court* (1889) as an example of a literary analysis using ethnicity. Revealing how the relationship between the Yankee and King Arthur's Court is cast in metaphors of other racialized historical relations, such as Southern slaveholders and slaves or white settlers and American Indians, his goal is to show that "[a] canonical text illuminates the symbolic processes that help to constitute ethnic contrasts" (Sollors, *Critical Term* 303). He notes that while "Mark Twain (MT) does not use the word 'ethnicity,' . . . his novel is full of ethnic matter" (291), by which he seems to mean the, mostly cultural, ways that two or more groups distinguish themselves from each other. It is not surprising that, as Sollors points out, the word Twain uses is *race* since *ethnicity*, as Sollors means it, did not exist in Twain's time. Through this substitution, Sollors forecloses on the possibility of a more discursively and historically situated critique. Was Twain

critiquing his contemporaries' conception of racial difference as he did in others of his works? And whether Twain was attempting to suggest that human differences are rooted in culture rather than biology has significant political consequences. These and other questions cannot be raised if ethnicity is used imprecisely and ahistorically to reference group difference in general.

14. Among the most helpful historical work on the subject is Dale Knobel's *Paddy and the Republic: Ethnicity and Nationality in Antebellum America*, which, as discussed in chapter 1, provides a good deal of evidence that the difference between native Anglo-Americans and Irish newcomers was perceived as a racial difference. Conzen et al. refer to Knobel's work and note that it shows "how Americans began viewing the Irish in ethnic terms by the 1850s once they began regarding character as the product of nature rather than nurture" (9). It is unclear why Conzen et al. would use the word "ethnic" here since the main difference between race and ethnicity is precisely that race is a function of nature rather than environment (nurture).

15. Much of my project is modeled after the kind of word histories Raymond Williams wrote, especially in *Keywords*. His etymologies trace the shifting nuances of highly significant words, showing how the terms both reflect and constitute the ideological struggles of British culture. My treatment of the word *ethnicity* similarly attempts to reconstruct the cultural and political ferment from which the term emerges and to which it contributes a crucial element of the ideological possibilities.

16. Though there are significant differences between them, examples of writers on American race who take a structural perspective include Blauner, Bonilla-Silva, Carmichael and Hamilton, Cox, Feagin, Omi and Winant, and Richard Williams. See chapter 2 of Bonilla-Silva's *White Supremacy and Racism in the Post-Civil Rights Era* for an especially lucid clarification of the distinctions among structural race theories and the other various approaches to the study of race in the social sciences.

17. Omi and Winant borrow terminological trouble here in attributing contemporary distinctions between ethnic and racial categories to a time in which these distinctions were still in their formative stages (the focus of chapter 3). Park, for example, like his contemporaries, never used the term *ethnic* but instead referred to his theory as "race relations."

18. While he describes their work as a "theoretical breakthrough" (30) to which his own scholarship is indebted, Eduardo Bonilla-Silva also usefully points to other limitations in Omi and Winant's formulation of racial formation. In addition to suggestions that their view of oppression is reductionist (leaving out reference to the capitalist and patriarchal aspects of the "racial state"), Omi and Winant emphasize representations at the expense of the collective and conflictual nature of racial identities. "By failing to regard races as collectivities with different interests," Bonilla-Silva observes, "their analysis of political contestation over racial projects seems to be quarrels over meanings rather than positions in the racial order" (31). Omi and Winant, Bonilla-Silva further notes, suggest that the hegemonic rearticulation of the U.S. racial state, following the crisis of Civil Rights, is a project of a right-wing, neoconservative coalition. They leave out, however, a comprehensive, structural analysis of the racial formation (31).

1

From the Invention of Race to the Rise of the Inbetween Peoples, 1840–1924

A PREHISTORY OF ETHNICITY

Although it is relatively standard to discuss nineteenth-century European American immigrants as ethnic groups, there is good reason to problematize such usage. *Ethnic* was, after all, relatively uncommon during the time and carried a very different sense than it does today. In fact, as Michael Banton pointed out in 1983, "Until recently, the adjective 'ethnic' has not been used very often in everyday English since the units to which it might be applied usually had alternative and better-established names, like nation, people, or minority" (*Racial* 64). While *ethnic* has, since the early twentieth century, referred to groups defined by culture rather than race, it should be recalled that in the nineteenth century it was the discourse of race that became virtually the only way to frame the question of human difference in America. The idea of group identities defined by cultural traditions and practices is a relatively recent innovation and neither the word nor the conception of ethnicity existed in the nineteenth century. Moreover, the fact that *ethnic* is still rarely used in conjunction with discussions of black culture and identity should pique our suspicion that something else needs to be explained in the exclusive use of this term for European Americans. What the use of *ethnic* with reference to European groups entails but rarely reveals is a history in which ethnicity is created initially as an exclusive privilege of whiteness.

30

More often, it retroactively assigns a stable white identity to groups who could not always take their own whiteness for granted.

And yet developments in the nineteenth century, especially in the area of racial ideology, frame the issue of the race-ethnic distinction and are crucial to understanding how ethnicity was created in the twentieth century. Among the pressing political and historical problems the emerging discourse of race is used to explain in the first half of the 1800s is the question of American national identity. Two distinctly different but overlapping theories developed to explain the nature of the American racial character. The first, favored by native-born Americans[1] of English heritage, proposes that Americans' boldness and unique love of freedom are the result of ancient Anglo-Saxon blood. Whether or not other, lesser races could enjoy the republican gifts that Anglo-Saxon Americans were destined to bring to the world became a question of considerable import. A second theory, frequently favored by non-English white citizens, asserted that an American was the amalgamated mixture of the best of all the races of Europe. The exclusion of Indians, blacks, Asians, and Latinos from both traditions narrowed considerably the conception of who an American might be. But the gap between the theories left the question open for a considerable number of European Americans who could not trace their ancestry to the shores of England or the forests of Germany. Massive immigrant waves of precisely these populations in the nineteenth century would raise the racial question to a crisis point that would not be resolved until the next century. In the process, the new immigrants found themselves in an ambiguous racial category that was neither black nor quite white. Their eventual social assimilation and the gradual, begrudging conferral of white privilege created a theoretical need to explain the nature of their new identity that, as we shall see in subsequent chapters, would eventually be filled by the formulation of ethnicity.

CREATING RACE IN AMERICA

Richard Williams offers a historical account of the shifting relations in the meanings of race and ethnicity in the United States. His argument corroborates Pierre L. van den Berghe's observation on the political basis of the race/ethnicity distinction: race imposes an intransigent position in which mobility is relatively circumscribed while social groups designated ethnic, by contrast, will enjoy greater, although perhaps limited, access to privilege and choice (van den Berghe, *Race* 22). Furthermore, Williams argues that both race and ethnicity are created as a function of the need to legitimate structural inequities in the relations of production. Williams argues that race is employed first since it is already available within the English ideological repertoire at the inception of the North American conquest, though it formerly expressed class, national, and regional differences rather than skin color or biological features. The meaning of race had to be adapted and refashioned for a new situation in North America. Williams explains that the export of humans from Africa was not preconditioned by racist European bias but rather such a bias was created as a justification for using Africans to fill the slave labor slot.

In other words, the determinations for using Africans, rather than Europeans or indigenous peoples (though both served the purpose at various times), to fill the labor needs of a slave economy in seventeenth-century North America did not include skin color. Instead, the overdetermination of Africa as the source for slaves depended on a conjunction of circumstances in Europe, West Africa, and North America in the first half of the seventeenth century. These conditions included: the shift in power relations in the North American colonies from Puritan to Cavalier control that favored large plantations and slave labor rather than small farms with indentured servants; the decline of traditional West African trade routes from the Sahara and the Mediterranean to the Atlantic coast; hierarchical power relations that made it efficacious for the African elite to trade humans for European resources; and a decline in the supply of indentured servants from Europe. Williams's concern is to show that Africans were not imported as slaves because they were black but rather that the slave labor slot had already been created and was filled by Africans for a variety of reasons, none of which had anything to do with skin pigmentation. The dichotomies of identity, black and white, based on color differences and their relative values, inferior and superior, were only fabricated later as a justification for the inequitable structure of labor assignations.

The construction of an Irish identity in the United States furnishes Williams with the paradigm for the way ethnicity in general is created. While Williams's attribution of both race and ethnicity to the periods he describes are premature, his argument is instructive in locating within the dynamics of socioeconomic forces a position for European immigrants between African slaves and native Americans. His work is useful in suggesting the ways in which race and ethnicity, or at least their preconditions and precursors, are interlocked and bound up with questions of power. He argues that what he calls ethnicity is created in a process that is "similar to the process by a which a sector of the African population became Black" (88). Within the context of the development of a world economic system, it is a matter of a complex coordination of multiple determinants in Europe and North America that a significant segment of the lower status Irish population immigrated when it did and was incorporated into a specific labor slot in the United States. By the mid-nineteenth century, emerging industrialism was replacing merchant capital and the rise of factories was overtaking production in the home. These developments brought with them the need for low wage, unskilled labor. Furthermore, the resistance of native-born, skilled craft workers to the emergence of industrialism made it advantageous for capital to displace them as the core of productive labor. At the same time, conditions in Ireland, such as the Great Famine and displacement of small farmers, created a surplus population desperate for the sort of immediate remuneration that wage labor could supply. Thus, similar to the case of African slavery, only a unique set of international circumstances, the creation of a specific kind of labor market in one place and the appearance of a population suited to fill it in another, resulted in the emigration of a sector of the Irish to the United States between 1840 and 1860.

The transition from Ireland to the United States resulted in the Irish moving "from being the lower race (Irish and Catholic as opposed to English and Protestant) into the lower slot of the upper race (Irish and White as opposed to African and Black)" (Williams 87). The result of the introduction of the Irish into the relations of production is also, for Williams, responsible for the creation of ethnicity. In a system where free labor had already been marked off from unfree labor by the color line, another index of vertical stratification became necessary to discriminate between skilled and unskilled labor where color difference did not exist. As Williams writes, "Because the entire society was already premised upon skin pigment as the most fundamental mark of classification, there were not two distinct conceptions of race, but rather class and then ethnicity (religion, language, culture) became the mark of vertical classification within that social system, which was built upon the free labor slot" (86). Thus race exists prior to ethnicity and becomes its precondition (2).

Williams makes a compelling case for seeing race and ethnicity in the broader context of the social structure in which they operate and the related idea that they are inextricable from dynamics of social and economic power. His work is very suggestive in supplying the historical background for the hierarchical asymmetry between the two terms already asserted by writers such as van den Berghe and Takaki (as discussed in the introduction to this book). And we can adopt his insight that race is the precondition for ethnicity in the sense that the latter takes shape within a social and ideological framework organized by racial difference. But Williams is less than precise in his application of terms because his study does not include a history of the uses of the words *ethnicity* or *race*. While he is on more defensible ground when he argues that the processes he is describing results in the seventeenth-century creation of white and black identities, he too easily equates these with racial categories. Williams's assumption that these racial identities themselves remained fixed, such that the Irish are always in the same unchanging white race as Anglo-Americans, is likewise problematic. In fact, native Americans, at the time in which Williams refers, would not always have agreed with his assumption that the Irish were white or, at least, white like them. On the matter of the origins of race more generally, Michael

Banton's history of its changing meanings leads him to the conclusion that "it is a serious misconception to assume that the idea of race was generated in the interaction between whites and blacks in the New World" (*Racial* 38). While it may sound counterintuitive or like splitting hairs to insist on a more complex and mediated relation between skin color difference and the concept of race, it is important to the history of ethnicity to diagram these developments carefully.

It is fair to say that the roots of race may be traced as early as the sixteenth century, when Europeans began conceptualizing fundamental differences between themselves and the peoples of the New World and Africa. Scholars further suggest that such divisions, as well as a hierarchy that presumed European superiority over all others, in large measure responded to the need to rationalize the massive theft of land, lives, and labor that became the basis of Western expansion.[2] There is also broad scholarly agreement that the creation of ideologies of difference followed, rather than preceded, the point of contact and the practical, acquisitive purposes they served.[3] But to say that the concepts of difference before the late eighteenth century were racial is probably premature. To be sure, *race,* in the sense of bloodline and descent, has been in the English language since the sixteenth century. But it was not in common usage until the mid-1800s. Citing Winthrop D. Jordan's classic study, *White Over Black,* Banton points out that before 1776 there are no examples in North America of the use of *race* to designate groups of people. Moreover, English settlers did not begin to refer to themselves as white until after approximately 1680, instead of simply *Christians, English,* or *free;* and the term *Negro* was not supplemented with *black* or *African* until the eighteenth century (Banton, *Racial* 37). Joe Feagin reminds us that an ideology of color developed gradually, whereby the various shades of brown and tan European skins were called "white" and the various shades of African skin colors were reduced to "black." Undoubtedly guiding these heavily coded color choices, with their associations of good and evil respectively, was an evolving hierarchical social system based on black slavery (Feagin 75).

Not until the late 1700s and early 1800s did race become central to the conception of human difference. More specifically, it was race in the sense of a fundamental, biologically based division between human types. Audrey Smedley has further detailed the five-part definition of race that became the predominant way of understanding human difference in the nineteenth century. When Americans began to think in terms of race, when it entered popular consciousness and organized Americans' sense of self and their relation to others, it included most or all of these conditions:

1. racial divisions are distinct and universally applicable to all humans;
2. racial categories are hierarchical;

3. the races are characterized by distinct physical features and mental, moral, and behavioral traits;
4. race is heritable;
5. the races are permanent features of God's design for the natural world. (Smedley 26–27)

Race thus carried a fairly specific set of boundaries during the time in question. And while Williams offers many useful guidelines for analyzing the social and historical circumstances in which ideologies of race and ethnicity emerge, his attention to the historical specifics of those ideologies is less than precise. His focus is rather more on the dynamics of class exploitation in the sphere of production. Left out of his analysis are the ways racial and ethnic categories operate in social life beyond the economic. In part, perhaps, this shortcoming stems from the familiar tendency to see racial categories as merely the side effects of stratification within the evolving relations of production and the division of labor.[4] In any event, Williams's structural approach is useful in suggesting that race makes ethnicity possible or, in other words, that ethnicity is a function of the wider arena of American racial politics. But plotting more precisely how this might be the case requires a greater attention to the terms' appearance and meaning in discourse.

THE ENVIRONMENTAL THEORY OF DIFFERENCE

Even though much of what Williams provides should be kept, a more precise understanding of the development of ideologies of identity requires greater attention to the textual detail of the historical record. And what that record reveals is that biological conceptions of race do not come to dominate theories of identity until the third or fourth decade of the nineteenth century. Until then, it is rather the biblically supported theory of monogenesis, the narrative of human origins, that explains how all peoples derive from a single Adamic source, that organized Europeans' understanding of their relation to Africans and the indigenous people of North America. Groups were different and hierarchical as a result of events since Creation, such as sin or "improper unions" (Banton, *Racial* 37), or differences in their natural environments. Biblically based monogenesis was further reinforced by Enlightenment notions of the universal nature of humanity.

Thus, in the mid-eighteenth century, the emerging theory of polygenesis, that non-Europeans were inferior because they derive from a separate origin, was ridiculed and denounced as heresy by the leading minds of the day. In his history of the concept of race, Thomas F. Gossett argues that the biblical influence was still so strong in the first part of the nineteenth century that "the idea that the Negroes might be a 'distinct race' was then associated with atheism and blasphemy" (44). Even Linnaeus, for example, whose early eighteenth-century system of classifying would provide the basis for the "scientific racism" of the nineteenth century, considered the major groupings of humans merely varieties within the same species. Likewise, Johann Friedrich Blumenbach, who would in the 1770s provide the West with the standard four- or five-part division of humankind (into Caucasian, Mongolian, American, Ethiopian, and Malay), never doubted the unity of the human species. Thomas Jefferson, however, may have anticipated the thinking of the next generation in his famous remarks from 1787, that the mental, moral, and physical inferiority of "the negro" is "not the effect merely of their condition of life" but "the difference is fixed in nature" (340, 337). Yet the tentative way in which he finally frames his assertions suggests the tenuous hold such thinking had in the late eighteenth century: "I advance it, therefore, as a suspicion only, that the blacks, whether originally a distinct race, or made distinct by time and circumstances, are inferior to the whites in endowments both of body and mind" (Jefferson 341).

For Jefferson's contemporaries, physical differences between groups of people could best be accounted for by environmental factors such as climate, diet, and even altitude. The Reverend Mr. Samuel Stanhope Smith was the most influential authority on race in America in the late eighteenth century, and his book, *An Essay on the Causes of the Variety of Complexion and Figure in the Human Sciences*, was the "first major American work on racial differences" (Horsman 99). Smith was articulating the consensus of the period: human differences are sufficiently complex that the attempt to divide humanity into distinct races is a waste of time (Gossett 40). It is, in fact, Smith argues, "contrary to the laws of true philosophy to resort to the hypothesis of different original species of men in order to explain varieties which can otherwise be accounted for by the known operation of natural causes" (22).

OVERCOMING MONOGENESIS

Thus the concept of race in the sense of a distinct species-like division between humans had yet to dominate within the discourse of human differences in the early nineteenth century. Nor yet can we too hastily leap with Williams from the construction of a particular Irish identity in the nineteenth century to the assumption that this was an ethnic identity in any meaningful contemporary sense. As a matter of chronology, neither the word nor, by extension, the concept of ethnicity will emerge until a great deal later. It might be said that the "environmentalism" of the late eighteenth and early nineteenth centuries' conception of difference foreshadows, in a sense, twentieth-century conceptions of ethnicity, insofar as they assume a common humanity whose distinctions are a mere matter of variations resulting from nurture rather than nature. But it must be noted that the environment in question was generally the natural, rather than the humanly or culturally constructed, world. Nor did the word *ethnic* then refer to the kind of cultural variation that Williams means to indicate, but rather it reflected the religious framework within which identity was still configured in the late eighteenth century. *Ethnic* referred to the Other beyond the Judeo-Christian pale. According to dictionaries of common American usage from the first half of the nineteenth century, the primary sense of the word refers to those who are neither Christian nor Jew, that is to say "heathen or pagan." And, as the meaning of the word shifts in the first half of the nineteenth century, it moves even further away from its contemporary sense as a marker of the cultural. That is, by the mid-nineteenth century, *ethnic* acquires a secondary meaning in which it is synonymous with *race*, or "relating to the races or classes of mankind" (Webster). At the same time, *ethnography* and *ethnology* enter the lexicon as the "science which describes the different races of men, or a work on that science" (Webster).[5] Thus, the term that will eventually provide the base of *ethnicity* reflects the general shift in the early decades of the 1800s in which the ideology of human differences is increasingly racialized.

Yet the scientific theory of race which asserts that human variation is a matter of fundamental divisions on the order of separate species, as well as the assumption that such distinctions are hierarchically ordered, met its strongest theoretical resistance from the concept of monogenesis. Given the firm grounding that monogenesis enjoyed in scriptural authority, the question is how it could have been overcome by the 1840s when scientific race reaches its definitive position over American understandings of human difference. One reason for the usurpation of monogenesis is that the Enlightenment, which provided philosophical support for the idea of the unity of humanity as well as its infinite perfectibility, provided, at the same time, a double edge insofar as it accelerated the secularization of Western thought. Reginald Horsman argues that by "separating science from theology [Enlightenment thinkers] opened the way for science to reach entirely different answers from those of [Christian orthodoxy]" (46). Moreover, while the pursuit of knowledge in the eighteenth century through efforts to identify and classify revealed the interconnectedness of Creation, the same project in the nineteenth century demonstrated the divisions between the world's categories (Horsman 46).

But while the rise of polygenesis is part of the broader currents in American and Western thought, the assault on monogenesis was supplied, at the same time, by practical considerations proper to early nineteenth-century American political and economic development.[6] Namely, Indian resistance to western expansion and the defense of slavery in the South were compelling inducements for the articulation of a theory that proved the inherent difference and inferiority of both Indians and blacks. As Horsman asserts, "In the West violence engendered by the white advance was used to condemn the Indians who had been provoked to resist; in the South the degradation engendered by slavery was used as a justification for continuing the enslavement" (115). In fact, the theory of polygenesis, which is a corollary to race science's principle of distinct species, coincides with the first European encounters with the New World inhabitants in the early sixteenth century (Horsman 45). So compelling was the need to provide a theoretical rationale for the permanent inferiority of blacks and Indians that, as Horsman suggests, even committed monogenesists found ways to reconcile race science with Scriptures (133–34). Horsman proposes that the theory of monogenesis, often too sensitive an issue to be confronted head-on, was not so much overturned with the rise of race science as it was overlooked and carefully sidestepped. Direct assertions of polygenesis remained controversial through the mid-nineteenth century even while the assumption of inherent differences between the races became a matter of common sense. Even the majority of abolitionists, whose arguments had previously relied on monogenesis and the environmental explanation of difference, by mid-century accepted the fundamental assumptions of the racialists' ideological terrain. The slavery debate of the 1830s was fought "between environmentalist defenders of a single human nature and proponents of deep-seated racial differences," but by the 1840s, both sides "tended increasingly to start from a common assumption that the races differed fundamentally" (Fredrickson 101).

RACIAL NATIONALISM

That even most abolitionists by the 1840s had abandoned the assumptions of an undivided human race provides a gauge for the power of the emerging discourse of racial difference. They accepted the premise of fundamental racial distinctions and counterposed the essential nature of the Negro, based in a childlike and truly Christian innocence, against the immoral brutality of enslaving them. This position is the origin of what George Fredrickson calls "romantic racialism," the acceptance of racial essentialism without the kind of hierarchical ordering that ranks the races in terms of superiority and inferiority. Instead, each race has its own unique gifts that characterize it and distinguish it from all others. This ideology, whose articulation is associated with the philosophy of Johann Gottfried von Herder, was increasingly popular in the early nineteenth century in America and Europe and provides another stream for the ascendancy of race theory. Most frequently, it was used to advance the ideal of American national unity. Ironically, despite the fact that Herder held the Enlightenment conception of the unity of humanity, his theories were taken as further support for the fundamental division between peoples. His work also became the basis for the identification of nation with race and helped to transform the concept of nation from a political structure to a distinct cultural and biological unity rooted in the "Volk," or the unique "tribal community" of a nation's common people (Horsman 27).

While the ideology of romantic nationalism provided one discursive source for the racialization of American identity, we must also include the rise of Jacksonian, whites-only democracy in the early nineteenth century as another major contributor to this process. What is interesting to note in this context is the seemingly paradoxical conjunction of popular egalitarianism with explicit white supremacy. Fredrickson argues that while the Jacksonian movement was not the only cause for the rise of democratic ideology in the antebellum North, it nevertheless promoted democratic ideology "to an extreme almost unparalleled in American political history, while at the same time condoning a form of anti-Negro demagoguery that anticipated the Southern race baiters of a later era" (90). Fredrickson explains this apparent contradiction by suggesting that the basis for the conception of a classless popular order is precisely the presence of the Negro in America. Old world distinctions of class become trivial and "artificial" in the encounter with the Negro's radical, "natural" Otherness and inferiority. In the view of Jacksonian propagandists, "this consciousness of the insignificance of differences among whites, when compared to the gulf that yawned between the races, produced the Virginia 'democrats' of the Revolutionary era, who had laid the foundation of egalitarian ideas and practices in the United States" (Fredrickson 93). Such an ideology appealed not only to the Southern defenders of slavery, who based their arguments on the natural hierarchy of the races, but also to the most marginalized elements of American society, such as the poor and immigrant Irish. The ideology of equality and democracy rooted in a common whiteness, that is, "undoubtedly had an appeal not only to the Southern advocates of *Herrenvolk* egalitarianism but also to frustrated and deprived groups in the North who were seeking a way to maintain, against all evidence to the contrary, an image of themselves as equal participants in American society" (Fredrickson 94). Another way to put this observation is to say, as Fredrickson does, that had equality existed in fact, rather than merely in the image projected by ideology, or had existing inequality been recognized as such, "then presumably there would have been less inducement to view the Negro as beyond the pale of humanity and outside the American community" (96). The apparent oxymoron of the white racist egalitarianism of Jacksonian democracy also constitutes one of the many instances in which the black presence provides a reference point for the nullification of differences among European Americans.

Romantic nationalism and Jacksonian white herrenvolk democracy thus converge to further racialize the conception of American identity. In so doing, both ideological frameworks also manifest what Fredrickson identifies as the underlying "psycho-social" desire for homogeneity. Indicative for Fredrickson of this urge is the romantic racialist, antislavery constituency who rejected the more radical abolitionist demand for the eventual inclusion of emancipated blacks into the union. The antebellum "free-soil" movement, which would become the basis for the Republican party, likewise espoused a homogeneous society and opposed slavery primarily on the basis that it entailed the continued presence of blacks in a "white man's country." Each of these political tendencies provided support for the highly popular "colonization" movements, which proposed, repeatedly throughout the nineteenth century, various schemes to export and expel the nation's blacks to Africa or South America. Thomas Jefferson, for example, had suggested in 1785 the deportation of America's freed slaves, and the importation "of an equal number of white inhabitants" from other parts of the world to fill the vacancies (336). Lincoln had gone further and was formulating a policy in 1862 to relocate America's blacks to Panama when he abandoned the plan as impractical (Fredrickson 150). His justification, like that of Jefferson's, was that the peaceful coexistence of two such distinct races as white and black was simply unthinkable. Thus, as Fredrickson argues, "a hope for homogeneity by some means other than intermarriage has been an important element in white racial speculation throughout all or most of American history" (131n). The origin of the "psycho-social force" for homogeneity, he suggests, is a supposed homogeneity of white Americans' European homelands (Fredrickson 131). Unlike Latin American colonies in the New World, Northwest European societies' conception of racial uniformity rejected the possibility of intermarriage. As a result, Fredrickson suggests, "one would expect that in English North America the white desire for homogeneity would be reflected most dramatically in expectations of Negro removal or elimination" (131). Even those groups most consistently opposed to colonization, such as slaveholders and those who otherwise depended on the exploitation of blacks, experienced a kind of "pseudo-homogeneity" by regarding racial Others as foreign elements. The "egalitarian ethos" of Jacksonian ideology "seemed to require that the Negro be regarded, not merely as an alien, but as a creature not quite human" (Fredrickson 132).

While a desire for racial homogeneity in American society was in evidence in the early nineteenth century, Fredrickson seems to ignore his own evidence for plotting the emergence of this desire with greater historical specificity than he implies is possible. Any transhistorical desire for homogeneity should have been satisfied with the previous paradigm, which guaranteed the unity of humanity in both Enlightenment philosophy and the Adamic myth of monogenesis. Moreover, the claim that the desire for racial purity is rooted in ancestral memory cannot be reconciled with recent scholarship that demonstrates the heterogeneous social and political formations European immigrants left behind. As Conzen et al. suggest, "Immigrant groups themselves were by no means homogeneous; they were divided by varying combinations of regional origin, dialect, class, politics, and religion" (5). And as John Higham notes, the European peasants and villagers (like the Africans) arrived not with national identities but with more localized identities defined undoubtedly through their difference from a welter of other local identities. In other words, "They were not Germans but Wurttembergers, Saxons, and Westphalians; not Italians but Neapolitans, Sicilians, Calabrians, and Genoese; not Chinese, but members of particular districts and clans" (Higham, *Send* 177). Similarly, Anglo-Americans derive from a region whose history is organized around a variety of heterogeneous group divisions. Fredrickson never questions the stable givenness of whiteness nor the equation of a blanket whiteness with all of Europe. But as we shall see, the racialization of all group identities and the contingencies of nineteenth-century social development created a host of problems regarding not only racial divisions between Europeans but also the question of exactly who was white and, therefore, who was American.

Thus the issue of a social compulsion for racial purity becomes a question of the specific terms in which it is conceived and the historical conditions that frame the options. In the case of the desire for racial homogeneity that emerges in white America in the opening decades of the nineteenth century, we can specify at least four primary preconditions. First, a desire for racial purity presumes a conception of race that can become impure by the admixture of other, fundamentally different races, a formulation that does not become widely available until the third or fourth decade of the nineteenth century. That is, racial homogeneity only makes sense in relation to racial diversity, an unthinkable thought before the popularization of polygenesis as a way to explain how the human race might be subdivided into separate sub-races. Second, a popular wish for the racial uniformity of the nation depends on a popular conception of nation and national identity. Despite a relatively brief period of national unity during the Revolution, the formation of a United States, as Winthrop Jordan reminds us, was by no means a foregone conclusion nor was it universally desired (315). Third, as Fredrickson himself clearly demonstrates, the articulation of the white racial character of American identity only appears once the elements of a racial discourse become available and are deployed in response to abolitionists' claims for black freedom, equality, and citizenship. Finally, the waves of European immigration in the 1830s and 1840s, predominantly from Ireland, raised alarms about the boundaries of whiteness and thus the racial basis of American identity. If the Irish question did not change the desire for white homogeneity, it demonstrates that the specific formulation of the whiteness desired is not obvious and contingent on a multiplicity of factors.

"OUR ANGLO-SAXON-AMERICAN RACE"

Even if we cannot assume the idea of some kind of transhistorical human desire for social homogeneity, much less in what that homogeneity might consist, evidence suggests that such a desire becomes a historical force in the first part of the nineteenth century and is articulated through the emerging discourse of race. The discourse of racial difference, which asserted that humans could be divided into separate subspecies and, for many writers, ranked hierarchically, had many uses including the defense of slavery and western expansion. Eventually, by the 1840s, it had become so pervasive and so deeply embedded in the foundations of American thought that, ironically, racial ideology was used as well to argue against practices like slavery and the policy of western expansion. But the new racial theories were also thoroughly intertwined with the question of American national identity. In this aspect, American discussions about race borrowed heavily from European sources where race theory was likewise bound up with questions of nation. But historical circumstances specific to America framed the issue of national identity in a unique way. First of all, the question of American identity was only raised as a result of the Revolution and its success. As Jordan points out, it is only with independence that a need to define the "national self" arises at all (335). In the Revolutionary period and after, the issue takes on paramount importance: "The country emerged from the war politically independent but precariously unified, and the most crucial question of the postwar years was that of national union" (Jordan 335). The Revolution provided a partial answer to the question of American identity over which there was general consensus. That is, most Americans agreed that the country should be based on republican principles; its government should be "non-monarchical, balanced and checked, and representative of the people in whom resided ultimate sovereignty" (Jordan 332).

But the formulation of Americans' "republican genius" was only a political answer to the question of the national character. Clarifying the cultural distinctiveness of Americans presented a considerable problem because of their contradictory relation with England; Americans were politically independent but, at the same time, economically and culturally dependent. Originally, the majority of settlers to North America "had often thought of themselves primarily as colonial Englishmen" (Jordan 335). Even the non-English European immigrants were absorbed by the pervasive English influence. As one observer surmised in 1745 upon his observation of the assimilation of his Swedish countrymen, "the English are evidently swallowing up the people" (qtd. in Jordan 338). Jordan notes that "by the Revolutionary era, many of the non-English peoples in the American colonies had lost much of their cultural distinctiveness to the voracious dominance of English language, customs, and institutions, and their original genetic character to English numerical superiority" (338). In the period following the Revolution, Americans were dependent on England in the most fundamental ways. They spoke English and the majority of American institutions, such as "family, churches, learned societies, and representative government," were based on English models (Jordan 336). Yet, with the Revolution and political independence, the traditional self-image of Americans as English colonials was suddenly invalid. Thus, as Jordan notes, "to proclaim convincingly non-Englishness as an accomplished fact was at once essential and impossible; the clash between political independence and the inertia of cultural heredity made for uncertainty and ambivalence" (336). The question became how Americans might resolve this contradiction so central to the definition of their national identity: "to deny that they were English without denying their English heritage" (Jordan 336).

For a time, the terms of the environmental theory for group difference provided one approach to the dilemma. The theory allowed Americans to accept their English heritage but attribute to the New World those forces that had remade the colonial Englishman into something new and better and that would continue the improvement (Jordan 336). Drawing on the "environmentalist posture" in this manner made it possible for Americans to satisfy "the need both to embrace and repudiate their own Englishness" (Jordan 336). But as the environmental explanation of difference gave way to racial explanations in the early decades of the 1800s, so too did environmental explanations of American identity cede their place to racialized conceptions. In the process, the particular problem of delineating American distinctiveness in the shadow of England seems to have become less prominent despite continued hostilities with the mother country. In fact, as the larger problem of American national identity is increasingly perceived as a racial project in the early nineteenth century, white Americans begin to emphasize their common Anglo-Saxon ancestry with the English. Such an identity was clearly in evidence among the Revolutionary generation who distinguished the English people from the English government, acknowledging an affinity with the former and contempt for the latter. Reginald Horsman notes that "in the very act of revolution the Revolutionary generation believed they were reinforcing their links with their Anglo-Saxon ancestors while separating from the government of Great Britain" (23). American intellectuals of the Revolutionary period, such as Thomas Jefferson, believed in a mythic, freedom-loving Saxon people whose ancient democratic institutions offered the highest ideals for the fledgling nation. Jefferson believed that Americans descended from the Anglo-Saxons and hoped the government of the new nation would restore the Saxon liberties of English government that had existed before the corrupting influences of the Norman invasion of 1066 (Horsman 20).

In the late eighteenth century, Americans conceived their links to their Anglo-Saxon forebears as a matter primarily of institutional continuity rather than race. The first instance Horsman finds of "Anglo-Saxon" used in an expressly racial sense in America is not until 1826 (165). In the twenty years that followed, however, a conjunction of forces inspired the rapid and widespread acceptance of a racialized conception of Americans' Anglo-Saxon identity. As Horsman notes, "The use of *Anglo-Saxon* in a racial sense, somewhat rare in the political arguments of the early 1830s, increased rapidly later in the decade and became commonplace by the mid-1840s" (208–9). This sudden shift was the overdetermined result of several ideological and political developments. Among those developments was, of course, the rise of racial discourse that divided and ranked the races. Despite disagreements between European Americans, most concurred on the superiority of the Caucasian race and, for those who accepted further subdivisions, the superiority of the Anglo-Saxon branch of the Caucasians. As scientific race developed, "in western Europe and America the Caucasian race became generally recognized as the race clearly superior to all others; the Germanic was recognized as the most talented branch of the Caucasians; and the Anglo-Saxons, in England and the United States, and often even in Germany, were recognized as the most gifted descendants of the Germans" (Horsman 43–44). Romantic nationalism, for its part, with its ideas about the unique essence of each national identity, allowed Americans to imagine their society and destiny as the expression of an Anglo-Saxon racial essence. The rise of an influential racialized linguistics in the early 1800s also disseminated, in a learned scholarly guise, a flattering myth about the noble origins of Americans' ancestors. German philologists, working from the assumption that racial patterns could be traced through linguistic affinities, provided Americans with an image of themselves as the children of "a specific, gifted people—the Indo-Europeans—who spilled out from the mountains of central Asia to press westward following the sun, bringing civilization, heroism, and the principles of freedom to a succession of empires" (Horsman 32).

With such grandiose ideological elements available, it required only a dire political conflict to apply them to the formulation of national policy. Horsman argues that the conflicts in the Southwest, especially the Mexican War of 1846–1848, were the "catalyst in the overt adoption of a racial Anglo-Saxonism" (208). Having beaten the militarily weaker country and marched into the "halls of Montezuma" in Mexico City, the issue became the disposition of the Mexican territory. A major factor in the decision not to annex all of Mexico, as opposed to merely its northern half, was American repugnance at having to accept Mexicans, a "mongrel race," into the white nation. Opposition to American expansion came from those Americans who "did not want to bring large numbers of non-Anglo-Saxon peoples as equal citizens within the American union" (Horsman 231). In support of expansion, the famous phrase "manifest destiny" had been coined in 1845 to rationalize the annexation of Texas, and it quickly became part of the discourse about the innate racial tendency of Anglo-Saxons to conquer their inferiors. Previously, territorial expansion had been further justified as the sacred mission of the American Anglo-Saxons to free humankind by sharing their traditions and institutions of liberty. This argument retained the Enlightenment optimism about universal human improvability. Increasingly, however, it was argued that only Saxon blood had the capacity to withstand the rigors of the democratic enterprise. To the myth of manifest destiny was appended the subplot involving all other races: they were doomed either to eventual extinction, like the Indian, or to become the servants of the superior race, like the Negro. By the mid-1840s, it was generally assumed that the prerequisite for free government was Anglo-Saxon heritage. As an American politician of the time surmised, it "seems to be something in our laws and institutions peculiarly adapted to our Anglo-Saxon-American race, under which they will thrive and prosper, but under which all others wilt and die" (qtd. in Horsman 227).

THE AMERICAN RACE: THE OTHER AMERICAN WHITENESS

While the rapid ascendancy of racialized Anglo-Saxonism laid its claims to the quintessential definition of American national identity in the first half of the nineteenth century, such a view did have its dissenters, even among white Americans. A second tradition of the American racial identity had quietly grown up alongside the Anglo-Saxon version. This alternative conception did not dispute that America was exclusively a "white man's country," but it provided a different historical myth of origin and a different racial constitution. Sometimes referred to as the "American race," and later the Melting Pot theory,[7] this tradition proposed that the uniqueness of Americans rested on the fact that they were derived from the best of all the Europeans, rather than merely one strain. St. John de Crèvecoeur is often credited with one of the earliest descriptions in 1782 of this conception:

> Whence came all these people? They are a mixture of English, Scotch, Irish, French, Dutch, Germans, and Swedes. From this promiscuous breed, that race now called Americans have arisen. . . . What then is the American, this new man? He is either an European or the descendant of an European; hence that strange mixture of blood, which you will find in no other country. I could point out to you a family whose grandfather was an Englishman, whose wife was Dutch, whose son married a French woman, and whose present four sons have now four wives of different nations. . . . Here individuals of all nations are melted into a new race of men, whose labours and posterity will one day cause great changes in the world. (qtd. in Jordan 336)

While this kind of amalgamation was, in fact, occurring, Crèvecoeur was expressing a distinctly uncommon view for his own time (Jordan 337–38). As noted above, the overwhelming influence of English culture and language gave Europeans the impression they were being Anglicized rather than melted into a new breed.

Thus, as Jordan notes of late eighteenth-century Americans, they "had good reason for thinking of themselves as modified Englishmen rather than as products of a European amalgam" (339). The sudden rise in German and Irish immigration in the 1830s and 1840s, in fact, provided further impetus to emphasize the narrower, Anglo-Saxon basis of American racial ancestry. Anxieties about the European newcomers were tempered insofar as "most Americans had faith that the multiplying Anglo-Saxons could easily absorb other European stocks, particularly those of Teutonic origin; but already some were indicating a desire to preserve their own status and economic interests through a strong emphasis on racial exclusiveness" (Horsman 225). Moreover, by the late 1840s, as race science became more elaborate and its racial categories and divisions more refined, it became common to distinguish between the various branches of the Caucasian race and to sort them hierarchically, usually with the Anglo-Saxons at the top. The prominent American "ethnologist" Josiah Nott, for example, asserted that the highest forms of civilization were the result of German blood and that, by contrast, "the dark-skinned Celts are fading away before the superior race, and that they must eventually be absorbed" (qtd. in Horsman 131). In some instances, it was granted that all Germanic peoples had the innate spirit of liberty that distinguished them from other races, but within that group, "only the Anglo-Saxons had shown the ability to transform the gift into effective political institutions" in order to conquer and rule the world (Horsman 174). The identification of forms of government with racial characteristics, as if the one were the expression of the other, would also have profound implications for questions of American identity and citizenship. For if Americans were Anglo-Saxons and Anglo-Saxons were now the only people capable of maintaining republican government, on what grounds could any group other than Anglo-Saxons be admitted?

Yet, at the same time, Crèvecoeur's vision of a broadly European Americanism had a strong appeal to "some nationalists and to Irish-American politicians who hated the English" (Horsman 93). American animosity toward Britain throughout most of the nineteenth century was qualified by expressions of racial kinship but also provided impetus for a conception of white American identity that was less closely related and superior to England. The alternative, European amalgam of the American race was equally as contemptuous of inferior races and often attributed to itself the same qualities as the Anglo-Saxons (Horsman 146). Nor was the American race any less organized around a compulsion for white racial homogeneity. Though it was an uncommon formulation, in 1846 Thomas Hart Benton offered "Celtic-Anglo-Saxon" as the more exact plotting of Americans' racial category. The difference between the two conceptions of American identity was that, on the one hand, "Anglo-Saxonists said that the Americans were Anglo-Saxons, and that Anglo-Saxons were the best endowed of all the Caucasians": on the other hand, "proponents of an American race said that the Americans were superior to the English in race as well as in institutions" (Horsman 251). The confluence of historical events and the emergence of racial discourse resulted in the contestation of American identity between two competing conceptions:

> By the late 1840s most Americans either thought of themselves as the descendants of English immigrants, speaking English, bound together by a common culture and a talent for government, or they thought of themselves as a superior, distant "American" race, drawn from the very best of the stocks of western and northern Europe. The former argument was clearly in the ascendancy, but there were indications by the early 1850s that the idea of the Americans as a distinct race might challenge the Anglo-Saxon theorists. (Horsman 301–2)

This challenge would be postponed until the twentieth century, however, as the immigrant sources in the second half of the nineteenth century shifted to southern, central, and eastern Europe and created difficulties for proponents of the "American race" alternative.[8] As Horsman suggests, "Even those who had been attracted by the idea of a superior 'American' race balked at the idea of the creation of a 'mongrel' America with traits drawn from a mass of new immigrants" (302). But in the mid-nineteenth century, the existence of conflicting interpretations of American racial identity placed non-English European Americans in an ambiguous position. One discourse rejected them while the other held out the vague promise of inclusion.

RACIALIZING THE IRISH

Perhaps the first of the European groups to be caught in this contradictory racial space, created in the contradictions and inconsistencies of competing racial ideologies, were the Irish immigrants who began to arrive in significant numbers in the 1830s and 1840s. Though Germans, too, increased their numbers in the same period, they seem largely to have escaped the racial crossfire that was to be the Irish experience. Among other advantages, they could claim a racial kinship with the Anglo-Saxons that eased their passage to American citizenship.[9] But what the qualities and capacities were of the Celtic tribe was a matter of some dispute for a highly speculative, disorganized, and ultimately groundless pseudoscience. And despite Richard Williams's other useful contributions, it is of no use to suggest that the Irish staked out an "ethnic" position in America since it should be clear that nothing quite like such a category in any contemporary sense was thinkable. Having displaced Enlightenment universalism, biblical monogenesis, and the theory of environmentalism, race science was the dominant discourse within which one had to think and, to be taken seriously, within which one had to speak. The application of the term *ethnic*, besides being simply anachronistic, also assumes a later development in which the word would be attributed to those European groups who had secured their whiteness. As such, it obscures the ideological conflict over non-English Europeans' racial positioning. For if only Anglo-Saxons had the right stuff to maintain American republicanism, then all other races, including those from Europe, were not only lesser racially but were inherently unqualified for American citizenship. For some native Americans, this logic led to the conclusion that other groups, such as the Irish, were not only unfit for American citizenship but were also less than white.

Particularly instructive in this regard is Dale T. Knobel's study of the popular discursive construction in the mid-nineteenth century of "Paddy," the Irish American stereotype. Knobel charts the transformation of this figure within the context of the American debate on nationality and the capacity of certain groups, such as the Irish, for citizenship. Despite his careful demonstration of the effects on the Paddy figure as the racial paradigm displaces that of environmentalism, he believes that his project involves the "ethnic" identity of the Irish.[10] Knobel shows the shift in American beliefs about those traits that rendered the Irish unfit for republicanism, such as Catholicism. At first, Irish shortcomings were regarded as the unfortunate result of the Irish homeland that could nevertheless be reformed in the processes of Americanization. The dominant assumption before the mid-1840s of a common human origin meant that human differences were subject to change as a function of environment. In such a context, Irish Americans were no less capable of assuming the proper character for citizenship than Anglo-Americans.

But within a few years, as we have seen in the case of the "Anglo-Saxon-American race," nationality was seen as an essential and inherent quality of a people. As Knobel writes, "More and more often after the mid-1830s, throughout the various popular media, discussions of national character turned into discussions of physical character, inheritance, and 'race'" (107). The proliferation of studies that followed the rise of "ethnology" during this period, such as phrenology, craniology, and physiognomy, all helped to ingrain the ideology of a correspondence between the physical features of a group or individual and characteristics that were mental and moral. For example, phrenologists uniformly asserted that the superiority of Caucasian heads provided a scientific explanation for their triumph over other groups, as in the case of the British in Asia. Some extended such ranking of head differences to support the idea of Anglo-Saxon superiority over other Caucasians. George Combe, one of the most popular and influential phrenologists of the mid-nineteenth century, argued that "the Celtic race was 'far behind the Teutonic,' and the belief was common that the Anglo-Saxons had the most perfect cerebral organization, an organization that placed them above other Caucasians as well as far above the non-Caucasians of the world" (Horsman 58). By the start of the Civil War, the division between the Irish "race" and that of the Anglo-American was considered irreducible and rooted in the physical reality of "blood." Knobel claims that while the discourse of ethnology was appropriated by Southern white supremacists to justify racial slavery, it remained at the service of its initial purpose: "analyzing the distinctions between the 'races' or 'nations' of western and central Europe" (111).

Despite Knobel's careful documentation of the antebellum process by which Irish Americans are constructed as racially Other, he never questions that the Irish are an "ethnic" group during the period and, correlatively, "white."[11] More recent scholarship, however, has thrown doubt over the historical boundaries of whiteness and which side immigrant groups, such as the Irish, were on.[12] David Roediger's groundbreaking work, for example, starts from the evidence that Irish Americans' relationship to whiteness (as well as blackness) was highly ambiguous and unstable in the antebellum period, and the forces that brought the Irish within the bounds of whiteness were multiple and overlapping but never guaranteed. For example, the Democratic Party's need to enlist immigrant votes involved supporting Irish claims of whiteness. The desperate situation of the newly emigrated Irish poor made the security of white privilege too valuable to refuse.

But Roediger insists that the extension of white privilege to the Irish as well as their efforts to seize it should not be reduced to economic, or even political, expediency. Indeed one of Roediger's most important contributions to whiteness studies is his exploration of W.E.B. DuBois's insight that despite their low wages in financial terms, workers obtained a valuable "public and psychological wage" from white identity (qtd. in Roediger, *Wages* 12). For example, Roediger suggestively describes how the Irish path to whiteness involved an anxious projection of their own traits onto blacks that the Irish feared might jeopardize their success as an urban proletariat. Through cultural practices like minstrelsy, the Irish could both embrace and disown a continuity with nature that they both longed for and, to conform to the demands of industrial labor discipline, needed to reject. As Roediger argues, "The Irish immigrants addressed their own divorce from connections with land and nature's rhythms in part by attempting to define preindustrial behavior, and even longing for the past itself, as 'Black' behavior" (*Wages* 153).

The point is that the Irish transformation into equal and unambiguous members of the white race was never secure. Recent scholarship that considers whiteness as much a historically transitional, constructed identity as any other racial category is recovering the degree to which becoming white for groups outside the original Anglo-Saxon core involved a complex series of political, economic, and ideological negotiations. The ambiguous racial position of the Irish in the antebellum period, somewhere between black and white, seems to have been largely resolved in the post–Civil War period as they are incorporated into American institutions as allies of white supremacy. And with the social developments that reconstructed the racial formation to secure the whiteness of the Irish came corresponding theories in the social sciences. For example, in the 1860s Swedish ethnologist Anders Retzius proposed a new way to measure skulls (calculating the "cephalic index" by dividing the length into the breadth) which, he argued, gave us two types: long heads, or the "dolochocephalic," and short heads, or "brachycephaloe." Since the long skulls were typical of northern and western Europeans, while everyone else had short ones, Celts and Saxons were scientifically part of the same race (Gossett 75–76; Knobel 176). Despite such scientific victories, however, it would still be premature to say that the Irish had moved from being a racial group to an ethnic one. They had merely secured a place within the white race by forcing it to redefine its boundaries.

RACIALIZING THE NEW IMMIGRANTS

Several scholars have drawn a comparison between the position of the Irish in the antebellum period and that of the "new immigrants" from south, central, and eastern Europe in the late nineteenth century.[13] Perhaps the process by which the Irish closed ranks with their former Anglo-Saxon antagonists was accelerated by the arrival, in roughly the same period, of immigrants who made the Irish look whiter by comparison. Following John Higham,[14] Barrett and Roediger have suggested that the new immigrants were "in-between" people because of their ambiguous status, like the Irish before them, as neither fully white nor clearly of color. From a heterogeneous collection of popular and official historical sources, including "laws; court cases; formal racial ideology; social conventions; popular culture in the form of slang, songs, films, cartoons, ethnic jokes, and popular theater," Barrett and Roediger observe "that the native born and older immigrants often placed the newer immigrants not only *above* African and Asian Americans, for example, but also *below* 'white' people" (4). The massive waves of immigration from southern and eastern Europe in the 1880s revitalized the discourses of ethnology to once again police the boundaries of whiteness and to take up the task of racializing the arrivals.

The presence of the new immigrants initiated the next crisis of whiteness by forcing the issue of where racial boundaries were to be drawn. And again, along with the answer to the recurring question of who could and could not be Americanized, as in the case of the Irish, it is the racial character of the nation that was at stake. Even though the crisis was eventually resolved through another reconstruction of whiteness, understanding the invention of ethnicity requires us to examine Higham's claim that native Americans' reaction was "the extension to European nationalities of that sense of absolute difference which already divided white Americans from people of other colors" (*Strangers* 132). As we shall see, the contradiction between their excluded racial position and the fact of the new immigrants' eventual assimilation created the need for a new concept of difference.

Despite the development of racial ideology in the first half of the nineteenth century, new theoretical and scientific developments prevented what had already been devised from being recycled in the second half of the nineteenth century. Higham's account suggests that the ideology of the new immigrants' racial difference had to be gradually crafted in the decades before and after the turn of the century in a piecemeal manner out of the most authoritative intellectual fashions of the day. Higham argues that the production of a popular racist ideology suitable to new conditions needed to draw from the intellectual developments of the period: "A rather elaborate, well-entrenched set of racial ideas was essential before the newcomers from Europe could seem a fundamentally different order of men" (*Strangers* 133). However, the intellectual climate of the period from the 1870s to the turn of the century did not make it easy to develop a plausible racist ideology. The problem was that while the spread of Darwinism reinforced the conception that biological laws governed human society, the idea of adaptation also gave much support to environmentalist approaches that, as we have seen, are antithetical to the sense of race as a permanent essence. Increasingly, however, the idea of the survival of the fittest was interpreted by elitist ideologues to imply that human history was determined by the struggle of race against race and that the flood of aliens posed a threat to Anglo-Saxon existence.

One of the more extreme expressions of this sentiment came from E. A. Ross who, in *The Old World in the New* (1914), inflated the concerns about a proportionate rise in the immigrant population into the notion of "race suicide" for the Anglo-Saxons. He feared that because of immigration, "the blood now being injected into the veins of our people is 'sub-common'" (Ross 285) and would eventually lead to the dissipation of the noble Anglo-Saxon race. The problem was that the new immigrant was less evolved than the native stock and, in civilized contexts, it became apparent that "clearly they belong in skins, in wattled huts at the close of the Great Ice Age" (Ross 286). This estimation was confirmed for Ross by a physician who notes, "The Slavs are immune to certain kinds of dirt. They can stand what would kill a white man" (qtd. in Ross 291). Having internalized nineteenth-century scientific racism, Ross can read the racial inferiority of the émigrés directly from their appearance and teaches his readers to do the same:

> To the practiced eye, the physiognomy of certain groups unmistakably proclaims inferiority of type. . . . narrow and sloping foreheads were the rule. The shortness and smallness of the crania were very noticeable. . . . There were so many sugar-loaf heads, moon-faces, slit mouths, lantern-jaws, and goose-bill noses that one might imagine a malicious jinn had amused himself by casting human beings in a set of skew-molds discarded by the Creator. (Ross 286)

Perhaps more inflammatory than many of the anti-immigrant works, Ross's contribution was part of an effort to raise the alarm that the infusion of the new immigrants threatened to pollute the American stock. Such work set the terms of debate for any thinkers who would challenge the racialized denigration of the immigrants. One such challenger whose work is instructive, perhaps, in its failure to capture the attention of a significant audience, is Horace Kallen. Responding directly to Ross's vitriolic attack, Kallen's strategy in his 1915 essay, "Democracy Versus the Melting-Pot: A Study of American Nationality," is to deny that assimilation operates in the manner assumed by either the proponents of the melting pot or those, like Ross, who feared its dangers. Kallen's work exemplifies the fact that *race* and *ethnic type* are still interchangeable terms because key to his argument is that one's ethnic ancestry is a primordial essence that is "the unalterable data of human nature" (Kallen 91). Thus, despite claims on either side of the melting-pot debate, ethnic identity cannot but remain intact. An American can change many aspects of his or her life, but "he cannot change his grandfather" (Kallen 78). Even with social mobility, the European immigrant "remains still the Slav, the Jew, the German, or the Irish citizen of the American commonwealth. Again, in the mass, neither he nor his children nor his children's children lose their ethnic individuality" (Kallen 79). The only question is how to bring order to the "cacophony" of enduring diversity, to which Kallen supplies the metaphor of the harmonious "orchestration of mankind" (92).

It must be noted here that Kallen never meant, however, to extend the metaphor of "a multiplicity in a unity" across the color line, "for there seems to be some difference of opinion as to whether negroes also should constitute an element in this blend" (75). "Thus 'American civilization,'" Kallen suggests, "may come to mean the perfection of the cooperative harmonies of 'European civilization'" (92). Kallen thus rejects, as Higham notes, the Darwinian struggle between the races that animated the xenophobic hostility of writers like Ross (Higham, *Send* 209). However, Kallen's concept of "cultural pluralism" offers a compromise to placate the miscegenation fears of native elites like Ross while simultaneously envisioning a way that southern and eastern European immigrants might be included as equals in the mainstream of American white supremacist hegemony. In the conflict between the two traditions of American identity, Kallen, in effect, proposes a compromise that incorporates features of both. Like advocates of the melting pot, Kallen, who was Jewish, is working within the tradition of the "American race" that is often favored by non-Anglo-Saxon European Americans. Kallen's novel twist, however, is to deny the melting that Crèvecoeur had initially described.

Significantly, however, while cited frequently today in the context of multiculturalism, at the time, Kallen's "doctrine of cultural pluralism made little impression outside of Zionist circles" (Higham, *Strangers* 304). Any other conception of national unity outside the terms of a homogeneous Americanization was still decades away from general acceptance. Moreover, the momentum toward racialized exclusion of the new immigrants overruled the possibility of such a compromise as Kallen proposed. It was not until the importation of English eugenics theory that Anglo-Saxon racism found a form by which it could begin to popularize its anti-immigrant ideas in a way that gave it a more scientific credence than it had yet achieved. Eugenics confirmed the idea of inherent biological qualities and its concerns about the unchecked breeding of inferior and degenerate stock meshed with anxieties about race suicide. Its reformist thrust and claims for the betterment of mankind echoed the spirit of the Progressive Era. But eugenics examined heritability only at the level of individual families, not national or racial groups, and so failed, finally, to deliver an ideology that explained the racial difference of the new immigrants.

Higham argues that the work of William Z. Ripley was instrumental in providing the elements necessary for a full-blown anti-immigrant racism. While professor of economics and geography, Ripley published *The Races of Europe* in 1899, borrowing from the work of contemporary European ethnologists. His concern was with avoiding either environmental or racialist extremes in the debate on the influences of human development and sought rather to understand the relation between the two and the proportions of each in specific circumstances. As one reviewer at the time put it, Ripley's consideration of the influences of physical and social environment, alongside race, "enables him to avoid some points of controversy and to reconcile some others in the dispute between those who interpret any civilization solely in terms of race, and those who consider that race counts for nothing" (Lindsay 127). In fact, "it is the chief service of Dr. Ripley's book that it has brought so many of these debatable questions concerning racial and environmental influences within the scope of scientific classification, and subjected them to positive tests" (Lindsay 127). Yet, as Higham points out, his most influential contribution to the discourse of human difference was his explanation of the racial differences between European groups. He denied that Europeans derived from the same Aryan or Caucasian racial origins. The fact was that "no continental group of human beings with greater diversities or extremes of physical type exists" (Ripley 103). Using a combination of cephalic index, stature, and the color of hair and eyes, Ripley argued that Europeans are divided into three distinct races, each with their own distinct histories: the tall, blond, longheaded Teutonics from the north (of which the Angles and the Saxons were subdivisions); the stocky, roundheaded Alpines from central Europe; and the dark, longheaded Mediterraneans from the south.

As we have seen, the Caucasian or white race had been subject to various racial subdivisions since some of the earliest writings of the American ethnologists but rarely, as in the ambiguous case of the Irish, had these white subdivisions disturbed the four or five major racial divisions laid down since the time of Linnaeus. Ripley's move, however, was to dispense with the notion of the white race on the grounds that such a category is scientifically imprecise. Given the latest findings, Ripley concludes that the phrase "white race" is a "misnomer" (103). He is not unaware that this may run counter to some of his readers' assumptions: "It may smack of heresy to assert, in the face of the teaching of all our text-books on geography and history, that there is no single European or white race of men; and yet that is the plain truth of the matter" (Ripley 103).

While Ripley makes a distinction within what others might consider a unified white race, he does not rule that any subgroup is more or less white. Skin color, he argues, is not a reliable racial marker compared to that of hair and eye color and head shape. Members of "the so-called white race" vary so greatly in skin shades that their "real determinant characteristic is, paradoxically, not the skin at all but the pigmentation of the hair and eyes" (Ripley 61). What struck a chord with his more opportunistic contemporaries and popularizers was Ripley's scientifically plausible explanation for challenging the new immigrants' claims to whiteness. (The fact that Ripley's theories undercut Nordic whiteness with the same blow could simply be ignored.) The most popular expression of the "scientific" racializing of eastern and southern Europeans, in a way that placed them at ambiguous margins of whiteness, comes with Madison Grant's notorious and influential *The Passing of the Great Race* (1916). Grant borrows Ripley's terminology for dividing Europeans into three distinct races (the Nordics, Alpines, and Mediterraneans) and hierarchizes them according to moral value. It is the tall, blond Nordic who is "the white man par excellence" and the only purely European group, while the "swarthy" Alpines and Mediterraneans are "western extensions of Asiatic subspecies" (Grant, *Passing* 27, 167). The Nordic group is the "great race," also ominously "the master race," foreshadowing the later, twentieth-century consequences of racial divisons between Europeans. The Nordics are the race characterized by their tendency for aristocratic leadership, for scientific and geographical discovery, and they are also the race chiefly responsible for civilization. Grant was, of course, merely recycling the older theories of Anglo-Saxon racial superiority but with the veneer of late-breaking science. And borrowing from Ross's idea of "race suicide," he warns that the mixing of racial groups always results in the breeding out of the higher type. Thus Grant's primary concern in the book is that the "racial civil war" (i.e., World War I) added to the unchecked immigration of inferior races, threatening the Nordics with eventual extinction. America's current immigration policies "are sweeping the nation toward a racial abyss" (Grant, *Passing* 263). "If the Melting Pot is allowed to boil without control," Grant warns in his closing lines, then the ideal American type "of Colonial descent" is doomed (*Passing* 263).

The idea that the new southern and eastern European immigrants were racialized as not exactly white, a sentiment that Barrett and Roediger find disseminated throughout a range of discourses of the period, reaches its most pronounced articulation under Grant. Higham attests to the significant influence Grant's book had over the racial ideology of the time. It was from *The Passing of the Great Race* that the "resurgent racism of the early twenties drew its central inspiration" (Higham, *Strangers* 271). Influential within both scholarly and popular circles, "more than anyone else he taught the American people to recognize within the white race a three-tiered hierarchy of Mediterraneans, Alpines, and Nordics, to identify themselves as Nordic, and to regard any mixture with the other two as a destructive process of 'mongrelization'" (Higham, *Strangers* 271–72).

THE JOHNSON-REED ACT AND A NEW WHITE RACE

The culmination of efforts like Grant's to racialize the new immigrants as nonwhite, as if they threatened the racial purity of the American gene pool, was the sweeping immigration restrictions of 1921 and 1924. On the one hand, the opposition came from immigrants themselves and industrialists who watched wages rise in the economic boom that began in the early 1920s and enjoyed the cheap labor pool of unrestricted immigration. On the other hand, some groups, such as the American Federation of Labor and "100 Percent American" groups like the American Legion, were pushing for total exclusion of southern and eastern European immigrants. The Republican congressmen who were sponsoring the legislation were motivated by the ideology of "racial nativism" and were much inspired at the legislation hearings by the testimony of ideologues like Grant.[15] Yet, they could not propose total exclusion, much less on the basis of Nordic superiority, in light of the powerful opposition represented by capital and, as Higham argues, a commitment to appearances of democratic justice (319). The Johnson-Reed Act of 1924 thus strove to maintain the "racial status quo" by limiting immigration from Europe (all Asian immigration was entirely eliminated) to 2 percent of the number of foreign-born residents of each nationality. But since the basis selected for calculating the numbers was the 1890 census, prior to the height of the new immigration, the flow of eastern and southern Europeans was effectively constricted to a trickle while the passage of western European "Nordics" was unaffected.

Barrett and Roediger see the legislation as "a triumph of racism against the new immigrants" (14). It seems clear that the Johnson-Reed Act was an effort to preserve the racial status quo on the part of those who acted out of a particular sense of white racial consciousness and who saw their privileged position threatened by the changing complexion of America. Higham shows that the discourse of "race suicide" and the construction of racial divisions between native, Anglo-Americans and the new immigrants played a major role in the immigration restrictions. At the same time, however, the measures effect a compromise within the hegemonic negotiations of what Omi and Winant call the racial state.[16] There were signs that the enthusiasm for racial nativism was on the wane and, had the legislation been passed only a year or two later, Higham argues, the restrictions would have been much less severe. A booming economy from 1923 to 1929 restored the old confidence in American institutions to assimilate and Americanize the newcomers and relieved much of the concern that they were a threat. "The idea [of racial nativism] remained," Higham suggests, "while the energy drained away" (*Strangers* 326). Even Grant by 1920 conceded a subordinate place within whiteness to the Alpines and Mediterraneans. While the Mediterraneans have only been "imperfectly Nordicized" ("Introduction" xxvii) and thus are unreliable guards against impending Mongol incursions from the east, the Alpine groups have been more fortunate. Grant reassures his readers that "nevertheless, long before the opening of the Christian era the Alpines of western Europe were thoroughly Nordicized, and in the centuries that followed, the old Nordic element in Spain, Italy, and France has been again and again strongly reinforced, so that these lands are now an integral part of the White World" ("Introduction" xxvii).

Thus, at the same time that Johnson-Reed represents the apex of the new immigrants' "inbetween" racialization, several indications suggest that resistance to the admission of the new immigrant to whiteness was weakening. Immigration restriction might consequently be seen as a compromise of the white formation, particularly in light of the demands by some Americans for a total immigration embargo of all but western Europeans (on the grounds of "race suicide" no less). Eastern and southern Europeans would be admitted but the "Nordics" retain hegemony. If we recall the Naturalization Act of 1790, which admitted only the "free white person" for U.S. citizenship, the Johnson-Reed Act also represents a significant, though highly qualified, step toward drawing the boundary of whiteness around all of Europe, rather than within it. That is, the acceptance of even a restricted proportion of Europeans from racially suspect regions for naturalization under U.S. law virtually institutionalizes their whiteness. At the same time, such legal admittance codifies the identity of whiteness and Europe. As Mai M. Ngai has recently argued, rather than the traditional scholarly consideration of Johnson-Reed as an end point, it might also be interpreted as the inauguration of the legal foundation of a new racial configuration. While she concedes that, "at one level, the new immigration law differentiated Europeans according to nationality and ranked them in a hierarchy of desirability," Ngai also points out that, "at another level, the law constructed a white American race, in which persons of European descent shared a common whiteness that made them distinct from those deemed to be not white" (69–70). The exclusion of all non-European immigrants, such as Japanese, Chinese, Mexicans, and Filipinos, renders them permanently foreign and unfit for Americanization and "[erases] them from the American nationality" (Ngai 72). Johnson-Reed's new white racial basis of American national identity suggests a kind of compromise fusion between the two separate traditions of American whiteness that emerged in the late eighteenth century. On the one hand, Johnson-Reed partially capitulates to the old Anglo-Saxon supremacy by determining that it would predominate in the future character of American identity. On the other hand, by admitting the formerly inbetween peoples of outré Europe, at the expense of all other racialized nations, the act envisions an "American race" composed of that European amalgam (though not of equal parts) that Crèvecoeur had described so long before.

CLASS MOBILITY AND THE NEW IMMIGRANTS

Gary Gerstle suggests that by the 1920s the emerging politics of Teddy Roosevelt's "New Nationalism," the precursor of modern liberalism, were, like the Johnson-Reed Act, setting the terms for a new American racial formation. Roosevelt had often taken the controversial position of supporting American citizenship for anyone who could claim European ancestry, including southern and eastern Europeans, on the strict condition that they absolutely Americanize and forswear any allegiances to their former homelands (Gerstle 53). Thus, despite the traditional strength of the Anglo-Saxon (now Nordic) racial schema, growing support for the European amalgam tradition (now the melting pot) that espoused the potential whiteness of all Europeans, made it possible for the new non-Anglo immigrants to recognize themselves as members of the American race. Gerstle suggests that these overlapping but incommensurate conceptions of white American identity, in which they were white in one but less than Nordic white in the other, presented the new immigrants with an illogical but promising syllogism: "If Nordics were white, and the new immigrants were white, why couldn't the new immigrants become Nordic?" (167). In cases in which the determination of whiteness was at issue, the

federal judiciary consistently ruled on the identification of Europe and whiteness, even when the court had to contradict the logic of former rulings or
the leading scientific evidence of the day. As Barrett and Roediger observe,
"Even when much of the citizenry doubted the racial status of European
migrants, the courts almost always granted their whiteness in naturalization
cases" (10).[17] Indeed, the growing acceptance of the new immigrants' whiteness was the function of an overdetermined coordination of economic, legal,
political, and cultural changes. Karen Brodkin Sacks, while looking specifically at the case of Jewish immigrants, puts the question well that should be
asked of each group that would later be seen, and see itself, as white:

> Like most chicken and egg problems, it's hard to know which came first. Did
> Jews and other Euroethnics become white because they became middle class?
> That is, did money whiten? Or did being incorporated in an expanded version
> of whiteness open up the economic doors to a middle-class status? Clearly both
> tendencies were at work. (105)

Along with this dialectic of race and class mobility, scholars have also noted
the importance of Americans of color in the racial transformation of the new
immigrants. Primarily, it is the performance of anti-black racist behavior that
has typically lent a sense of whiteness to those whose racial position was
otherwise in question. Fredrickson, it will be recalled, noted a similar appeal
that racist Jacksonian democracy held for the marginal groups, such as the
Irish, in the early nineteenth century. A major factor in the class mobility of
the new immigrants in the early twentieth century was labor union membership, and the consistent exclusion of black workers undoubtedly helped to
teach the European newcomers the price of color. Phillip S. Foner recounts
the repeated attempts of black workers to pressure the American Federation
of Labor (AFL) to force locals to admit them. At a national convention in
1919, John Lacey asked the AFL leadership, "If you can take in immigrants
who cannot speak the English language, why can't you take in the Negro,
who has been loyal to you from Washington to the battle-fields of France?"
(qtd. in Foner 153). Though Herbert Hill begs the question of the new immigrants' whiteness by reading back over them an anachronistic "ethnicity,"[18]
he shows that "the embrace of white supremacy as ideology and practice
was a strategy for assimilation by European working class immigrants" (6).
As James Barrett notes, "The fact that newer immigrants played little part
in the race riots of the World War I era suggests that it took some time for
them and their children to make these prejudices their own, but their prominent presence in post-World War II racial conflicts demonstrates that many
learned their lessons only too well" (1,006).

Finally, Conzen et al. likewise support the claim that becoming white for
racially borderline immigrants included performing anti-blackness. But these
collaborative authors of "The Invention of Ethnicity" also inadvertently pro-

vide a useful example of the problems that arise from the anachronistic use of ethnicity to analyze a period preceeding the availability of the term. They observe that "European Americans quickly learned that the worst thing one could be in this Promised Land was 'colored,' and they quickly distanced themselves as best they could from this pariah population" (14). To this point the authors add, "The invention of ethnicity also served that function: to define the group in terms of what it was *not*" (14). In other words, the immigrants themselves created an identity they hoped would be recognized as not "colored." By the invention of ethnicity, they mean the content, not the concept, of ethnicity. But the question of an identity's relation to the color line is a racial matter. There would seem to be no justification for the invocation of ethnicity in this case except that it has become the habitual term for nineteenth-century immigrants. Its use here seems merely to obscure social and political dynamics.

Ironically, their own argument depends on the invention of the *concept* of ethnicity, which functions to eliminate the racial ambiguity of those European Americans to whom historians like Conzen et al. can now refer, with confidence, as "white ethnics." They do not feel the need to explain what it was that allowed only European immigrants the designation "ethnic." They note, "In the second quarter of the nineteenth century Americans themselves were engaged in a self-conscious project of inventing a national identity, and in the process found themselves also inventing the category of ethnicity—'nationality' was the term they actually used—to account for the culturally distinct groups in their midst" (6). The writers seem to justify the use of *ethnicity,* despite the fact that it was not the word Americans really used, on the assumption that what Americans actually perceived were cultural differences between groups.

But, as discussed above, by the second quarter of the nineteenth century what we might today recognize as cultural differences were then seen and discussed as racial differences. Indeed, as we have found in the case of Anglo-Saxon identity and Knobel's history of the Paddy figure,[19] the perceptions of malleable cultural differences (or those attributable to environment) congealed by the 1840s into those of immutable biological race. Conzen et al. observe that, at this time, "Anglo-Saxon descent alone offered a secure grounding for a national identity, or so it began to seem to many Americans" (9), a point mentioned above. But "descent," or biological genealogy, was the reason why it was not culture that was at stake but bloodline, which determined who was and was not capable at birth of republican citizenship. As we have seen with other writers as well, such as Knobel, Richard Williams, and Herbert Hill, there is a habit of scholars to misinterpret mid-nineteenth-century America's perception of immigrant differences as "ethnic" (i.e., cultural) differences and to mistake this moment as the discovery or invention of ethnicity. However, to reiterate the point, given the historical record, this moment is better understood as the arrival of the discourse of race science and the first "scientific" division of the white race. It is not until a century later, in the 1940s, as we shall see in chapter 3, that ethnicity is invented in order to resolve the division within whiteness by rewriting racial divisions as cultural. Old divisions within the white race are henceforth forgotten. Ironically, it is this revision (and this forgetting), effected by the invention of ethnicity, that misleads contemporary scholars to retroactively interpret racial divisions in the mid-nineteenth century as merely "ethnic" or cultural.

CONCLUSION

At least since the Naturalization Act of 1790, which specified "free white persons" as the only proper candidates for naturalized citizenship, whiteness and American identity have been closely associated. When the discourse of race rose suddenly to dominate the ideological paradigm of human identity and difference by the 1840s, the link between whiteness and Americanism only solidified. The interlocking theories of monogenesis and environmentalism initially offered hopes of molding and Americanizing those who, like the Irish, arrived unschooled and unsuited to fulfill the demands of republican participation. But as it developed, race science eventually reified racial categories into permanent conditions and did away with all distinctions between the Anglo-Saxon race and Anglo-Saxon civilization. Changing those without the inborn instincts for freedom, such as the Irish or Negroes, or bestowing the divinely granted gift of freedom on racial others, such as the Mexicans, ran counter to the hard truths of science and history.

Yet the existence of another myth of American whiteness that expanded its membership from Anglo-Saxons to Europeans never entirely closed the door of American whiteness to the Irish and, with the help of overriding historical contingencies, they eventually were grudgingly admitted. Richard Williams is correct that the case of the Irish set a kind of precedent in the history of American identity "slots," but it would be skipping crucial discursive and historical steps to see that slot as the creation of ethnicity. Such a concept would require an immense theoretical and discursive apparatus over the course of decades, as we shall see, to assemble and rise to the point at which it could claim sufficient intellectual space beside the imperium of race science. Williams's assertion that the Irish occupied "the lower slot of the upper race," however, is provocative. Further attention to such an intraracial division suggests that if the Irish establish a precedent, it is that of a racial position which is at once European and distinct from black but, for a certain moment, distinct from white as well. This racialization process would repeat itself more virulently in America's encounter with the new immigrants who arrived at the end of the nineteenth century from the remoter regions of the

European continent. They would test the boundaries of whiteness and the limits of the American race and fail.

And yet again, economic and political expediency would wear down the disdainful principles of racial purity and gradually the swarthy Europeans would force the door of American whiteness to open a little wider. Yet, the difference of eastern and southern Europeans from the Anglo-Saxon natives was not erased with the new white racial formation configured in the John-son-Reed Act. Race science had left its traces on them. Somehow, if they were white, the new immigrants were differently white. What was lacking was a language to describe that difference and name the nature of those who seemed so surely on their way to whiteness. In a sense, a kind of gap had opened up between experience and discourse that race science could not close. But, as we shall see in the next chapter, race science, which had ruled the intellectual meaning of human difference in the nineteenth century, would be under substantial attack in the twentieth century. The emerging fields of cultural anthropology and sociology would expose the scientific pretensions of race theory as the superstitions of a bygone age. If it did not entirely clear away and replace those racial predilections, the sociology of race relations, as it would come to be known, would prepare the intellectual space for the possibility of differences within the white race that would, still later, be named ethnicity.

NOTES

1. As per historiographical convention, I use *native American* to mean European Americans born in America, usually of English or Western European ancestry and of more than one generation native-born. This group generally felt a sense of entitlement and ownership of the country, especially in relation to the nineteenth-century immigrants. By *Native Americans*, I mean the indigenous peoples who have called the continent home since before the European conquest.

2. See, for example, Blauner, Cox, Feagin, and Omi and Winant.

3. In addition to Williams, Fields makes the argument that the creation of the concept of race followed the institution of slavery, rather than there being a preexisting racial bias that determined Europeans' choice of Africans to enslave. On the point that ideas about race respond to and explain historical, material relations, rather than cause them, see Blauner, Cox, Feagin, Bonilla-Silva, and Omi and Winant.

4. The Marxist treatment of race has frequently been accused of reducing race to an epiphenomenon of economics and class. Within such a framework, race has no autonomous reality but is a matter of false consciousness. For a brief example of a critique of the Marxist analysis of race, see Bonilla-Silva 24–25. See also Blauner and Omi and Winant.

5. According to the twenty-nine dictionaries spanning 1806 to 1996 consulted for this study, the first and secondary meanings of *ethnic* switch places by the turn of the nineteenth century: *ethnic* increasingly refers primarily to the races, followed by

the sense of "pagan or heathen." This order of meanings, as well as the synonymy between *race* and *ethnic*, is maintained with few exceptions until the 1960s. Only in the 1970s is the sense of *ethnic* as "heathen or pagan" considered rare or antiquated. Nor does the nominative form *ethnicity* appear in dictionaries of standard English until the 1970s. The first recorded textual instance of *ethnicity* according to the *Oxford English Dictionary* is from 1772 and, like all related variations (such as *ethnicism*, *ethnish*, and *ethnize*), refers to the issue of heathenism.

6. For a more detailed account of how densely complicated and intertwined the arguments around race, polygenesis, slavery, and the colonization of American blacks were with social and political developments in the late eighteenth and early nineteenth centuries, see Dain. Dain's work is especially helpful in situating the debate between monogenesis and polygenesis in a rich historical context.

7. The well-known Melting Pot theory likewise advances an image of American identity as the fusion of the various European peoples into a new American type. It is most often identified with Israel Zangwill's popular stage play *The Melting Pot* that debuted in 1908.

8. By the second half of the twentieth century, the American race, in the form of the Melting Pot theory, would far eclipse Anglo-conformity as the most popular version of American identity—that is until the appearance of multicultural pluralism. Celebrations of the Melting Pot, however, generally suppress its original exclusive whiteness.

9. Benjamin Franklin complained that the Germans in Pennsylvania were aliens turning the region into New Germany (Jordan 102). He also considered them, as well as most Europeans, among those of a "swarthy Complexion" (Jordan 143). Jordan notes, however, that by "the latter part of the century much of the concern and resentment about Germans in Pennsylvania abated as they became less isolated" (338). Germans also had the advantage over the Irish of not having the long history of British domination.

10. The details of Knobel's study show that what he is illuminating is the cultural work that effectively racialized the Irish immigrant within the span of a few decades of the nineteenth century. And yet, in his preface, Knobel writes, "In attempting to recapture the antebellum image of the immigrant Irish and to place it in relation to Anglo-Americans' groping for satisfactory criteria of republican nationality, this book is guided by certain premises about ethnicity, interethnic relationships, and ethnic stereotypes" (xi). Why he frames and refers to his analysis as a matter of ethnicity is a question throughout. A study of Irish American ethnicity, strictly speaking, would examine how the group defined and practiced their evolving sense of identity. But Knobel's project is to look at the terms in which American society constructed Irish American identity during a certain period (a time before the concept of ethnicity was available). Knobel's substitution of *ethnicity* for the historically more accurate *race* probably stems from the contemporary scholarly bias, to which I am trying to call attention, which reserves *race* for groups of color and *ethnic* for Europeans presumed white, regardless of historical location.

11. Knobel's work also presents an interesting example of the way the contemporary distinctions between race and ethnicity are read back into historical periods before such distinctions were operative. By his own definition, *ethnicity* seems to

mean a conception of group identity not reducible to other characteristics like religion or political character. But the anachronistic application of the term to a period that had no such concept makes statements like the following somewhat confusing: "During the antebellum period of American history, ethnicity was a concept bound up tightly with the popular understanding of nationality. Americans' conception of what constituted an ethnic group and their perception of what seemed to be the most important indicators of ethnicity were channeled by the connection of nationality with 'character' and by changing notions about the seat of 'character' itself" (Knobel 179–80). The use of *ethnic* seems to further imply that the Irish never lost their racial kinship with Anglo-American whites. But it is precisely this racial dissociation that Knobel's work demonstrates. Such a contradiction suggests that the implications of Knobel's arguments can only be pursued once the historical stability of whiteness is questioned.

12. For detailed histories of the racialization and whitening of the Irish, see Allen and Ignatiev.

13. As Knobel writes: "Ought we to take elitist antebellum oratory . . . as seriously as we regard the anguished rhetoric of another generation of American intellectuals at the end the nineteenth century . . . who lamented the dilution of Anglo-Saxon blood by discordant material—a rhetoric which helped prepare the way for national immigration restriction legislation in the early 20th?" (74–75). Similarly, Barrett and Roediger state: "The best frame of comparison for discussing new immigrant racial consciousness is that of Irish Americans in the mid-nineteenth century. Especially when not broadly accepted as such, Irish Americans insisted that politicians acknowledge them as part of the dominant race" (31). Stow Persons notes that the first phase of racism against immigrants from Ireland and Germany had settled into a kind of complacency when a second phase began with a new focus: "Towards the end of the century, however, with the shifting of the sources of immigration to central and southeastern Europe and to Asia complacence yielded again to anxiety, and earlier racist theories of Anglo-American superiority were revived and amplified" (77).

14. In *Strangers in the Land*, Higham describes "in-betweenness" (169) of the eastern and southern European immigrants in the American South in the late nineteenth century who failed to practice the southern codes of white supremacy and whose "whiteness was easily open to question" (168).

15. Another expert witness, Dr. Harry H. Laughlin of the Eugenics Record Office of the Carnegie Institution of Washington advised the Committee on Immigration and Naturalization in 1922, that "the surest biological power, which the Federal Government now possesses, to direct the future of America along safe and sound racial channels is to control the hereditary quality of the immigrant stream" (757). In his study on the "racial degeneracy" of various immigrant and native groups, Laughlin found the highest rates of "social inadequates" among the foreign-born and from southern and eastern European stocks; the lowest rates were among those who had been in America more than two generations (754).

16. Omi and Winant define the "racial state" as the coordination of a society's dominant institutions, which regulate, maintain, and legitimate the structure of hegemony based on racial oppression (83–84).

17. The Naturalization Law of 1790, which restricted naturalization to "free white persons," created a subsequent problem for the courts in interpreting what the

framers meant by *white*. Their decisions, usually but inconsistently defining *white* as "Caucasian" or European, involved legal, logical, and linguistic contortions that attest to the irrationality of racial categories. For discussions on the ways that the courts ruled, see Jacobson ("Whiteness of a Different Color" 231) and Haney-Lopez.

18. Hill's powerful historical account of the systematic exclusion of American workers of color from the trade union movement is, nevertheless, another example of the tendency to beg the question of the new immigrants' whiteness. Their arrival in great numbers to the U.S. urban industrial labor market at the end of the nineteenth century slightly precedes that of African Americans from the South in significant numbers. The gradual acceptance of the immigrants into the trade unions, after an initial period of exclusion, occurs at roughly the same time that the Great Migration brought African Americans. If we allow the ambiguous racial status of the Europeans, we can ask whether it was the presence of blacks, rather than the presumed whiteness of the new immigrants alone, that provided the missing element of the latter's acceptance. In other words, could it have been that in the context of turn-of-the-century urban America, the "swarthy" new immigrants appeared the more likely candidates for "Americanization" because they were whiter than blacks, rather than merely white? Did the dramatic increase in the black urban population increase the need for allies in the defense of white privilege?

19. Conzen et al. draw on Knobel's work on the Irish in this context and follow his lead in periodizing "ethnic" as a product of the nineteenth century. They also exhibit the same kind of contradictions in the use of the term. They write that "Dale Knobel has traced, for example, how Americans began viewing the Irish in ethnic terms by the 1850s once they began regarding character as the product of nature rather than nurture" (9). It is not clear why "racial terms" would not serve better here, either in Knobel or Conzen et al., given that character is seen as a matter of "nature" rather than socialization (not to mention that *race* was the term used during the period in question). In both Knobel and Conzen et al., the referent of "ethnic" alternates between biology and culture, depending on context, but it should be evident that even if such a dichotomy was available in the nineteenth century, the distinction is sufficiently important that the two referents cannot be used interchangeably.

2

Whiteness and the Limits of the New Environmentalism in the Social Sciences, 1895–1921

The period between 1890 and 1920 has been called the "nadir of American race relations" (Loewen 154) because of the institutionalization, both North and South, of the oppressed status of people of color and those groups excluded from whiteness as it was then defined. The period's racist developments included the official establishment of "separate but equal" apartheid with the Plessy decision (1896), the extension of the Black Codes begun in 1866, and the reemergence of the Ku Klux Klan. The success of the Johnson-Reed Act in 1924, that restricted immigration to western Europeans, depended as well on the authority that racist ideology commanded. But scholars of the concept of race note that the 1920s also brought significant changes in the social sciences, including new discourses that began to displace scientific racism. Writers devoted to the issue were beginning to explore the possibility that group character, formerly theorized as inherited and innate, could better be explained by environment. Prior to the dominance of race science, writers before the early nineteenth century had considered physiological variation as a result of climate and geography; the return to "environmental" considerations of group character in the first decades of the twentieth century began to develop the idea of the social circumstances as a significant influence in group difference.

Gradually a new paradigm emerged, dubbed the "ethnicity paradigm" by Omi and Winant, which, among other things, recontextualized the nineteenth-century notion of race. While several writers do seem to have questioned its utility and scientific credentials, the biological concept of race was not entirely discarded from the mainstream of academic discourse. Instead, the emerging notion of what we would today call the social construction of racial identity was paradoxically incorporated into social sciences in a way that still preserved the older notion of the races as fixed biological categories. We will see in the next chapter that the invention of the concept of "ethnicity" further institutionalizes the coexistence of these irreconcilable ideas, race as cultural and race as natural. But my intention in this chapter is to show that the invention of "ethnicity" for this purpose was made possible by the work of a generation of thinkers who were reconceptualizing an environmental approach to identity. The so-called "ethnicity paradigm" attributed to the contributions of such major figures as Robert Park and Franz Boas made way for cultural perspectives but without entirely doing away with the biological determinism bequeathed them by nineteenth-century race scientism. Chief among the historical conditions that scholars cite for the shifting theoretical framework are the need for cheap labor as immigration declined during World War I and the Great Migration that brought thousands of African Americans from the South into the Northern ghettoes to fill that need. John Stanfield argues that the "radical changes in perception and real changes in black status, wrought by capitalist interest in black labor and the dramatic black migration north in the 1910s, sowed the seeds of the environmental paradigms that would dominate social scientific and race relations research" (11). Despite the progressive character of the new approach, it did not eradicate biological justifications for racial hierarchies but, as Stanfield argues, "the rapid demographic shifts of black populations and consequent flux in race relations created a demand for more flexible ideologies and practices in order to preserve Jim Crow" (9).[1]

Chiefly, the Chicago School of Sociology and the creation of cultural anthropology in the work of Franz Boas established the terms of this paradigm shift from biological to social foundations.[2] Boas's detailed studies of developing peoples forcefully raised the possibility that a social group's distinguishing characteristics could be explained more lucidly with reference to its cultural traditions rather than its biological features. Gossett goes so far as to suggest that because his meticulous work gradually rendered racial explanations of culture obsolete, and because he was outspoken on racial issues, "it is possible that Boas did more to combat race prejudice than any other person in history" (418). The Chicago School and the work of its central figure, Robert Park, are generally credited with the shift to the "ethnicity paradigm" that governed academic discourse on race until the 1960s. Yet, despite the efforts of Park, Boas, their students, and others of the period to dislodge the preeminence of its claims, many of race science's basic premises were nevertheless retained. Several writers, especially those of color, published work (available to Park and Boas) that seriously questioned the validity of race as a biological category. However, neither Park nor Boas, nor the fields over which they presided, ever fully repudiated the reality of natural racial categories, especially in the case of fundamental differences between white and black. Boas's efforts to overturn race science are monumental. But, as Vernon J. Williams Jr. has shown, at the same time, Boas never entirely gave up the assumption of biological race nor the conviction of blacks' general intellectual inferiority relative to whites. Park, despite the fact that his work loosened the grip of biological determinism by suggesting ways that groups transform as a result of changes in social conditions, also based his theories on fundamentally biological principles and never questioned that races and racial hierarchies exist in nature. Work that more decisively broke with scientific racism was ignored while the schools of thought initiated by Boas and Park shaped their respective disciplines largely because they were white and commanded academic authority. My argument is that their work became hegemonic because it incorporated the new environmentalism and, at the same time, accommodated biracial social stratification. This state of affairs helps to explain why the progress of cultural determinism as it evolved into the discourse of "ethnicity," as we will discuss in the next chapter, became the exclusive property of those groups that could claim a place on the white side of the color line.

THE BOASIAN PARADOX

Any criticism of Franz Boas must be preceded by an acknowledgment of his pivotal contributions not only to the field of anthropology but also to the history of antiracism. His generous support of black scholars such as W.E.B. DuBois, Zora Neale Hurston, and many others; his extensive body of work attacking the scientific racism of his day; his participation in groups such as the NAACP; along with his authoritative position as an academic and public intellectual helped to transform the ideology of race in progressive directions. One of his earliest works, a report to the Senate Immigration Commission, effectively undermined the racial ideology governing the discourse of the new immigrants. In *Changes in Bodily Form of Descendants of Immigrants* presented to the Commission in 1911, Boas reports on empirical studies of physiological changes in immigrants and their children. Comparing natives from eastern and southern Europe with the children of immigrants from those countries, Boas "found much more than was anticipated" (*Changes* 2): that physiology is not nearly as fixed and stable as race science had insisted but instead adapted rather quickly to environmental conditions.

Boas's study specifically targets those features on which scientists had previously invested the most hope of grounding the validity of race, those characteristics which were assumed to be the most permanent and thus revealing of racial type, such as stature; eye, skin and hair color; physiological development; and especially head measurement and proportions. The results of Boas's study showed that most of these features change to some degree, varying from one "type" or group to another, in proportion to the length of time in America. Boas is emphatic that the surprising results of his research "can only be explained as due directly to the influence of environment" (*Changes* 2). Especially notable to Boas, and subversive of the scientific racist paradigm, are his findings with respect to changes in head shape or the "cephalic index." The heads of east European "Hebrews," for example, show a shift from round to long (as a ratio of width to length) while the southern Italian type goes from long- to shortheaded. Comparing the two groups, Boas notes that they are "[approaching] a uniform type, as far as the roundness of the head is concerned" (*Changes* 5). While he later expresses skepticism about the possibility of a uniform type (*Changes* 76), he argues that physiological change is the result of changed environmental and cultural conditions. In the case of cephalic index, he speculates that the variations are a result of nutrition and differences in infants' cradling and "swaddling" (*Changes* 70–72).

As we saw in chapter 1, in the difficult task of isolating features sufficiently consistent within a population to count as reliable racial evidence, racial scientists placed a great deal of stock in craniology. The collecting and measuring of skulls supposedly representing various racial types had become the preoccupation of many scientists and had become a field of study in its own right in the nineteenth century. And head shape was one of the primary features distinguishing the three races of Europe (the Nordics, Alpines, and Mediterraneans) in the schema developed by Ripley and popularized by Grant in *The Passing of the Great Race* (1916). Empirically verified changes in head shapes from one generation to the next challenges the assumptions that racial features are permanent and reliable markers of racial identity, core tenets of race science. Boas does not directly challenge the validity of race as a scientific concept in this text, but he is aware of the significance of this conclusion with respect to the framework of the discipline:

> This fact is one of the most suggestive discovered in the investigation, because it shows that not even those characteristics of a race which have proved to be the most permanent in their old home remain the same under the new surroundings; and we are compelled to conclude that when these features of the body change, the whole bodily and mental make-up of the immigrants may change.
>
> These results are so definite that, while heretofore we had the right to assume that human types are stable, all evidence is now in favor of a great plasticity of

human types, and permanence of types in new surroundings appears rather as the exception than as the rule. (*Changes* 5)

While the subversiveness of Boas's conclusions does not seem to have affected the Senate's legislation of the Johnson-Reed Act a decade later, nor the popularity of Grant's thesis about the racial superiority of the western European "Nordic," it nevertheless made an impression on his academic peers. Michael Blakey notes that Boas's study "shook evolutionary physical anthropologists" (77).

Yet it should be noted that while Boas removes a foundational premise of race science, he supports another at the same time, that of the identification between external and internal characteristics of "types." That is, one of the key features of scientific racism is that the physical features of a racial group are linked to typical mental and moral features of that group. The "plasticity" of bodily form within racial groups indicates to Boas a corresponding plasticity of intellectual capacity. His results indicate that "we may conclude that the fundamental traits of the mind, which are closely correlated with the physical condition of the body and whose development continues over many years after physical growth has ceased, are the more subject to far-reaching changes" (*Changes* 76). That is, while Boas subverts the idea of the permanence of racialized features, he nevertheless maintains the racist principle that physiological and mental traits are connected. Boas implicitly attacks the assumption about the permanence of racial characteristics as well as the basis for race science's intellectual hierarchies, but by basing his challenge on race science's mental-physical linkage, he leaves this assumption in place.

However, it is possible that Boas was writing with his audience in mind and may have thought that his impact on the Senate's legislative decisions might be greater if his approach was staged within the framework of the prevailing paradigm. We might consider this explanation because in the same year that he was maintaining the racist link between inner and outer qualities before the Immigration Commission, he was attacking the idea in one of the most celebrated publications of his career, *The Mind of Primitive Man* (1911). In this work, he explicitly sets out to challenge the assumption of a connection between physical traits and the mental capacities of a race. He concludes that "neither cultural achievement nor outer appearance is a safe basis on which to judge the mental aptitude of races" (*Mind* 18). Instead, it is environment that accounts for any differences between groups. In the face of the prevailing scientific race theories of his day, Boas boldly declares that "it seems to me that not the slightest successful attempt has been made to establish causes for the behavior of a people other than historical and social conditions; and I consider it unlikely that this can ever be done" (*Mind* 259). By the same reasoning, the explanation that "the White race" is currently more socially "advanced" than the others is not a matter of superior biology but rather "historical events appear to have been much more potent in leading races to civilization than their innate faculty" (*Mind* 16). Going further, Boas attacks the widespread assumption that racially based differences allow the ranking of superior over inferior groups. For if achievement is not a matter of race but historical accident, "it follows that achievements of races do not without further proof warrant the assumption that one race is more highly gifted than another" (*Mind* 16).

Boas considers the radical possibility that if there is no meaningful relation between biology and culture, then the entire practice of racial division can be abolished from scientific practice and "it will be permissible to treat mankind as a whole and to study cultural types regardless of race" (*Mind* 18). Boas is, in fact, skeptical of the idea of race itself. The concept, "as applied to human types, is vague," and it has "a biological significance only when a race presents a uniform, closely inbred group, in which all family lines are alike" (*Mind* 254). These conditions obtain in some cases, such as "in pure breeds of domesticated animals," but never, Boas notes, in the case of humans (*Mind* 254). The complicated mixture of all human groups, especially Europeans and Americans, is why those fears are unfounded that misapprehend the threat eastern and southern Europeans pose to American racial purity. Instead, "an unbiased review of the facts shows that the belief in hereditary racial characteristics and jealous care for purity of race is based on the assumption of non-existing conditions" (*Mind* 259).

Boas thus suspects that racial anxieties about the new immigrants are "to a great extent imaginary," and he rejects that there is any "need of entering into a discussion of alleged hereditary differences in mental characteristics of various branches of the White race" (*Mind* 264, 259). And yet, he has "no doubt that these people of eastern and southern Europe present physical types distinct from the physical type of northwestern Europe; and it is clear, even to the most casual observer, that their present social standards differ fundamentally from our own" (*Mind* 262). Contradictorily, Boas gestures back to the language and assumptions of race science in his discussion of the new immigrants and especially in his ambivalent assessment of the "Negro problem," problems Boas considers "from a biological viewpoint not essentially different" (*Mind* 268). On the one hand, he is adamantly convinced that "the traits of the American Negro are adequately explained on the basis of his history and social status" and that there is no reason, therefore, for "falling back upon the theory of hereditary inferiority" (*Mind* 270). Nor is there any scientific evidence that justifies the Negro's exclusion from any rights or occupation of modern civilization and that "there is every reason to believe that the Negro when given the facility and opportunity, will be perfectly able to fulfill the duties of citizenship as well as his White neighbor" (*Mind* 271). On the other hand, however, Boas cannot relinquish the idea that there are fundamental racial divisions. He feels it necessary to state "with some emphasis that it would be erroneous to claim as proved that there are no differences in the mental make-up of the Negro race taken as a whole and of any other race taken as a whole, and that their activities should run in exactly the same lines" (*Mind* 270). While he stresses that "no proof of an inferiority of the Negro type could be given" and that there is "nothing at all that could be interpreted as suggesting any material difference in the mental capacity of the bulk of the Negro population as compared with the bulk of the White population," yet it does seem to Boas that it is "barely possible that perhaps the race would not produce quite so many men of the highest genius of other races" (*Mind* 268). Boas's historic attack against the dominant race science is perhaps all the more striking in that it is undercut by this kind of ambivalence over some of the central principles of race science.

Indeed, as Vernon Williams has pointed out, praise for Boas seldom includes a consideration of his blind spots and, in this case, his concessions to the race science he otherwise challenged so thoroughly throughout his life. Williams has called the "Boasian Paradox" the contradiction in Boas's work between, on the one hand, his egalitarian and liberal impulses and, on the other, his continual reliance on the assumptions from physical anthropology about black intellectual inferiority (6) as evidenced in *The Mind of Primitive Man*. To take another example, among his major contributions to antiracist scholarship include his work on the reconstruction of conceptions of the African heritage. Long regarded as a legacy of barbarism, the distorted history of a primitive Africa rationalized slavery as a civilizing influence and black subordination as the inevitable result of blacks in a superior white society. Supporters of this mythology, a given among white writers, even included prominent black figures such as Booker T. Washington. Boas published work and supported other scholars and studies that refuted the notion of a historical African barbarism in favor of the idea of Africa as the origin of civilization. At the same time, however, he accepted the nineteenth-century precept of blacks as having smaller crania, on average, in comparison to whites, and thus a tendency for less intellectual capacity and a lesser likelihood to produce great and influential thinkers. He insisted nevertheless that none of this justified the unequal treatment of blacks as a group, school segregation, or lesser entitlement to the rights of citizenship. Yet, along with his considerable efforts to establish a more progressive framework for evaluating the significance of group differences, the Boasian Paradox also left the notion of race and natural black inferiority essentially intact.

WILLIAM I. THOMAS AND THE BEGINNINGS
OF THE SOCIOLOGY OF RACE

Boas's innovative work not only reshaped and influenced the field of anthropology but was significant in the work of scholars in other fields as well. One of those scholars was University of Chicago sociologist William I. Thomas whose career Vernon Williams argues "paralleled that of Boas" (43). In such works as *Sex and Society* (1907) and his article "The Scope and Method of Folk-Psychology" (1895), Thomas was among the first white scholars to question race science's correlation between physiological features and intellectual or moral character. In the essay on folk-psychology, Thomas attacks the practice of racial classification, especially the methods involving the weighing and measuring of the brain and skull, and he reviews the work that failed to show any correlation between brain size and morality. Yet, in the same article, Thomas relapses into contemporary assumptions about race, noting that "it is important to recognize that the form and spirit of the art, literature, ethics and politics of different races are to be regarded as an expression of the temperament even more than that of the intelligence of the people" ("Scope" 443). But the article is noteworthy, if contradictory, in that it does lodge strong objections to race science unusual for the time. Thomas asserts that "the classification of races has itself thus far proven an *ignis fatuus* [false hope]" and notes that "the question is no nearer solution than when Blumenbach one hundred and twenty years ago made the classic division of five which still stands in school books" ("Scope" 438).

Moreover, Thomas's work established a theoretical perspective for a generation of sociologists, including Robert Park. Scholars suggest that *The Polish Peasant in Europe and America* (1918) in particular, which Thomas coauthored with Florian Znaniecki, can be seen as the model for the Chicago School's sociological approach (Banton, *Idea* 107; Persons 46; Zaretsky 10). Its contribution is its combination of previously separate traditions of empirical studies and social theory (Zaretsky 10) in order to shift the foundation of what the authors call "social psychology" from primordial essence to social practices and institutions. The unity of the Polish family, for example, is determined by ongoing, concrete practices rather than any presupposed element of heredity. Thomas and Znaniecki argue that "common descent determines, indeed, the unity of the group, but only by virtue of associational ties established within each new generation" (66). They also seem to be among the first to use the phrase "ethnic group" in a sense that does not refer to a collective identity rooted in a biological or primordial essence. Though the phrase seems to remain synonymous with *racial*, both terms strain in *The Polish Peasant* against their traditional senses. It is the immigrant institutions, or "local associations," such as the parish, mutual help associations, and parochial schools, rather than genes, blood, or germ plasms that are responsible for "racial" group solidarity within the American social framework:

> The nationalistic Polish tendencies of the local associations have thus not a political but a racial significance. Their aim is to preserve the cultural stock brought by the immigrants to this country—language, mores, customs, and historical traditions—so as to maintain the racial solidarity of the Poles as an ethnic

group, independent of their political allegiance and of any economic, social, or political bonds which may connect each of them individually with their American milieu. (Thomas and Znaniecki 253)

Here then is the sense of group cohesion that is the product not of natural blood ties but the result of ongoing social practices that must be maintained in the face of disintegrative forces of the new "American milieu" if the ethnic group is to be sustained.

Because of *The Polish Peasant*'s influence on the Chicago School and its most famous proponent, Robert Park, Zaretsky claims it is "probably the single most important work establishing sociology as a discipline in America, and Thomas is arguably the single most important figure in this effort" (10). Park himself acknowledged that "probably nothing has been more influential than the publication of the monumental work by W. I. Thomas and Florian Znaniecki, *The Polish Peasant*, in directing the attention of sociological students to the possibility and the importance of studies in the field of race and culture" (*Race and Culture* 198).

ROBERT PARK AND THE INSTITUTIONALIZATION OF A SOCIOLOGY OF RACE RELATIONS

It is the work of Robert Park that is generally acknowledged as having mapped out the framework of the discourse on race in the social sciences for the next generation. Though he was not alone in the effort, Park, more than any other single figure, transformed the study of race from the biologically based discourse of the "race problem" (or "the negro problem") to a discourse of "race relations" that embedded race within the terms of social and historical processes. That is, following Emancipation, as James B. McKee writes, debates on "the race problem" within the emerging field of sociology assumed that blacks were permanently and biologically inferior to whites and that their freedom posed a problem of social control and how best to utilize their labor (103). Park, however, recontextualized the discourse on race within the broader consideration of social relations on an international scale. As Higham observes, Park was "the outstanding pioneer in the study of race relations," the effect of whose work was that "the purely sociological study of race relations was launched as a comparative examination of the multiethnic societies in various parts of the world" (*Send* 217). And unlike most of his contemporaries, who regarded blacks as an innately inferior people mired in an irredeemably backward culture, Park recognized that black culture provided the basis for solidarity and race consciousness that he compared to east European Slavic peoples struggling at the time to become, in words he attributed to his mentor Booker T. Washington, "a nation within a nation."

However, as some scholars have noted, Park's comparative international framework and his considerations of black racial consciousness were progressive innovations that did not become central to the sociological mainstream. Indeed, the legacy of the Parkian race relations approach to human difference is appropriated solely for European Americans through the concept of ethnicity, cutting short the subversive potential for a rigorous critique of biological race. While it is the subsequent use to which his work is put that should be our ultimate concern, an account is necessary of Park's theory that shows how it lent itself to a restriction of the new environmentalism. Namely, an account of Park in this context shows how the newly emerging environmental theory of cultural difference, in his work as in that of Franz Boas, could, paradoxically, contribute to race science and the maintenance of the color line.

The inconsistent, unsystematic, and changing nature of Park's writings have, however, left scholars a wide latitude to interpret and debate exactly what his own positions were. John H. Stanfield's Park, for example, is an inveterate Eurocentric apologist for "a biracial society which should advocate racial justice, but not racial equality" (Stanfield 43). James McKee's Park, on the other hand, was a bold innovator in sociology whose most original contributions, such as his international scope, a benevolent attitude toward black people, and the notion of conflict in race relations, set him apart not only from his predecessors but his own contemporaries and followers who were too conservative or narrow to keep up. Vernon Williams reviews the ongoing debates surrounding Park's work and notes that the two primary issues of contention have been whether Park supported the theory of racial determinism and where he stood on the issue of assimilation. Scholars have found support in Park's work to base diametrically opposed positions on each of these questions. Williams accounts for this ambivalence in Park by suggesting that he, like Boas, was a "transitional figure" (96, 108), at times reproducing the previous paradigm of race science and social Darwinism and, at other times, embracing the newly emergent cultural relativism.[3]

Indicative of the transitional nature of Park's work is his apparent attempt to reconcile the traditional assumptions of the nineteenth-century racist scientists with the environmentalist approach, grounded in social interaction, of thinkers such as Thomas and Boas. In the work that would become the "bible" for generations of sociology students, *Introduction to the Science of Sociology* (1921), Park suggests that human beings are the product of "a double inheritance," or two claims to identity imposed at once by both culture and race. One of these factors, constituted by "habits, accommodations, sentiments, attitudes, and ideals transmitted by communication and education" is called the "social tradition"; the other is inherited biologically and is a group's racial "temperament" (*Introduction* 140–41). The concept of racial temperament, as James B. McKee notes, was not Park's but his colleague W. I. Thomas's contribution to sociology. The idea, however, was a standard principle of almost all racist thought since the nineteenth century, and one of its most enduring holdovers in sociology's efforts to reconstruct the notion of race as a social rather than biological phenomenon (McKee 92). Park's use of it at this point in his career indicates his conviction that biological race is the more determining of the human influences. He admits that a group's "racial will" is shaped by social experience but adds that the impetus for social experience is preconditioned in the first place by race:

> My assumption is that [racial] temperament is the basis of the [social] interests; that as such it determines in the long run the general run of attention, and this, eventually, determines the selection in the case of an individual of his vocation, in the case of the racial group of its culture. That is to say, temperament determines what things the individual and the group will be interested in; what elements of the general culture, to which they have access, they will assimilate; what, to state it pedagogically, they will learn. (*Introduction* 141)

Because of its fundamental position in determining human character, race is also the basis on which the nationality of a people takes shape, "a nationalistic group being merely a cultural and, eventually, a political society founded on the basis of racial inheritances" (*Introduction* 141). The distinction for Park is that a nationality is a "racial group which has attained self-consciousness" (*Race and Culture* 219). Nationalities, then, have their own essential and distinct characters, and Park's speculations on the natures of each reproduce many of the same terms presented in the traditions of nineteenth-century racist science and racial nationalism. For example, just as for Grant and Stoddard, for Park the Anglo-Saxon is the "pioneer and frontiersman" among the races. The Jew is the intellectual and the East Indian "a brooding introspective" (*Introduction* 139). George Fredrickson suggests Park's stereotype of the Negro "set the tone for subsequent appreciation of black cultural achievements" (327). It is a variation on the tradition of what Fredrickson calls "romantic racialism" (101), which shares the assumption with scientific race of a fixed, essential character for each race, but casts it in terms that are meant to be flattering. That is, for Park, the Negro's racial temperament consists of "a genial, sunny, and social disposition, in an interest and attachment to external, physical things rather than to subjective states of introspection, in a disposition for expression rather than enterprise and action" (*Introduction* 139). In a notorious analogy that enlists retrograde stereotypes of both gender and race, the Negro's natural predilection for "expression rather than action" renders "[him], so to speak, the lady among the races" (*Introduction* 139).[4]

Despite the fact that Park reproduces many of the tendencies of the historical discourse on racial essentialism, he is also credited with helping to dislodge the preeminence of social Darwinism. As Banton notes, "Though starting with notions of racial temperament and innate dispositions, his teaching came to concentrate on racial hostility as the product of the norms of social distance and prejudice which individuals learned when they were socialized into their communities" (*Idea* 109). And as McKee argues, Park was one of the major figures in the general shift in the social sciences that took race out of its biological context and placed it within a framework of social relations. His conception of the "race relations cycle," while it may not be his only contribution to sociology, became through the work of his students one of his most well known (McKee 111). The theory allows for the possibility that inborn biological traits can be modified through intercultural encounters such as migration. Park argues that when "society grows and is perpetuated by immigration and adaptation, there ensues, as a result of miscegenation, a breaking up of the complex of the biologically inherited qualities that constitutes the temperament of the race" (*Introduction* 141). While it might be argued that Park's mention of "miscegenation" restricts racial modification to the biological, he allows for other factors in the dynamics of social interaction, such as communication and competition, to "modify the effects which would be produced by racial factors working in isolation" (*Introduction* 142).

The ruling metaphor of Park's "race relations cycle" is biological and organic so that as a natural process, it is always and everywhere the same when a smaller body meets a dominant one: "By a process of nutrition, somewhat similar to the physiological one, we may conceive alien peoples to be incorporated with, and made part of the community or state" (*Race and Culture* 209). His cycle of interaction consists of four major modes or phases: competition, conflict, accommodation, and assimilation. The process is universal in the sense that it explains all human dynamics and, because it seems drawn from the natural world, it carries scientific authority. An encounter between populations begins in conflict and competition, and the outcome is that the weaker group is subordinated. It is either assimilated or accommodates itself to its subservient role. In the case of slavery, for example, "intimate and friendly relations between master and slave were established" because "each caste and class lives within the limitations of its own world and accepts the definition imposed upon it as if it were a part of the order of nature" (Park, *Race and Culture* 234). In some cases, though, the process ends in assimilation as the smaller group is absorbed into the body of the larger social organism.

Scholars disagree, however, over whether Park had only the new immigrants in mind or thought the general process of assimilation applied to African Americans as well. Some readers of Park focus on his assertions that, as a consequence of the assimilating process, race in every case would recede as a significant social marker of difference and be superseded by class conflict (*Race Relations* 45). Because the process was governed by natural principles that came into play in any situation of intercultural contact, Park can be read as identifying the situations of American blacks and European immigrants. It is especially notable for the present discussion that Park took the specific contribution of *The Polish Peasant* to be the recognition of a parallel between the two groups. In assessing the influence of their work, Park notes that:

> Thomas and Znaniecki were the first, or almost the first, to call attention to the fact that the situation of the European immigrant in the United States can be defined in terms that imply its logical relation to that of the Negro, even though the Negro, in the Americas, North and South and particularly in the West Indies, is not an alien or an immigrant but has become, in the course of some three hundred years' residence, an indigenous race intimately related by blood to the Indian who preceded him. (*Race and Culture* 198–99)

This highlighting of an analogy between European immigrants and American blacks is significant because, as Banton argues, "the recognition of this 'logical relation', obvious though it may seem now, was of fundamental significance for establishing a sociology of race relations" (*Idea* 107).[5]

On the other hand, there are those scholars who read Park as having placed more emphasis on the permanence of a biracial society and black subordination. Park seems to have been aware of the emerging critiques of race as a scientific category but dismisses such a line of inquiry. He admits that race is "clearly nothing scientifically definite, since ethnologists themselves are not agreed upon classification of the human family along racial lines" (*Introduction* 634). However, the lack of scientific verification of racial difference does not deter Park's faith in its reality:

> The really important matter is one about which there need be little dispute—the fact of racial differences. It is a practical question of differences—the fundamental differences of physical appearance, of mental habit and thought, of social customs and religious beliefs, of the thousand and one things keenly and clearly appreciable, yet sometimes elusive and undefinable—these are the things which at once create and find expression in what we call race problems and race prejudices, for want of better terms. In just so far as these differences are fixed and permanently associated characteristics of two groups of people will the antipathies and problems between the two be permanent. (*Introduction* 635–36)[6]

Park reiterates the basic assumption of nineteenth-century race science by including that the most reliable classification will be based on color with the knowledge that "the color [is] accompanied by various and often widely different, but always fairly persistent, differentiating physical and mental characteristics" (*Introduction* 636). Moreover, physiological difference provides the stimuli for an involuntary reaction to individuals of different races: "Race prejudice may be regarded as a spontaneous, more or less instinctive, defense-reaction, the practical effect of which is to restrict free competition between races" (*Introduction* 623). The result is a "vicious cycle" for the ostracized groups of "isolation, prejudice; prejudice, isolation" (*Introduction* 625). Because they bear the marks of their race, the Japanese, Chinese, and Negroes "cannot move among us with the same freedom as members of other races" and so, unlike the European immigrant, "they are bound to live in the American community a more or less isolated life" (*Introduction* 625).

Yet, despite the inequalities between center and periphery of any racially divided social structure, Park's theory suggests that racial groups will accommodate themselves to their respective positions. His model for race relations when they do not lead to assimilation seems to be the Southern slave plantation where all parties function harmoniously within the system of relations as, again, a biotic organism seeking equilibrium. Slaves, and their post–Civil War descendants, learned to embrace their subordination and even develop affection for their white superiors. Speaking for Southern blacks of his time, Park's text reassures his readers that they are not concerned about voting, separate schools, and public transportation, and "[the Southern Negro] neither knows nor cares anything about 'social equality'" (*Introduction* 639). Acceptance of "this relation of superior and inferior as a mere matter of course" is simply a function of natural adaptation, "an inherited part of his [the Negro's] instinctive mental equipment" that comes with the process of accommodation (*Introduction* 639).

The way that the *Introduction* naturalizes even the most exploitative racial inequality clarifies Vernon Williams's account of Park as a transitional figure. The aspect of his work for which he is most often remembered introduces the emerging environmental understanding that social groups modify as a result of changing social conditions. On the other hand, he also reproduces many of the fundamental premises of biological determinism that rationalize a racially hierarchized social structure. We can see why his race relations cycle is sufficiently adaptable to account for the possibility of both assimilation, in the case of European immigrants, as well as a permanent biracial social structure, in the case of groups of color. Most scholars agree that Park deserves credit for having departed from much of the biologically based and disparaging conceptions of blacks reiterated by his contemporaries. His race relations cycle reconceived race as a function of social relations, rather than biology and evolution, and was a major factor in the general shift in the human sciences to open the issue of race to social analysis. But, as McKee points out, his model relied upon evolutionary assumptions in which blacks were seen as a premodern people in confrontation with the forces of modern civilization. Thus, whether his intention or not, Park reinforced the general tendency in academic discourse that replaced biological with cultural inferiority (McKee 106).[7]

Moreover, as we will see in the next chapter, Park's race relations cycle sets the precedent for the development of ethnicity as a reference for the cultural construction of identity in the case of European Americans without dis-rupting the authority of biological race. But while Park never distinguished race from ethnicity, later writers, including Omi and Winant, rename Park's theory the "ethnic" instead of "race relations cycle." In his study of Park and the Chicago School, Stow Persons elects to "use the term *ethnic group* in a comprehensive sense to include both racial groups and Caucasian ethnic groups" (23n). Yet Persons notes that Park himself rarely used the term *ethnic group* and then only in his later writings, and "it was only appropriate that when Thomas and Park proposed to analyze the experience of both types of groups within a common frame of reference they should use the single term *race* in all contexts" (23n). Persons does not explain why it was "appropriate," but the primary reason must be that Park was not aware of any term other than *race* in which to frame group or national difference. As we shall see in chapter 3, *ethnic*, in the contemporary sense that Persons or Omi and Winant use it, to mean cultural identity, was only used sporadi-cally in the social science literature. J. Deniker had first suggested the use of *ethnic* in 1901, and writers like Alain Locke and William I. Thomas use *ethnic* in contexts that anticipate its later use. But the now-familiar sense of the term would not become accepted in the sociological discourse until the 1930s, when sociologists would explicitly begin to pair *race* with *ethnic* to indicate a clear dichotomy between groups identified either by biologi-cal or by cultural difference, respectively. In popular discourse from 1800 through the mid-twentieth century, the primary sense of *ethnic* indicated a religious difference, that is, "heathen or pagan," "neither Christian nor Jew." By the mid-nineteenth century, the term had gained the additional sense as a synonym of *race* and maintained that sense through Park's time. The 1930 edition of the *New Century Dictionary of the English Language*, for example, is representative of other similar volumes published from the 1920s through the 1940s in defining *ethnic* as "pertaining to, or peculiar to a race; pertaining to races, their origin, characteristics, etc." (518).

THE HORIZON OF CONCEPTUAL POSSIBILITY

But even without distinct terms, it is necessary to recognize that Park had the option of a more fully developed critique of race. It is important to acknowledge that there was at the time a developing discourse by which to investigate the scientific claims for race and to articulate national, cultural, or phenotypic group differences in terms other than biological inheritance. As previously mentioned, Franz Boas and Park's colleague William I. Thomas were already exposing the fallacies of race science by the turn of the cen-tury, though neither was able to escape entirely from the assumptions of biological determinism. Nancy Leys Stepan and Sander Gilman have shown that other writers within what they call the "critical tradition," particularly writers of color, had been challenging scientific racism since its beginning in the nineteenth century. Though frequently biblically and morally based, and thus unlikely to gain serious credence against the authority of science, by the end of the nineteenth century the critical tradition had begun to challenge the discourse of race on its own scientific terms. Such a move was rhetorically necessary because, as science increasingly defined the parameters of legitimate debate, scripturally based arguments had lost their previous validity. A key text in the effort of the critical tradition, as Mia Bay argues, is W.E.B. DuBois's *Philadelphia Negro* (1899). Although the book is marked by the pervasive influence of biological determinism, DuBois's empirical method outlining the complex social forces acting on the lives of African Americans marks "the early erosion of his scientific belief in Darwinian laws" (Bay 54). Even before his work began to show the influence of Boas, his famous "Conservation of the Races" in 1897 shows DuBois noting the limitations of race as a scientific concept and reaching for a more sociocultural conception. We must acknowledge that humans are divided into races, he argues, even if the "essential differences" between them are difficult to discern ("Conservation" 39). However, it is not the physical differences that interested DuBois: "The deeper differences are spiritual, psychical, differences—undoubtedly based on the physical, but infinitely transcending them" ("Conservation" 41). DuBois's conception of race continued to evolve such that by the end of World War II, as Thomas C. Holt suggests, he had developed a historical and economic understanding of race as a modern product of European imperialism (Holt 72–73).[8]

Along the same lines, in a series of lectures delivered at Howard University in 1916, Alain Locke expanded on the idea of race as a modern invention growing out of the "race practice" of Western imperialism. He argues that race has many meanings, and it appears that one of Locke's primary goals in his lectures was to rearticulate dominant biological race to a sociological framework. He begins by arguing that the biological sense of race amounts to an "ethnic fiction" that has made "a fetish of biological purity" (Locke 11). Locke cites Boas as having shown that racial groups are subject to constant change and flux as historical circumstances change (76). The supposed objective science of race is, in fact, a reflection of power, "a philosophy of the dominant groups" and utterly without any scientific merit (Locke 3). The idea of inferior and superior races is merely a reflection of historically situated power relations: "So that [the] people that [have] not been successful in acquiring dominance, the people that have not been able to force their [identity] upon another group, will be called the inferior people" (Locke 22–23).[9] But Locke argues that race does have an important social function which is to foster "historical group sense and to stimulate men into that sense of corporate destiny" (87). This Locke calls "social race" or, as he explains at the end of the lectures, "civilization type" (88). That is, every society creates its own, sometimes arbitrary type and it is the duty of every individual and group to achieve "culture-citizenship" by conforming to that type (Locke 99). Locke's rearticulation of race recalls race's older identification with nation but liberates it from its biological underpinnings and emphasizes its cultural elements: "So that really·when you conform or belong to a civilization type, [(when you are an American in all your beliefs, mores, and social customs, for example)], you are of the same race in any vital or rational sense of race" (79). He expresses optimism about the possibility of eliminating racial conflict as a result of modern industrial development and his strategy of rearticulating the meaning of race. He argues that "a change will come about . . . through a substitution of better meanings for the meanings which are now so current under the term" (Locke 84–85). In fact, Locke predicts that "the ideal of race will be revolutionized in a very short while"—within his own generation or the next (85).

With his historical and cultural approach and thoroughgoing repudiation of race science, Locke was among the first American writers to develop the emerging environmental perspective in the social sciences. This critique lends his frequent use of *ethnic* the sense of cultural identity, one of the earliest uses of the term in this contemporary sense. Locke's lectures on race are also noteworthy for the ways in which he is able to bring Franz Boas's ideas to bear on issues confronting black intellectuals. Jeffrey C. Stewart argues, "Locke was the intellectual who most fully comprehended the implications of Boas's theories for African Americans" (xxiv).

Stewart adds, however, that Locke's treatment of race differs from Boas in significant ways. First, while Boas contradictorily retained, as we have seen, ideas about race as biological inheritance, Locke argued that any classification of human beings based on "anthropological" features was impossible since one could find more variation within the same racial group than between two different races.[10] For this reason, among others, Locke had no use for the biological sense of race, which had "lapsed" (12), and so argued that only a socially situated theory could restore the usefulness of race to the social sciences: "Consequently, any true history of race must be a sociological theory of race. [It] must be a theory of culture stages and of social evolution" (11). Second, Locke developed the concept of race within the political and historical framework of modern imperialism and so "moved beyond the cultural relativism of Boas" (Stewart xxv). Locke argued that "there is very little difference" whether one lives within or without modern imperialism because both are aspects of the same larger structure. Locke warns that we lose "considerable perspective" if we dissociate domestic from foreign practices of imperialism since "to be subjected to economic subordination and social prejudice is similar to being subject to political dominance and commercial exploitation" (33). Both situations are instances of "race practice" for which we require a corresponding "race theory." Finally, Boas considered, like many of his contemporaries, that the solution to race problems was complete assimilation of the subordinated groups. Locke, on the other hand, maintained the crucial importance of race as a device to foster group solidarity. While he argues that assimilation is ultimately desired and that it is accomplished by conformity to the national civilization type, such a merger could occur only paradoxically through collective cultural effort by the "submerged" racialized group.[11]

THE WHITE POLITICS OF THE NEW ENVIRONMENTALISM

Despite the fact that Locke's lectures developed critiques of race in 1916 that strike us as remarkably innovative and contemporary, the lectures received no evident response at the time and were, in fact, unpublished until 1992. Nevertheless, they are useful as indexes of the limits during the period of the theoretically possible. While the work of Boas and Park became paradigmatic in their respective disciplines by the 1930s, a comparison with Locke and others of the same era indicates the degree to which Boas and Park, as "forward"[12] and progressive as their thought was, compromised between theoretical development and dominant power structures. Boas is justly recognized as perhaps the most influential figure in the refutation of biological determinism but at the same time, as we have seen, preserved the idea of black physiological inferiority and the idea that racial differences were real at the level of biology. Park as well, despite developing a counter-theory to social Darwinism in his race relations cycle, nevertheless reproduced tenets of the race science that preceded him. As John H. Stanfield remarks:

> Park's positive conclusions assured that after interracial contact and subsequent conflict, competition, accommodation, and assimilation, America would still be dominated by whites. Such a view appealed to conventional public views supporting permanent racial separation and white domination. (53)

Thus, as Stanfield suggests, understanding the development of knowledge requires an examination of the underlying social and institutional conditions. In this light, one of the primary motivations for the critique of scientific racism in the first place is a kind of disciplinary self-justification for the newly emerging fields of the social sciences. John Higham has observed that the critique of race after World War I "had a special appeal to social scientists, since it helped establish the autonomy of their subject matter. . . . Now to refute racial determinism was, in effect, to declare the independence of the social from the natural sciences" (*Send* 216). At the same time, the self-inflicted limits to the critique owe something to the exclusive whiteness of the practitioners. African Americans, who have typically been the most rigorous thinkers within the "critical tradition" of intellectual antiracism, as we have seen in the case of Locke, were largely excluded from dominant post-secondary institutions as undergraduates but more so as graduate students and almost completely as professors (Banks 70). Their work was routinely rejected for publication, often with the justification that the writers were not "accredited" or, as people of color, their work would be "interested" or biased and therefore unscientific (Stepan and Gilman 88). The ironic exclusion of black voices in the early development of race relations sociology, however, served its purposes in supplying justification for continuation of the biracial hierarchy. Indeed, the conception of the field of study as "race relations" further reveals its larger intentions as Stephen Steinberg has suggested. The phrase is itself an "artful obfuscation" of the reality of oppression under an image of mutuality (Steinberg 58).

As we shall see in the next chapter, the concept of ethnicity arises on the theoretical foundation prepared by the emerging fields of sociology and cultural anthropology. That is, ethnicity depends on a theory and a language of human group difference whose reference points are specific practices and histories rather than physical bodies. This is why ethnicity could never have emerged as long as race science monopolized conceptions of difference. Yet ethnicity will be forged exclusively for differences within whiteness. It is not surprising that the forces guiding the development of "ethnicity" into the exclusive hands of whiteness were the political and disciplinary forces of whiteness itself. And because of its exclusive whiteness, ethnicity will not disturb assumptions about racial differences but, contradictorily, will accommodate a hierarchy of differences tied to biology. In so doing, the concept of ethnicity helps naturalize a reconciliation between the incommensurate theories of human difference based on biological race, on the one hand, and those based on culture, on the other. What we need to note here is that the contradictions inherent in the concept of ethnicity are a legacy of the theory on which it is based. Such limitations stem from the failures of both Boas's and Park's schools to found their respective disciplines without carrying forward the old biases of the very race science they were attempting to supersede. If ethnicity's cultural frame of reference could sit quietly within a structure of fundamental biological difference, it was because such formidable examples had already shown it how.

NOTES

1. George M. Fredrickson argued along similar lines a decade earlier by drawing a connection between the social changes of the Great Migration and the new environmentalism in the social sciences. He suggests that there was a structural incentive for a new sociological approach to race that was "conservatively geared to the need of an increasingly complex, industrialized, and bureaucratized society for 'social

engineering' as a means of neutralizing the potentially disruptive tensions of group life" (325).

2. Pierre van den Berghe expresses the general consensus on this shift, that "by the 1920s and 1930s, the United States had become the centerstage of the social sciences, and the students of Franz Boas in anthropology and Robert Park in sociology began to spread the gospel of extreme cultural relativism and determinism that held sway through the 1960s" (*Ethnic Phenomenon* 2). Zaretsky echoes this narrative but places the origin a generation earlier: "The disciplines of sociology and anthropology both took shape in America in the years between 1890 and 1915 by gradually disengaging themselves from this kind of [social] theory, which essentially viewed social history as a subspecies of biological evolution. [William I.] Thomas's early work in sociology parallels Franz Boas's in anthropology: both men sought to replace biological concepts of evolution with specifically sociological (Thomas) and cultural (Boas) mechanisms of change" (10).

3. Oliver Cox had a much less generous way of putting it: "Shorn of its censual and descriptive support, Park's theory of race relations is weak, vacillating, and misleading; and to the extent that it lends 'scientific' confirmation to the Southern rationalizations of racial exploitation, it is insidious" (474).

4. His unpublished notes indicate further essentialist identifications Park considered between African Americans and (presumably white) women: "Man has got what he wanted by tackling things; going at them directly. The negro and the woman have got them by manipulating the individual in control. Women and Negroes have required the machinery of rapid and delicate adjustment to the words and temper of men." This passage comes from the "Unpublished notes on the Negro," Robert E. Park Papers (qtd. in Stanfield 53).

5. Much of the foundation for Park's identification of European immigrants with African Americans may have been laid early in his career under the tutelage of Booker T. Washington at the Tuskeegee Institute. Park's recollections suggest it was there, as Washington's aid, that he took the circumstances of Southern African Americans as the model for all other group relations:

> I think I probably learned more about human nature and society, in the South under Booker Washington, than I had learned elsewhere in all my previous studies. . . . I was not . . . interested in the Negro problem as that problem is ordinarily conceived. I was interested in the Negro in the South and in the curious and intricate system which had grown up to define his relations with white folk. I was interested, most of all, in studying the details of the process by which the Negro was making and has made his slow but steady advance. I became convinced, finally, that I was observing the historical process by which civilization, not merely here but elsewhere, has evolved, drawing into the circle of its influence an ever widening circle of races and peoples. (*Race and Culture* vii–viii)

In his later work, "The Nature of Race Relations" (1939), Park seems to reverse this relation, suggesting European colonization and immigration as the model for all other forms of group interaction (35).

6. Several of the following quotes are from the section titled "Conflict and Accommodation" on pages 634–40 of the Park and Burgess's *Introduction*. Park notes that he "adapted" this section from an article by Alfred H. Stone, but the fact of its interpolation without editorial comment in a work intended for use as a graduate text-

book strongly suggests that Park identifies with its views or at least considers them au courant in the discipline.

7. McKee also makes the case that Park's followers took his race relations cycle too dogmatically, as if each phase inevitably followed from one to the next. Park's relatively few uses of the race relations cycle included variations that did not always lead to assimilation. McKee also points out that subsequent sociology did not share Park's interest in conflict as a key feature of race relations, a predilection that would contribute to its difficulties explaining the Civil Rights Movement. Once again, the polyvalency of Park's work made a selective interpretation of key issues possible in ways consistent with prevailing ideological preferences: "The Park of the race relations cycle ending in peaceful assimilation was acceptable to sociologists, but the Park of national minorities struggling for new racial accommodations was not" (McKee 146).

8. Eric J. Sundquist suggests that while DuBois never entirely relinquished the idea that racial categories were biologically justified, he nevertheless increasingly emphasized the priority of the cultural and political aspects of race over any biological considerations (37). See also Anthony Appiah's far less sympathetic assessment of DuBois's use of race in which he argues that DuBois "was unable to escape the notion of race he had explicitly rejected" (135). For Appiah, race is only illusion because it lacks scientific credence and so dismisses the consideration of race as ideology or, as DuBois employed it, the basis of solidarity and collective action.

9. Locke's lectures, never published during his lifetime, were edited by Jeffrey C. Stewart from flawed transcriptions. Except where required for my own grammatical consistency, brackets are reproduced exactly as they appear and indicate "conjectural words or passages supplied by the editor" (Stewart lxv).

10. This point is made frequently in more recent attacks on the idea of race—that more variation exists within a race than between any two races. As Locke put it: "To put it in terms of a concrete example, one can find more variability in the [anthropological differences] between one class of Frenchmen and another class of Frenchmen than when you take an average European and [compare him with] an [average] African or a Malay" (5). Genetic evidence has since corroborated the point. See, for example, Corcos (173).

11. "Now, culture-citizenship is something which is to be acquired through social assimilation, not necessarily physical assimilation. . . . [It] must come in terms of group contribution to what becomes a joint civilization. . . . [It] will enable us . . . to qualify in terms not merely of imitation but of contribution" (Locke 99). This argument became one of Locke's guiding principles regarding the "New Negro" and the Harlem Renaissance.

12. Though I assume throughout this discussion that some racial theories are preferable to others, namely that the cultural construction of race and identity should replace race science, I am aware that it is difficult to avoid the impression that thought develops along a continuum toward enlightenment. Instead, however, it makes more theoretical sense to consider that, to use Locke's terms, the dominant race theories of any period, including our own, are appropriate to and determined by the limits of its social race practice and never fully autonomous (3–4).

3

Inventing Ethnicity in the Context of Race and Caste, 1930–1945

By the 1920s, the discourse of the social sciences, particularly the emerging fields of anthropology and sociology, was groping toward a new conception of human difference based on environment rather than biology but still unwilling to relinquish old assurances about the physical foundation of group identity. This chapter's argument is that the idea of ethnicity emerges in the 1940s out of this contradiction between the advancing cultural critiques of race pseudoscience and the reluctance of most white intellectuals, at the same time, to forgo the idea of the color line as an inherent and permanent feature of American social reality. Ethnicity signifies a cultural or "environmental" conception of identity, a perspective that accompanied the critique of biological race. However, the immediate circumstances of its invention served the paradoxical purpose of erasing turn-of-the-century ideas regarding the racial differences between European groups while leaving race and the black-white color line fully in place.

As stated earlier in chapter 1, there was considerable doubt in popular and academic thought in the decade before and after 1900 as to whether all Europeans, especially eastern and southern European immigrant groups, really were white. And if they were generally considered white by the 1920s and 1930s, the ambiguous concepts of race that identified it with nationalities left lingering doubts about whether all white Americans were members of the same race. *Ethnicity* enters the sociological lexicon as a means by which the concept of the white race eliminates internal divisions created by race science. The uncommon term *ethnic*, which had been used since the nineteenth century as a synonym for *race* as innate physical traits, was by the 1930s redefined and recontextualized in ways that made use of the newer ideas of group differences as a function of culture. As we have seen in chapter 2, scholars and researchers, chiefly Boas and Park, had begun to undermine the race science of the previous generation by attacking its premises and by exploring ways to understand group differences as a matter of social history rather than heritability. Ironically, however, *race* became paired with, rather than replaced by, *ethnic* in the sociological discourse despite the fact that the two terms bespeak contradictory and incompatible intellectual frameworks. The concept *ethnicity* can be seen then as the means by which the social sciences accommodate the potentially devastating new critique of the social construction of race while, at the same time, maintaining a firm ideological commitment to the racial status quo.

To understand how such a theoretical chimera as the race-ethnic compromise could exist and become naturalized within the common sense of sociology requires looking at several features of the sociological literature of the time. Though much of the change around the issue of race was instigated by the groundbreaking work of Boas and anthropology, it was sociology that was most committed to the development of a whole theoretical schema of race relations, and it was increasingly within the terms defined by sociology that race was debated (McKee 145). In fact, while anthropology was poking holes in the scientific evidence for biologically based racial categories, it was Park and the field of sociology that in the 1920s had reconstructed the discourse on race from a language of biology to one of social relations. However, as we have seen, even the staunchest proponents of cultural alternatives to scientific race, like Boas, Thomas, and Park, could not seem to help repeating in their own work some of the crudest shibboleths of the race-science paradigm. In general, there was a growing sense within the dominant sociological discourse of a fundamental difference between American blacks and European immigrants. The consensus among mainstream sociologists was that American black people, unlike the new immigrants, were primitives who had lost their own culture, language, and traditions and whose potential for assimilating into American society was limited.

Thus, the kind of comparisons that Park had considered within a global perspective, that saw American blacks and European immigrants involved in the same broader historical process of migration and intercultural encounters, were generally dismissed by his peers (McKee 146). Instead, sociology embraced the narrative of modernization, which interpreted history as the process by which traditional practices and cultures were swept away in the advance of rationalized, industrialized modern society. In the perspective of mainstream sociology, blacks were a traditional, premodern people whose chances for survival in the modern world were doubtful. Park himself developed his own version of this scenario (Stanfield 48–49).[1] Moreover, the sociological consensus held that European immigrants could be assimilated, or "Americanized," successfully, but that white prejudice against African Americans would prohibit their assimilation. White sexual anxiety over "amalgamation," it was generally agreed, posed an insurmountable barrier. However, even without white prejudice, many white scholars felt that blacks lacked the capacity to adapt to modern society. Thus, even though the credibility of race science became increasingly tenuous, many of its basic principles remained within sociology; the narrative of modernization facilitated the exchange of black cultural, instead of biological, inferiority (McKee 6–7).

Perhaps most instrumental in providing a framework that could contain both the new idea of ethnicity and the old racial ideology, despite their logical inconsistency with one another, was the rise of the caste model of race relations to a position of disciplinary prominence in the interwar period. Dating from the nineteenth century, the analogy of the caste system, borrowed from what American sociologists thought they knew about the social structure of India, became dominant in the 1930s sociological discourse. It was, in fact, within this model in the 1940s that the word *ethnicity* was first coined and given its initial meaning. By the 1930s, the Great Migration had brought millions of blacks from the South to northern urban centers, creating a new black industrial working class to fill the labor needs of burgeoning industrialism and thus profoundly changing the nature of race relations in the United States. Nevertheless, the caste model, rooted in the example of the traditional rural South, assumed the status of a generalized model for American race relations as a whole. Its incongruity with historical conditions thus foregrounds the ideological appeal of the caste analogy for a conservative sociology: it offers an image of inequitable and exploitative power relations that are nevertheless functional, stable, and free of conflict and coercion.

The caste perspective claimed its interpretive authority on the basis of three basic assertions. First, it offers an understanding of race as fixed, ascriptive, and unchanging. Though caste in its American incarnation makes allowances for class mobility, it does so without the possibility of altering caste hierarchies. Second, caste societies are characterized by endogamous marriage practices within caste divisions, characteristic of written and unwritten laws in American society. And third, the caste model sought to explain the system of rituals and attitudes whose purpose was to reinforce the inferiority of the lower caste. This aspect had an obvious application in relation to the codes of interracial contact in the South. Though the caste interpretation of American race relations met with thorough criticism, it nevertheless became the dominant mode in which American sociologists discussed and analyzed race for a period in the 1930s and 1940s. The language of caste offered a comforting vision of race relations in equilibrium, in which everyone knew and accepted their place, and the struggle for change was neither possible nor desired. And though the period was relatively brief, assumptions behind caste influenced the sociology of race relations until the 1960s when the reality of resistance and racial conflict could no longer be denied.

THE NEED FOR NEW TERMS

Thus reconstructing the circumstances of *ethnicity*'s origins is a matter of considering two lines of development in the social sciences. One of these paths is the rise of the caste model as the authoritative understanding of race in America. The other development is sociologists' search for a new language to address what appeared as the limits of biological race in light of new, cultural bases of human difference. We have already seen that Robert Park was prominent among those who tried to reconcile the older conception of group identity as seated in heritable physiological traits, often referred to as racial "temperament," with more recent ideas about the way social environment shapes individuals and group character. His discussions often gave a place to both kinds of forces and frequently weighted race with the more fundamental determination over culture. But as Persons notes, Park used race to describe all processes and phenomena of group formation. Since his perspective could accommodate both physical and cultural factors together in the same larger process, he never saw the need for terms that separated a group formed on the basis of race from another formed on the basis of culture. We have also seen that a few scholars had begun using the term *ethnic* in contexts that anticipated its future use to distinguish cultural groups from those considered racial. Since the nineteenth century, *ethnic* had been used interchangeably with *race*. But in *The Polish Peasant in Europe and America* (1918), William I. Thomas and Florian Znaniecki use the word *ethnic* in the context of a discussion of group character that stresses social practice over biological inheritance. And we have seen that Alain Locke's 1915 lectures on race are so theoretically rich and innovative that, without calling attention to it, his use of *ethnic* carries with it the sense of cultural identity virtually indistinguishable from the most contemporary applications. His uncompromising critique of biological race as historical and political fabrication renders his references to ethnic groups in the same context collectives by virtue of shared culture rather than phenotype.

However, it was a French anthropologist, Joseph Deniker, who explicitly raised the terminological question as far back as 1901 in his book *The Races of Man: An Outline of Anthropology and Ethnography*. Deniker begins by arguing that the zoological sense of *race* and *species* is neither useful nor appropriate in the classification of human beings. There is a great deal of confusion among scientists, Deniker observes, with their various racial schemas that divide humans into anywhere from two to thirty-four different varieties (280).

Instead, Deniker proposes that the scientific practice of classifying human beings should make a distinction between races and ethnic groups. The latter, he proposes, are defined "by virtue of community of language, religion, social institutions, etc., which have the power of uniting human beings of one or several species, races, or varieties, and are by no means zoological species" (3). Classification by race, on the other hand, is based purely on physical characteristics or what Deniker calls "somatological units," which are the "aggregation of physical characters combined in a certain way" (3). Human races or species differ significantly from their zoological counterparts in that there are no pure examples empirically available. "It is a very rare occurrence," Deniker explains, "to meet with an individual representing the type of the somatological unit to which he belongs" (3). Rather, most humans exist as members of ethnic groups that are the result of several somatological units combined and "include human beings of one or of many species, races, or varieties" (Deniker 3). The combination of a small number of races (Deniker proposes twenty-nine), "in various proportions, are met with in the multitude of ethnic groups" (281). Races in the case of human beings, then, are "theoretical" in the sense that they must be deduced from actual ethnic groups. Moreover, Deniker suggests that the study of race and ethnic groups are the proper objects of two distinct sciences. The former, which looks at physical or "somatological characteristics," is anthropology while it is ethnography, or ethnology, which "should concern itself with human societies under all their aspects" (9), and thus take up the study of ethnic groups. Because he accommodates both, despite their theoretical incommensurability and despite his own thesis that races exist not in nature but only as ideal abstractions, Deniker thus presages the later accommodation of ethnicity within an essentially racialized schema of human differences.

Even while Deniker was widely read and considered an authority on the subject of human classification, most authors for the next thirty years could not entertain the idea that distinct human races were not a matter of biological and empirical reality. Only a minority within scholarly circles acknowledged the holes in the arguments for race that were beginning to show by the turn of the century, or the influence of environment on human character. The word *ethnic* was beginning to pick up the sense of identity defined through social practice, as in the lectures by Locke, but no formal distinction of the sort that Deniker proposed between *race* and *ethnic* would become part of the discourse until the 1930s. Only the development of social, as opposed to biological, definitions of human difference, and the repeated use of *ethnic* and *race*, respectively, could establish the conditions for such a formalization to take place.

By the early 1930s, sociologists were sensing the deficiency in their terminology to reference emerging new perspectives. Donald Young's 1932 *Amer-*

ican Minority Peoples is an interesting case in point. He indicates the growing gap between the popular ideology of race and that of scientists. In the era of scientific race in the two decades before and after 1900, popular and professional understandings of race were fairly consistent. But by 1932, Young could complain that the "ordinary citizen" cares not at all about the subtle requirements of racial classification and whether members of various groups fit one definition or another. Young notes that "with superb disdain for the findings of the scientists, popular belief lumps biological, language, cultural, political, and other groups under the one heading of 'race,' and behaves accordingly" (Young xiii).[2] Young thus indicates that, for scientists at least, such distinctions between biological and cultural groupings were significant, even if this went unrecognized in popular arenas. And yet, while the distinctions were sufficiently important to name, Young indicates the inadequacy of the current terminology to do the job. He writes, "There is, unfortunately, no word in the English language which can with philological propriety be applied to all these groups, that is, which includes groups which are distinguished by biological features, alien national cultural traits, or a combination of both" (xiii).[3] Moreover, since the nineteenth century, *race* signified virtually any human group whether national, racial, cultural, even, in some cases, gender. It was generally interchangeable with *ethnic* (group) and *nation*. Young's description of the circumstances that call for a term other than *race* to refer to all groups is suggestive of a new kind of limit on the word. *Race* could refer to groups identified by physical features, but Young's work is a strong indication that by the early 1930s culturally or nationally defined groups responded to forces of group formation other than *race* and that required a new and different term. Significantly, however, *ethnic* was not yet that term.

CHOOSING *ETHNIC*

The consolidation of the sociological vocabulary of race relations in the 1930s, however, would institutionalize *ethnic* as a paired term with *race*. McKee cites the works of T. J. Woofter as instrumental in establishing the pair as a phrase, namely his 1931 essay, "The Status of Racial and Ethnic Groups" and his 1933 book *Race and Ethnic Groups in American Life*. Interestingly, Woofter does not clarify the terminological distinctions explicitly, though he does implicitly differentiate between *race* and *nationality*. Contrary to McKee's claims, however, Woofter uses *ethnic* interchangeably with *race* throughout his texts. Nevertheless, Woofter's pairing of the terms in his titles implies that they are not synonymous or redundant, indicating a new semantic development. The phrase, "race and ethnic," or some variation thereof, would become standard in the language of the sociology of race relations and would, as McKee notes, become "widely used as titles for books and college courses" (131). Moreover, their definitional relationship would become more precise in the 1930s and respond to the lack to which Young had referred by firmly situating *ethnic* as *race*'s cultural counter-term.

A key text in the stabilization of the race-ethnic distinction is Julian S. Huxley and A. C. Haddon's 1935 *We Europeans: A Survey of "Racial" Problems*. Significantly, however, Huxley and Haddon's focus, as the quote marks imply, is the questionable status of *race* as a concept, and they use the occasion to call for a moratorium on its use. Like Young, they note a widening gap between popular and scientific understandings of the idea. They note that "in spite of the work of geneticist and anthropologist there is still a lamentable confusion between the ideas of *race, culture* and *nation*" (Huxley and Haddon 107). On all the referents of *race*, including the major divisions of humankind, the population of a nation, a recognizable physical type, and so on—"on all these uses, scientific analysis, backed by the results of modern genetics, throws a pitiless light" (263). The evidence now shows that genetic variability and mutability are so complex and dynamic, even within putative racial groups, that "no single scheme of classification, in point of fact, has been devised which will provide a satisfactory pigeon-holing for the various human types in existence" (264). Elazar Barkan notes that "the main achievement of *We Europeans* was its endeavor to combine biological and anthropological data in one volume in a serious application of advanced theories of genetics to a comprehensive study of ethnic groups" (297). While not the only work of its kind in the 1930s, its sophisticated intellectual approach as well as popularity and influence make the book "among the most important of this genre which helped undermine the scientific basis for racism" (Barkan 296). For present purposes, however, the book is especially significant for the explicit distinction the authors draw between *race* and *ethnic*.

In showing that racial differentiation is inconsistent with recent scientific discoveries, the authors hoped to reach an audience beyond the scientific community. At pains to explain that *race* "is almost devoid of biological meaning as applied to human aggregates," they nevertheless knew that "it is extremely difficult to remove it from popular use" (Huxley and Haddon 144). Such incongruity suggests that race serves important functions elsewhere, other than science. It is, according to Huxley and Haddon, a pseudoscientific disguise employed "to rationalize emotion, and to bolster up the appeals of prejudice" by appealing "to the accuracy and to the prestige of science" (282). Race legitimates economic and political policies as if they were based on objective scientific principles. In fact, Huxley and Haddon suggest, "the violent racialism to be found in Europe to-day is a symptom of Europe's exaggerated nationalism: it is an attempt to justify nationalism on a non-nationalist basis" (287). Thus, perhaps the most pressing issue informing the text is the need to discredit the fascists' racial division of Europeans. Such division harnessed to the eugenic policies of the state was, of course, the logical conclusion of the discourse we have seen within the human sciences that sought to explain all religious and national group differences as a function of innate and hierarchical racial determinants. The work of Ripley, Grant, and Stoddard in the early part of the twentieth century, as noted in chapter 1, successfully popularized the racial ideologies that divided European groups into separate, hierarchical races. Stoddard, in fact, met with Adolf Hitler in 1940 and, though he felt the Nazis had taken them to extremes, regarded "many of their ideas as excellent" (Gossett 427–28).

Accordingly, Huxley and Haddon take special care to dismantle both the idea of an Aryan and Jewish race. The former they trace to the tradition of European philology, translated from Sanskrit and used to distinguish both a family of Indo-European languages and its speakers (Huxley and Haddon 147). When one of the most prominent philologists in the mid-nineteenth century, Max Müller, expanded the group of speakers into an "Aryan race," the idea was enthusiastically received in Germany and England and spread by writers and propagandists with no training to appreciate the scientific merits of the claim. To no avail were Müller's later attempts to qualify the point that he meant "neither blood nor bones, nor hair, nor skull; I mean simply those who speak an Aryan language" (qtd. in Huxley and Haddon 151). Likewise, Huxley and Haddon point out the Teutonic type is an arbitrary ideal whose claim to scientific status is suitable only for derision:

> Our German neighbors have ascribed to themselves a Teutonic type that is fair, long-headed, tall and virile. Let us make a composite picture of a typical Teutonic from the most prominent of the exponents of this view. Let him be as blond as Hitler, as dolichocephalic as Rosenberg, as tall as Goebbels, as slender as Goering, as manly as Streicher. How much would he resemble the German ideal? (25–26)

Completing the demolition of fascism's racial ideology, Huxley and Haddon explain why Jews are not a race but are of mixed descent and constitute rather "a society forming a pseudo-national group with a strong religious basis and peculiar historic traditions" (274). Even in *Mein Kampf,* the characteristics that Hitler lists as definitive of the Jewish racial type "are based not on any biological concept of physical descent—as to the essential nature and meaning of which he exhibits neither knowledge nor insight—but almost entirely on social and cultural elements" (Huxley and Haddon 28). Thus given the evidence, from a biological standpoint, "it is almost as illegitimate to speak of a 'Jewish race' as of an 'Aryan race'" (Huxley and Haddon 274). Further, the absolute racial division that the two concepts assume is itself questionable. Proving one's Aryan purity in Germany by demonstrating the absence of Jewish ancestors has shown itself to be difficult and frequently impossible (Huxley and Haddon 284). Rather, again, the social and political

factors are more revealing: competition during the Depression and the convenience of treating "the Jews as a collective scapegoat" explain better than
science the motives for anti-Semitism (Huxley and Haddon 284–85).

Huxley and Haddon reject, for lack of scientific evidence and because
of the harmful ends to which it is applied, the notion that there are any
racial differences between the people of Europe. "Racialism is a myth, and
a dangerous myth at that," they argue (Huxley and Haddon 287). Its social
function serves a need other than scientific inquiry: "It is a cloak for self-
ish economic aims which in their uncloaked nakedness would look ugly
enough" (Huxley and Haddon 287). Therefore, they recommend, "the word
race should be banished, and the descriptive and non-committal term *ethnic
group* should be substituted" (Huxley and Haddon 268), at least in the study
of European group differences, because "*so far as European populations are
concerned*, nothing in the nature of 'pure race' in the biological sense has
any real existence" (27, emphasis added). The distinguishing characteristics
that racialists such as Hitler have noted, suggest Huxley and Haddon, are
cultural rather than biological and physical differences are merely environmental adaptations. They urge "that we must avoid mistaking cultural for
innate differences; and cultural differences are the most obvious and greatest
differences between European ethnic groups" (Huxley and Haddon 123).
Because the term *race* has lost all specificity and should be dropped from
scientific language, Huxley and Haddon recommend a shift in language that
is crucial to the present study: "In what follows the word *race* will be deliberately avoided, and the term (*ethnic*) *group* or *people* employed for all general purposes" (108). While Huxley and Haddon include all racial divisions
in their condemnation, their chief consideration throughout the book is the
elimination of European racial divisions. Indeed, the title of the work, *We
Europeans*, speaks to the imagined community of a unified Europe made
possible by the scientific evidence that erases all racial dividing lines, at least
those separating Europeans from each other. In fact, Huxley and Haddon
make a point of attacking the tripartite racial schema advanced by Ripley
and Grant, as discussed in chapter 1, that divided and ranked the races of
Europe. Huxley and Haddon write, "The conception of three main European
'races': Mediterranean, Alpine, and Nordic, which is still commonly held
is too simple and has led to erroneous generalizations" (201–2). For Grant
they offer only passing ridicule: "When, too, we read in Madison Grant's
The Passing of the Great Race that the greatest and most masterful personalities have had blond hair and blue eyes we can make a shrewd guess at its
author's complexion" (Huxley and Haddon 18).

Huxley and Haddon thus reconstruct a unified European community by
removing the foundation for racializing group differences. At the same time,
they also redefine those differences by proposing *ethnic groups* where previously *race* had been used. Unlike Deniker, who had advocated a similar

terminological innovation thirty years prior, Huxley and Haddon are not content with the unempirical status of *race* and demand it be "banished" and replaced rather than merely accompanied by another new, more verifiable, concept. And yet, the first time that Huxley and Haddon suggest the switch, *ethnic groups* is inserted within parentheses, as if to be taken as optional or implicit, and they follow the phrase not by an explanation or definition but by a discussion of genetic variation. In this context, the "descriptive and non-committal" sense to which "(ethnic) group" refers purposefully eludes precise definition (268). It indicates only a kind of statistical approximation of human types in a way that *race*, rendered imprecise and pseudoscientific by popular misuse, no longer could. Their chapter on the "Main Ethnic Groups of Europe" looks very much like their many predecessors' obligatory inventories of the major races of Europe, such as Ripley's, complete with descriptions of prehistoric descent and definitive physical characteristics of head shapes, hair and nose types, stature, and so on.[4] No doubt this is why Andrew Lyons comments that the authors share a sense of *ethnic group* with Ashley Montagu that is "primarily biological rather than sociological in its reference [though] it does not refer to a biological division of the species" (Lyons 12). Yet, in a discussion on the classical historian Herodotus, Huxley and Haddon describe what they have in mind in selecting just that term. They observe that his use of the words *ethnos* and *ethnea*, though often unfortunately translated as *race*, rather suggested the senses "at times a tribe, at times a political unit, at times a larger grouping, and in using the word he guards himself against treating either type of unit as necessarily or even probably of common descent" (Huxley and Haddon 31). Furthermore, Herodotus "comes to the sensible conclusion that a group such as the Greeks, is marked off from other groups by complex factors of which kinship is one, but that at least as important are language, culture or tradition" (Huxley and Haddon 31).

In a move that has central importance for the present study, Huxley and Haddon identify with Herodotus's sense: "It is, in fact, what we in this volume label, non-committally, an 'ethnic group'" (Huxley and Haddon 31). Thus, through classical texts, they recover a definition of *ethnic* that had been largely suppressed since at least the nineteenth century. We have seen this meaning inchoate in writers skeptical of race science and explicit in Deniker. But the term was rare and its dominant meanings remained "foreigner" (i.e., "heathen, neither gentile nor Jew") and, in the later nineteenth century, "race." But Huxley and Haddon's rediscovery circumvents these conventions. Moreover, the restoration of the lost etymological heritage of *ethnos* responds to and resolves the particular historical crisis that Young had acknowledged: the environmental conceptions of group difference were exceeding the capacity of *race*, shackled as it was to biology alone. Here, the term *ethnic group* is explicitly joined to the cultural foundations of human difference in a way that marks it off from biological race. But, just as significantly, the context for this rediscovery is the problem of fascism, which had forced the issue by taking the logic of racial divisions among Europeans to its conclusion. Thus, the redefinition of *ethnic* responds to the crisis in the racial integrity of Europe and, by extension, "the white race." In an American context, the new immigrants, once an "inbetween people," could now find an unambiguous place, in the discourse of the human sciences at least, among the now racially unified European Americans.

But the implicit exclusivity of ethnic group status to Europeans alone reinforces the reserving of cultural definition to whiteness and does nothing to alter the standard identification of blacks as a people without a history or a culture and as the products of an inferior biological inheritance. Moreover, on the issue of "race-mixing," Huxley and Haddon are strangely equivocal. They assert in no uncertain terms that "disapproval of 'miscegenation' is primarily social, not biological" (280) and that any "biological reasoning" in prohibitions against intermarriage or restrictions on immigration, such as occurred in America in the 1920s, "is a cloak to fling over obscure, perhaps unconscious feelings" (283). Yet, at the same time, Huxley and Haddon assert that sometimes "the discouragement of 'racial crossing' may be the correct policy" (286). Part of their rationale for this stance is that mixtures of extremely divergent groups may cause social and cultural changes too great and too sudden for the social system to bear. For example, because of the "new genetic recombinations to be obtained," it might be advantageous "to undertake mass-crossing between say the British and the Bantu, or the Americans and the Chinese," but the resulting cultural changes would exceed what each society could sustain (Huxley and Haddon 282). At the same time, in language that is reminiscent of race science, Huxley and Haddon also explain that in considering race-mixing, "there is also the question of the biological results of wide crosses" (280). If such mixing involves ethnic groups with "low average level of innate intelligence, to allow crosses between them and more intelligent types is a retrograde step" (281).[5]

Huxley and Haddon would seem to hold a contradictory position similar to several of the white writers we have encountered thus far. They advance the most current theories to eviscerate racial difference in the case of Europeans but fall back on outmoded thinking, the very thinking they set out to destroy, to reaffirm racial difference in the case of nonwhites and non-Europeans. Barnor Hesse writes of an analogous state of affairs in the origins of the concept of racism. Its first appearance as a term of disapprobation was in German author Magnus Hirschfeld's *Racism* (1938), and subsequent rejections of race and racism from the same period, such as Huxley and Haddon's, were written by Europeans responding to Nazi anti-Semitism. For Hesse, the question is "how did the racialized experiences and violations of the Jews in Europe, rather than those associated with US Blacks or colonized 'non-whites' generally, come to dominate conceptually and frame paradigmatically the twentieth-century concept of racism in international relations?" (18). Why was it, in other words, that the Jewish situation in the 1930s and 1940s modeled and motivated European intellectuals to develop the concept of racism despite previously available examples in the treatment of African Americans and colonial subjects? Hesse's answer is that Nazism was a "profound disruption" (20) in the liberal framework of European imperialism insofar as it brought home for domestic use management techniques previously restricted to overseas colonies and people of color. Nazism and the persecution of the Jews, in other words, "conflated the distinction between European Nation and European Empire" and "erased the global colour line, distorting the extant colonial and racial distinction between European and 'non-European', white and 'non-white'" (20). As DuBois and Aime Cesaire noted at the time, given the omission of people of color and the colonized, such a formulation of racism was itself racist. Transposing Hesse's critique of the concept of racism, we may consider that one of the driving forces for the creation of the concept of ethnicity in America was a fundamental commitment to liberal imperialism as well as white supremacy.[6] Racialized divisions between European Americans and the colonized Other were acceptable, even necessary, to the colonial project while divisions within the European American population violated the order predicated on that same project.

Despite this contradiction (that should by now be familiar to students of the early attempts to break away from race science), the development of the concept of the *ethnic group* in the sense forged by Huxley and Haddon presented a way around the racial barriers preventing conceptual unification of the new immigrants with the rest of the white race. However, while often cited in retrospect for its controversial and influential theoretical and terminological innovation, the book had little immediate impact in British circles where it was first published. Barkan observes that "despite the challenge laid down by *We Europeans*, the scientific community was too divided on substance and policy to present any alternative for racist thinking" (308). Upon its American publication, the book was widely and prominently reviewed, including enthusiastic front-page spreads with banner headlines in both the *New York Herald Tribune Books* and the *New York Times Book Review*.[7] Its highly visible reception and forceful argument suggest that *We Europeans* was a significant contribution to the development of the race-ethnic distinction.

The scientific authority of the book also lent its weight to the theoretical shift that regarded differences within whiteness, first inscribed by the discourse of race science, as meliorable and ripe for reclassification as cultural. Evidence that this shift was taking hold is Carleton Stevens Coon's 1939 anthropology textbook, *The Races of Europe*. The book is dedicated to William Z. Ripley, author of the now "classic" 1899 text of the same title, which was influential in promoting the triple division of Europeans into the Mediterranean, Alpine, and Nordic races. However, despite Ripley's repudiation of the term *white race* as hopelessly unscientific, Coon uses it without hesitation or apparent need for explanation. It is also interchangeable with *Europeans* in his writing. The aim of Coon's *The Races of Europe* is, he explains, to "trace the racial history of the white division of *Homo sapiens* from its Pleistocene beginnings to the present" with "the main emphasis . . . placed upon the racial identification and classification of living white peoples" (vii). Ironically, much of the evidence he employs for his history is skeletal, from which he admits no conclusions about pigmentation can be drawn. Yet he never attempts a justification for the use of *white* as a designation for the racial category of European peoples, which suggests the definitive degree to which the color line had been drawn around Europe by 1939, at least in the American intellectual context. He explains that the popular appeal of Ripley's "facile" (Coon 285) tripartite classification was a result of its accessibility to the layperson who then added, beyond Ripley's intentions, the various psychological and moral characteristics.

WARNER AND CASTE

We should, of course, assume that the historical circumstances pressing on Coon's efforts to reunify the white "family" in 1939 were as compelling as Ripley's to divide it in 1899. But the special, exclusive allocation of ethnic or cultural identity to Europeans left the larger issue of race unresolved. Claiming only to follow popular usage as common and scientific understandings of race continued to diverge, sociologists came to recognize that groups of color were designated as racial, while newly initiated whites were deemed ethnic. The work that perhaps first and most extensively develops this race-ethnic distinction, suggested by Huxley and Haddon, is W. Lloyd Warner's *Yankee City* series which is cited, not coincidentally, as the first appearance of the word *ethnicity*.[8] The results of a collaborative study by social anthropologists from the Committee of Industrial Physiology at Harvard University, the *Yankee City* series examined in six volumes between 1941 and 1945 the social patterns and structures of a "modern community" in New England. Though the word first appears in passing on page 212 of volume 1 (1941), volume 2 (1942) introduces and defines the neologism *ethnicity* as "one of the several characteristics which modify the social system and are modified by it" (Warner and Lunt, *System* 73). While Warner (and Paul S. Lunt in this volume) recognizes a distinction between racial and ethnic characteristics, their coining of *ethnicity* at this point in the series encompasses both. Thus, "ethnicity may be evaluated almost entirely upon a biological basis or upon purely social characteristics" (Warner and Lunt, *System* 73). The difference between racial and social characteristics, however, is that they define the extreme poles of a spectrum on which all minority groups may be positioned depending on whether their predominant group differences, relative to the native Anglo-American, are defined as the one or the other. Thus:

> Negroes tend to be at the first extreme, since they are most physically variant of all groups in the community, and the Irish at the other extreme, since they are most like the native white stock. The Yankee City Negro's culture comes from a Yankee tradition, but the group's biological differences provide a symbol around which social differences are defined and evaluated. The Irish maintain certain social usages which differentiate them in varying degrees from the whole community. The other groups fall in between these two extremes. (Warner and Lunt, *System* 73)

This continuum of groups is revealing, suggesting that it is the Negro's phenotypic differences that "provide a symbol around which the social differences" of all the other groups are defined, regardless of culture. Irish differences are a matter of "social usage" because, compared physically to a field organized by the Negro, they are the most like the native white stock. Warner thus suppresses the history that would better explain the Negro's extreme and defining alienation in Yankee City. His facile assumption of skin color prejudice as the principle organizing group hierarchy naturalizes and mystifies racial discrimination based on color, dehistoricizes its basis, and obscures the nature and function of racial power relations.

The *Yankee City* series further develops its taxonomy of cultural and physical differences in volume 3 (1945) by plotting out "degrees of subordination" from the "present old-American stock" into six cultural variations for each of five racial types. Though racial and cultural differences are still part of the same continuum, "the racial evaluations made by the American host society are far more potent and lasting in the ranking of divergent peoples than those applied to cultural groups" (Warner and Srole 287). The reason for this distinction between cultural or physical differences is that the cultural or ethnic group includes all those who are implicitly white and part of "the Caucasoid racial group" but are inferior by virtue of "a divergent set of cultural traits" (Warner and Srole 286, 285). Racially different groups, on the other hand, "the Mongoloid and Negroid peoples," are deemed inferior by virtue of inherited physical traits. For example, "such physical attributes as dark skin, the epicanthic fold, or kinky hair become symbols of status and automatically consign their possessors to inferior status" (Warner and Srole 285).

Warner's distinction between ethnic and racial groups, as the difference between cultural versus biological differences from the native white norm, is still largely that which applies today and is the one delineated by van den Berghe in 1967. That is, ethnicity and race describe two modes of difference from the hegemonic group with implications for power relative to the nature of the difference. Moreover, the difference between cultural and racial traits is that the former are ephemeral. Ethnic group status is cast in Warner as a kind of probationary status, to borrow Matthew Frye Jacobson's felicitous metaphor,[9] while that of the racial group is more or less static and permanent. Cultural groups originate, paradoxically, in order to dissolve by forming "their own social world to nurse their members through a period of transition until these members 'unlearn' what they have been taught and successfully learn the new way of life necessary for full acceptance in the host society" (Warner and Srole 285). Inferior cultural traits, therefore, can and do change over time, while "the physical traits which have become symbols of inferior status are permanent" (Warner and Srole 285). Yet, Warner does not assume that this process is a function of what Park and others argued was an involuntary competitive reaction to the racial Other. Instead, Warner maintains that stratification is discursive and the subordination that is grounded in physical features is only as permanent as the discourse that deems it so: "Unless the host society changes its methods of evaluation these racial groups are doomed to a permanent inferior ranking" (Warner and Srole 285). As with most white sociologists through the 1960s, the possibility of a coordinated effort by the racial groups themselves to force such change does not exist for Warner.

The conclusion that Warner and his collaborators draw from the chart of racial and ethnic traits is that the black-white color line will become more pronounced and that the various groups will merge toward the predominant color on each side. "All of the six cultural types in Racial Types I and II [the Light and Dark Caucasoids] we predict will change from ethnic groups and become wholly a part of the American class order," while all six types in each of categories IV and V, Mongoloids and Negroids, "are likely to develop into castes or semi-castes like that of the American Negro" (Warner and Srole 295). The "ethno-racial groups" of Racial Type III, however, including the Spanish and Latin Americans, will split along the color line as it infinitely recedes: "Those of the more Caucasoid type will become a part of our class order and be capable of rising in our social hierarchy" while "the darker ones will probably become semi-caste" (Warner and Srole 295). As race in the sense of skin color becomes increasingly decisive in positioning groups in American society, "ethnicity" appears as a transitory phase in the larger process of assimilation. In due course, Warner and Srole portend, a new era in American social relations begins:

> The future of American ethnic groups seems to be limited; it is likely that they will be quickly absorbed. When this happens one of the great epochs of American history will have ended and another, that of race, will begin. (295)

On the issue of race, the pronouncement corroborates W.E.B. DuBois's famous prediction a half century before that the history of the twentieth century would be a history of the color line. *Ethnicity* re-enters the language in this work as a transitional state in which an underlying whiteness eventually blots out cultural differences. Michael Banton, writing from a later time when ethnicity would be a quality possessed by all groups, criticizes Warner for the use of this term because "without realizing what he was doing," he was merely borrowing the "folk concepts" of his subjects: "He took over the Yankees' assumption that they had no ethnicity since ethnicity characterized the people who had not yet been fully Americanized" (Banton, *Racial* 146). No doubt merely attempting to describe his data, Warner's adoption of *ethnicity* nevertheless effectively codifies the subordinate status of the eastern and southern Europeans, in a way that might remind us of a similar gesture in the Johnson-Reed Act. And Jacobson detects in Warner's taxonomy of "light" and "dark" Caucasians suspicious traces of "the earlier scheme of distinct white races" (*Whiteness* 109). But if Warner's categories retain a memory of the older racial division within whiteness, and the subordination of the darker Europeans, they are also heralding the resolution of that fragmentation. Warner's study works out in further detail what was ambivalent in Park, that assimilation would prevail among the European immigrant groups within a fundamentally black and white biracial social organization.

CASTE AS IDEOLOGICAL COMPROMISE

Warner's work consolidates and makes explicit what we have seen only gradually emerging within the discourses of anthropology and sociology for three or four decades. The widening disparity between the fortunes of African Americans as compared to the assimilating new immigrants indicated the need to distinguish the differences groups manifested with respect to their native white hosts. The declining repute of scientific race was eroding along two fronts, by the critique of racial classification itself, on the one hand, and the expanding theory of sociocultural determinations of difference, on the other. The resulting gap, as Young sensed, called for a new language. Most significantly Warner crystallizes the race-ethnic dualism that splits along the color line and paradoxically absorbs the cultural critique of race within a racialized order. As the division grew wider between social ("folk") practices of race and the social scientific discourse of race, Warner and other sociologists concerned themselves with how race was actually taken up in the "host society [and] its methods of evaluation" (Warner and Srole 285) regardless of the subtleties that made it untenable as anything but ideology or the rationalization of inequity. Ironically, ethnicity appears only as that quality that disappears in the process of assimilation to a greater whiteness, a purgatorial access to "our class order." Color, on the other hand, once it was detected, condemned one to inferior caste status. Such identification of racialized color with the sociological concept of caste is, in fact, one of the hallmarks of Warner's career; his oeuvre is often credited as the most complete elaboration of the caste model of race, the dominant paradigm for racial analysis in the late 1930s and 1940s. While Sean P. Hier reminds us that many other sociologists of the time, including Robert Park, promoted the caste perspective, Warner was the "central figure," and it was the "body of literature produced by a group of social anthropologists under [his] leadership" that formed the basis of the orthodox school of race relations during the period (Hier 294). Thus, a more detailed consideration of Warner's conception of race-caste relations is warranted by the further light such a study sheds on the origins of ethnicity.

The basis of the caste model is an analogy between East Indian society and race relations in the United States, often specifically the American rural South, justified by a set of similarities. Warner argues that the caste systems in India and the Deep South are homologous because both societies are organized into stratified social hierarchies such that privileges, rights, and duties are allocated unequally to various groups and assigned permanently from birth. Moreover, both systems prohibit marriage and mobility between social divisions and require complex symbolic rituals and behaviors that reflect relative ranks of individuals. In the work of Warner most devoted to arguing the utility of the caste model for the examination of American race relations, his 1936 essay "American Caste and Class" and his 1939 "Comparative Study of American Caste" (with Allison Davis), the question of the relations between caste and socioeconomic class are very much at issue. Both caste and class refer to types of status that "connote superior and inferior groups where there are one or more superordinate groups and one or more subordinate groups" (Warner and Davis 227). Both are status systems that cut across the social structure as a whole and affect all aspects of life.

Warner observes that class differs from caste, however, in two important respects: class allows exogamy as well as upward or downward mobility between classes. The class structure within the black community had developed a growing middle class by the 1930s, and Warner and other sociologists of the time who were interested in the caste framework set themselves the task of formulating its relation to economic groups. Robert Park, working within a narrative of modernity's relentless progress to eliminate the tribal vestiges of traditional society, such as racial division, had suggested that caste was, in fact, in decline. "Race conflicts in the modern world," he predicted, "which is already or presently will be a single great society, will be more and more in the future confused with, and eventually superceded by, the conflicts of classes" (Park, "Nature" 45). Warner, on the other hand, while recognizing that caste and class were similarly antithetical for most social scientists, presented a model accommodating them within the same system. The existence of an emerging black middle class, in which some members were economically above some whites, suggested to Warner that class mobility is possible within caste. In fact, if current trends continued, blacks could become equal or even "theoretically" the dominant caste (Warner 235). For the present, however, the "skewness" of caste and class lines "has placed the upper class Negro in a decidedly difficult situation" (Warner 236) because they simultaneously occupy positions of both inferiority and superiority with respect to lower-class whites. Such an individual, Warner informs us, feels "in his own personality . . . the conflict of the two opposing structures" (236). The psychological result of their contradictory structural location is that "[upper class Negroes] are always 'off balance' and are constantly attempting to achieve an equilibrium which their society, except under extraordinary circumstances, does not provide for them" (Warner 237). The "instability" that such individuals exhibit, as compared with their lower class counterparts, Warner hypothesizes, is the likely result of the instability of their social position.

Yet, there is little remedy for the difficulty of the upper-class black. "If it ever came to issue," Warner posits, whites would close ranks to secure caste dominance: "The supraordinate white class would maintain the solidarity of the white group by repudiating any claims by any Negro of superiority to the lower-class whites" (236). Thus, regardless of changes and variations in class, Warner insists that the caste system will remain in place and that the castes will remain apart. The system is so entrenched and pervasive that Warner dismisses any efforts aimed at reform such as anti-lynching legislation, education programs, or support of voting rights. Because the "disabilities of Negroes in all these respects are systematically maintained by the society, little improvement of their position relative to that of whites has been made during the past twenty years, in any of these respects" (Warner 245). Groups and agencies that have tried to improve black life by treating the various symptoms of the caste system have discovered "by grim experience" that such change is "hopeless" (Warner 245). Only holistic approaches can have any effect. Warner writes, "Such a social change would involve gradual but basic changes in the economic, occupational, educational, and class status of the majority of Negroes" (245). How such gradual changes might be brought about except through specific initiatives targeting specific inequities, Warner does not say.

COX'S CRITIQUE

While the caste model dominated the discourse of race sociology in the late 1930s and 1940s, there was some dissent. McKee notes that several scholars had lodged their objections to such a framework, including Park, Guy Johnson, E. Franklin Frazier, and Charles Johnson (McKee 174). The work of Oliver Cromwell Cox, however, represents the period's only sustained critique of caste as a model for American race relations. A brief consideration of his analysis reveals not only the theoretical limits of caste but also the political implications of applying it at the exclusion of other interpretations. Beginning in 1942 in a series of essays that were then collected in Cox's 1948 magnum opus, *Caste, Class, and Race: A Study in Social Dynamics,* Cox lays out his theory of race and class and, in so doing, thoroughly dismantles the arguments Warner offers to justify framing race in terms of caste. Cox systematically refutes each point of identification Warner proposes between the Indian caste system and race in the United States. Endogamy and marriage restrictions, for examples, frequently taken as proof positive of the race-caste argument, have a different meaning and function for U.S. race relations than they do within a caste system. Endogamy in a caste society is a self-imposed means by which each caste protects its integrity and heritage and thus is generally embraced by all castes (Cox 447). But attitudes about black and white intermarriage in America vary by race and regional cultures and traditions (Cox 448). Cox emphasizes that proscriptions on marriage are a feature of social systems other than caste, and "hence, the final test of caste is not endogamy but the social values which endogamy secures" (494).

Likewise Cox shows that the other social features justifying the race-caste identification fail to withstand scrutiny. The supposed permanence of the caste and race position, for example, overlooks that while its biological basis means individuals cannot change race, it is not impossible for individuals to change caste since such ascription is cultural and social rather than biological. "In fact," Cox notes, "this very distinction should raise the suspicion that different social forces are operating in the caste system from those in situations of racial adjustment" (494). Nor do the rituals of obeisance required of blacks to whites provide intended support since the same is required of lower- to upper-class whites and is common to many hierarchical social structures besides (Cox 496–97). While this strategy of isolating specific features of caste and identifying them with analogous aspects of race may at first seem persuasive, warns Cox, "in almost every case . . . the comparison is not between caste and race but merely a recognition of apparently common characteristics of all situations of superior-inferior or superordination-subordination relationships" (497). This piecemeal approach amounts to the proverbial blind men studying the elephant (Cox 498).[10]

To understand the system of color prejudice in America more precisely Cox advocates analyzing it not through an analogy with some other social system but in terms of its own historical origins and socioeconomic functions. Cox argues that theories of racial difference were unknown to ancient peoples and denies that any evidence exists to support the claim that race was involved in the inception of India's caste system. Instead, Cox dates the idea of race from the European conquest of the Americas, when a rationale was required for the exploitation of militarily weaker peoples, their labor and resources. As Cox writes:

> Our hypothesis is that racial exploitation and race prejudice developed among Europeans with the rise of capitalism and nationalism, and that because of the world-wide ramification of capitalism, all racial antagonisms can be traced to the policies and attitudes of the leading capitalist people, the white people of Europe and North America. (322)

Racial theories merely presented themselves as the most effective means for European and American capitalists to secure their economic interests. "The capitalist exploiter," Cox observes, "being opportunistic and practical, will utilize any convenience to keep his labor and other resources freely exploitable" (333). Slavery, for instance, "did not develop because Indians and Negroes were red and black, or because their cranial capacity averaged a certain number of cubic centimeters" (Cox 322), but rather because Africans and Indians became the most convenient labor source. Theories of race were then supplied to justify involuntary servitude (Cox 334).

Cox, in other words, argues along lines very similar to Richard Williams, as we saw in chapter 1, though some forty years earlier. He maintains that the continuity of race conflict from the seventeenth century to the present is traceable to the ongoing needs of capitalism. Race is a necessary component to the exploitation of labor and is one aspect of the larger process of "the proletarianization of labor, regardless of the color of the laborer" (Cox 333). Ideas about racial inferiority help to maintain blacks as a reserve supply of cheap labor and weaken the working class by keeping it divided against itself. The continued exploitation of the working class as a whole "has been done most effectively by the maintenance of antagonistic attitudes between the white and colored masses" (Cox 473). Thus race has been central in the ideological legitimation of capitalism. In other words, "race prejudice may be thought of as having its genesis in the propagandistic and legal contrivances of the white ruling class for securing mass support of its interest" (Cox 475). Far from originating in some instinctual reaction to color difference, then, race prejudice is a symptom of a specific social structure and the result of a specific history. That is, as Cox argues, "race prejudice is the social-attitudinal concomitant of the racial-exploitative practice of a ruling class in a capitalistic society" (476). As such, race prejudice can only be altered by addressing its underlying systemic foundation: "The articulate white man's ideas about his racial superiority are rooted deeply in the social system, and it can be corrected only by changing the system itself" (Cox 462).

Caste society and America's racialized society for Cox, then, are incomparable because they are structured in two entirely different ways. On the one hand, castes are integrated and interrelated into a complex, functioning whole. That is, "the caste system of India is a minutely segmented, assimilated social structure; it is highly stable and capable of perpetuating itself indefinitely" (Cox 502). On the other hand, whites and blacks in the South constitute two separate societies or, to the degree that it can be considered one, a society divided against itself (Cox 502). Far from being the fixed structure that Warner describes, resistant to reform or change, for Cox the racial arrangement in the South is "tentative," and "unlike the permanence of caste, it is a temporary society intended to continue only so long as whites are able to maintain the barriers against [Negro] assimilation" (503). In a caste system, each group and individual has a designated place and a purpose which is acknowledged by all other castes as indispensable to the welfare of the whole. The South, however, "[guards] against any development of an overt expression of indispensability of Negroes within the social organization" (Cox 504) regardless of their actual importance.

In short, Cox shares with Warner, correctly or not, the image of a caste society as a harmonious system that "carries within itself no basic antagonisms" (Cox 502). But for Cox, the Deep South is fundamentally conflicted such that "the social aims and purposes of whites and Negroes . . . are irreconcilably opposed" (502). Thus Warner's interpretation of the maladjusted upper-class Negro is not only misguided but presents, in fact, evidence that undermines his theory. Cox admits that "the biracial system in United States is . . . a pathological situation . . . [adversely affecting] the personalities of both whites and blacks" but also adds that "sensitivity to social wrongs need not imply derangement or an 'off-balance' personality" (498). The point is that Warner's identification of any maladjusted personality belies the caste hypothesis since "personalities developed in the caste system are normal for that society"; caste barriers are not challenged in an authentic caste society because "they are sacred to caste and caste alike" (Cox 498).

Moreover, for Cox, Warner's suggestion that the development of the black upper class may alter power relations between castes, to the point where blacks become equal or even dominant, without altering the caste division itself, "makes his theory particularly illogical and sterile" (Cox 495). The idea that blacks and whites could have nothing else differentiating them but skin color "is sterile because it has no way of confronting the real dynamics of race relations" (Cox 495). For Cox, such a perspective misses the underlying political function of racial ideology. To demonstrate that the caste concept is irrelevant to the study of race relations, Cox suggests "substituting in the writings of this school the words 'Negroes' or 'white people' where ever the words 'Negro caste' or 'white caste' appear and observe that the sense of the statement does not change" (507). And since, Cox concludes, the caste metaphor has been in use to discuss American race at least since the nineteenth century, the caste school adds nothing new to our understanding of race relations except "perhaps publicity and 'scientific prestige'" (506). It is nothing more than "old wine in new bottles" (Cox 507).

Given such unqualified and thoroughly documented repudiation of the caste hypothesis, it is notable that Cox's criticism influenced neither the sway that caste held over the discourse of race relations at the time nor further criticism of the perspective. Although reviewed widely and known to the sociologists he attacked, *Caste, Class, and Race* went out of print in 1949 after the first edition. In a study of its reception among students and faculty in the Department of Sociology at the University of Chicago, Herbert M. Hunter reveals that, while the book was not ignored, its overt political stance clashed with the ideal of the detached scientific observer then embraced by the discipline ("Introduction" xxxiv–xxxv). Sean P. Hier agrees: "Although Cox was primarily concerned with discrediting Warner's writings on 'race relations,' his general epistemological approach to social inequality contrasted sharply with the value-neutral, functionalist-oriented research program promoted by Robert Park" (293). The fact that Cox was black undoubtedly played a hand in his marginalization, although Hier asserts that "the academic exclusion of black intellectuals in the 1940s and 1950s was neither definitive nor absolute," as evidenced by the acclaim Cox's black colleagues received, such as E. Franklin Frazier and Charles S. Johnson (293). However, Mary Jo Deegan observes that black sociologists had to contend with what she calls the "Veil of sociology," or the experience of "multiple layers of discrimination" that could not be articulated within the hegemonic white sociological discourse (280). Deegan argues that though Cox was educated at the University of Chicago and therefore more accurately constitutes a "reflexive insider," Cox's refusal to accommodate himself to the "Veil," unlike his black colleagues, is largely responsible for his marginalization as an outsider. In addition to his blackness, his extensive use of Marx in *Caste, Class, and Race* established, perhaps inaccurately,[11] Cox's reputation as a Marxist during a period that was especially anticommunist. These aspects of his life and work set him at odds with the Chicago School, despite the fact that Cox was trained there at a time when the Department of Sociology at Chicago determined the dominant paradigm of the discipline. In fact, Hier argues, "the exclusive nature of the Chicago school, indeed the entire sociological orthodoxy, was strong enough to produce the rejection and systematic exclusion of a potentially threatening intellectual current such as the one offered by Oliver Cox" (303). Such marginalization from scholarly appreciation has been sufficiently effective; even today Cox's work is largely unknown or omitted from sociology textbooks and course syllabi, despite the fact that scholars of race relations and "world-systems theory" have recognized it as groundbreaking (Hunter, "Introduction" xxxviii; Hier 304). For the present study, Cox's work not only helps to identify the limits of Warner's work, but the marginalization of Cox's critique of race within his own field also suggests the function of academic race relations with respect to the racial formation. Cox makes a strong case that at least one of the effects of Warner's work, with which we might include the conception of ethnicity, is to obscure and rationalize racial oppression.

CONCLUSION

George Snedeker has suggested that race relations sociologists of the 1930s and 1940s widely adopted the caste model "to fill the void" in the absence of any other "theoretically satisfactory formulation available at the time" (221). Yet the disregard to which Cox's work has been subjected, for reasons other than its academic validity, should lead to a consideration of orthodox sociology's extra-academic interests (that is to say its political investments) that would motivate so thorough a rejection. Put more precisely for the present context, the question is not so much why Warner decided to conceptualize American race in terms of caste, but rather "why sociologists responded so favorably to such an idea during the volatile decade of the 1930s" (McKee 153). McKee argues that the appeal of the caste model rationalized a number of conservative impulses among mainstream sociologists. First, in the context of the Depression and the rapid changes brought about by the Great Migration and the Northern urbanization of African Americans, the image of the Southern caste order provided a comforting, if regressive, sense of stability. Warner's vision of caste is a system in permanent equilibrium, regardless of inequalities of race and class. As McKee writes, "Warner provided American sociologists with a comfortable assurance that change would not occur too abruptly, that racial disorder was not imminent, and he affirmed the 'hopelessness' of efforts to intervene with well-intentioned programs of social betterment" (157).

The way the caste metaphor conceptualized only the most glacial change, if any, through a gradual process of assimilation also spoke to the deep-seated conviction among white sociologists that blacks were incapable of initiating change through organized action (McKee 146). A tendency which would leave sociology especially ill-equipped in the coming decades was its aversion to the idea of black solidarity and the possibility of change through conflict and collective struggle. The majority of U.S. sociologists rejected the idea that blacks had a common culture or history that could provide the basis for organized action. The caste perspective satisfied these predilections and rationalized continued white paternalistic control of race relations. Issues of race remained the "white man's burden" for whites to solve in their own fashion for the benefit of blacks (McKee 147). The caste hypothesis, then, far from providing the disinterested scientific perspective of social science that it pretended to offer, is in fact implicated in the ideological maintenance of white supremacy. As Cox well understood, "by using the caste hypothesis, then, the school seeks to explain a 'normal society' in the South. In short, it has made peace of the hybrid society that has not secured harmony for itself; and in so far as this is true, its work is fictitious" (504).

In addition to the conception of a racial system in stasis, caste also lends a static sense to the idea of race itself. The caste metaphor as it is applied to race by Warner and his colleagues imposes a kind of reification to racial positions. An individual's race-caste is ascriptive and permanent, simplifying the often vexed issue, especially in the North, of where racial lines are drawn. Within the context of what I have been calling the crisis in the white race, caste responds with an idea of fixed, unambiguous clarity about racial divisions. The assimilation of European immigrants confirmed that the North was already heading toward a black and white biracial arrangement for which the South seemed an appropriate model. (All other groups of color would likewise find themselves on the wrong side of the dividing line.) In Warner's later *Yankee City* series, as we have seen, the difference between groups designated as caste or "semi-caste," on the one hand, and "ethnic," on the other, is stark. While "ethnicity" appears only to disappear into undifferentiated whiteness, those slotted by color for a caste position, by contrast, were condemned to permanent exclusion. As Jacobson puts it, by mid-century:

> ethnicity itself provided a paradigm for assimilation which erased race as a category of historical experience for European and some Near Eastern immigrants. Not only did these groups now belong to a unified Caucasian race, but race was deemed so irrelevant to who they were that it became something possessed only by 'other' peoples. (*Whiteness* 110)

Warner's formulation in *Yankee City* suggests a fusion of the dominant race relations theories of the day, the assimilation model for whites, and permanent racial subordination of the caste model for all peoples of color. As such, Warner's conception formalizes and resolves the internal contradiction that we saw in Park's work between his tendency to replace race science with social science while, at the same time, retaining the conviction that the inferiority of blacks was a fixed and natural condition.

By the 1940s, the spectrum of races and racialized nationalities had been reduced within the dominant discourse of sociology to the older division of Negroid, Caucasoid, and Mongoloid. With the production of *ethnicity*, divisions among Europeans had given way to a reconsolidated white race. Only two decades before, scientific theories of race had rendered the new immigrants of eastern and southern Europe an "inbetween people," a species apart from their native Anglo hosts. In the 1920s, the newcomers were sufficiently alien and threatening to inspire the reactionary Johnson-Reed immigration act which, it was hoped, would preserve the racial purity of the original American stock. (At the same time in Europe, scientific racism articulated state policy regarding human difference with its own ghastly results.) Yet, within two decades the once bewildering array of racial nationalities in

America and their corresponding physical traits were enfolded into the newly reconstituted, "multicultural" white race. In America, the races of Europe had become ethnic and in a short time would become, after World War II, "white ethnics."[12]

But, as Jacobson points out, "the social sciences did not create the social division between black and white; writers like Park . . . and Lloyd Warner were remarking on the impact of distinctions that predated modern sociology and that had long been maintained by law, by real estate and housing policies, by employment practices, and by a range of segregated institutions from movie theaters and churches to labor unions and military units" (*Whiteness* 105–6). Along with continued antiblack segregation, the assimilation of the new immigrants and their families intensified the increasingly biracial nature of American society. The mobility and assimilation of the new immigrants and their descendants, as Sacks has suggested, lent greater credence to their claims to whiteness, while greater whiteness made available more opportunities for advancement (105). Many of the recent arrivals from Europe and their children learned their whiteness between the wars and, as the boundaries of whiteness expanded to include them, social scientists needed a new language to account for the change.

Yet, for its part, more than merely reflecting racialization, sociology helped to maintain racial segregation by legitimating its logic with a scientific rationalization. The institutional marginalization of Cox and the promotion of Park and Warner reveal that the social sciences systematically rejected the lines of thought that analyzed race as a function of capitalism or that located its sustaining foundation in the ideological requirements of structural inequality. Such conclusions could be reached by those, like Cox and Locke, who understood the full implications of the new cultural theory's attacks on race science, which revealed that all racialized positions were matters of social invention. Instead, schemas that naturalized the inevitability and immutability of the biracial hierarchy found institutional and financial support. An ingenious crystallization of this view is the concept of race stratification as a caste system. As reassuringly stable as such a society is, it would only become more so as a result of the transient feature called *ethnicity*, which codified and minimized the fading differences among assimilating whites. And yet as thoroughly whitening as this process was, the conceptualizing of ethnicity as a quality that named the cultural rather than biological nature of identity made the idea theoretically available to those for whom it was not originally designed. As an almost magical quality that promised success to those who had once been barred, it became a valuable power to which those unintended others would lay claim. Ethnicity was invented to confer whiteness as well as mobility. Given the right circumstances, the contradiction of seizing ethnicity for blackness could conceivably unleash powerful forces and orient its bearer not just to succeed in the system, but to transform it.

NOTES

1. Stanfield points to Park's view that the civilizing process conformed the traditional, rural cultures of immigrants to the rational, urban order of civilization. At the same time, Park believed "the process of civilization required the dominance of one cultural group over another . . . a privilege belonging to those of European descent" (Stanfield 48–49). Those racially similar to the dominant group were likely to assimilate while with "widely different racial stocks, assimilation and amalgamation do not take place at all, or take place very slowly" (qtd. in Stanfield 49).

2. As the gap grew between the academic disrepute of race and its continued popular intransigence, the lack of an institutional analysis such as Oliver Cox's left most scholars who addressed it to conclude that the roots of race prejudice lay no deeper than the hearts and minds of the people. The apotheosis of this view was Gunnar Myrdal's monumental *An American Dilemma* (1944) which declared that "the American Negro problem is a problem in the heart of the American" (xlvii). Ruling out the sort of structural and historical understandings of racial oppression that Cox had explored, Myrdal instead chose to "constantly take our starting point in the ordinary man's own ideas, doctrines, theories and mental constructs" (l). Expressions of antiblack prejudice had once been a means by which the racially ambiguous new immigrants learned to signify their whiteness. By the 1940s, white racist attitudes, as a feature characterizing the recently reconstituted white race, therefore function as a kind of proof for its existence. I am here suggesting the reverse of what is usually assumed: white racist behavior is not created by the white race but, rather, constitutive of it.

3. Young's solution here is to codify within the sociological discourse the concept of "*minority*" as an umbrella term for all outgroups, regardless of the basis of their marginalization. As McKee notes, while the term had been used sporadically and without specificity in the sociological literature in the 1920s, Young's use of *minority* makes of it a central concept in the discourse and thus contributes to the general development of the period of instituting a lexicon of sociological terms (McKee 130–31).

4. Barkan's reconstruction of the collaborative authorship of *We Europeans* accounts for stylistic and intellectual inconsistencies in the work. While the book was largely Huxley's project, there were actually three other writers involved but not credited. The chapter in question, chapter 6, was in fact one of two written by Haddon, though he noted in a letter that his work was "subjected to a certain amount of amendation [*sic*]" (Barkan 303).

5. While Huxley and Haddon are very lucid about the use by politicians of biological language to hide other motives for racial policies, it is interesting that in their arguments in support of group segregation they retreat to language that echoes the terms used in nineteenth-century American discussions about black and white race-mixing:

Dismissing such cases [as the popular rejection of miscegenation on biological grounds], we are however confronted with the possibility that very wide crosses may give biologically 'disharmonic' results in later generations, by producing ill-assorted combinations of characters. Characters may be unduly exaggerated by the coming together of unfamiliar genes; or characters adapted to one environment may be forced to co-exist with those adapted to another. . . . Further, if it be true that some ethnic groups possess a low average level of innate intelligence, to allow crosses between them and more intelligent types is a retrograde step. These objections undoubtedly have some validity. (281)

Here the terms are reminiscent of Edward Alsworth Ross on "race suicide." My point is to underscore Huxley and Haddon's concern for eliminating racial difference between Europeans rather than racial differences *tout court*. This built-in limitation to their reconstruction of *ethnic* is relevant to understanding how the same limitation is inherent in the later derivation of *ethnicity*. This lapse into the crudest superstitions about miscegenation, even in a book that recommends the banishment of the concept of race, demonstrates again just how tenacious racial assumptions were and how reluctant white scholars were to give them up (especially when it came to discussions of peoples of color). Accounting for this double standard requires further theorization of the kind provided by Barnor Hesse, discussed in the next section.

6. The connections between the new immigrants, whiteness, and American imperialism are developed in Jacobson ("Malevolent"). He argues that contradictory forces made claims on the identities of European immigrants (the Irish, Jews, and the Polish), one from race and the other from American imperial adventures. Looking at the immigrant press's reactions to the Phillipines and Cuba in the Spanish American War in 1899, he finds identification on the part of the immigrants with the oppressed in the face of U.S. imperialism because they made the analogy to their own anti-imperialist national histories. On the other hand, they also contradictorily identified as European whites against the dark people of these countries. As Jacobson suggests, "That race emerged as the dominant motif by which others resolved this tension suggests the extent to which, for European immigrants, becoming American depended on becoming 'Caucasian'" (175).

7. See Jennings and Kaempffert. The eighteen reviews listed in *Book Review Digest* are generally quite positive and take the major import of the work, of which they overwhelmingly approve, to be an attack on the scientific pretensions of biological racial classification. As E. C. MacDowell writes in the *Nation*, "Read this book and thereafter hesitate to speak of *races* of men!" (354). Kaempffert, however, is skeptical that "really scientific anthropologists will accept 'ethnic group' any more readily than 'race' precisely because it has no biologic significance" (14). In missing Huxley and Haddon's point so thoroughly, Kaempffert's comment suggests how difficult it was to shift the paradigm of race science.

8. Locating the origins of *ethnicity* is no simple matter. Often a reliable reference on such matters, the *Oxford English Dictionary* notes the first use of the word in an entry from 1772 but, as one might expect, it carries the sense of "heathenism." That work does not cite another instance until 1953. No less an authority than Pierre L. van den Berghe claims that *ethnicity* was coined in the late 1960s during the "ethnic binge" when it became fashionable to "cultivate and cuddle ethnic identities and 'roots'" (*Ethnic Phenomenon* 4). A search of the Library of Congress reveals that the

first book title to include the word was not until 1968, after which there is a surge, including van den Berghe's own *Race and Ethnicity: Essays in Comparative Sociology* in 1970. My sources for its modern origin in Warner are Sollors's forward to *Theories of Ethnicity* (12–13), his *Beyond Ethnicity*, and Arthur Schlesinger Jr.'s "The American Creed: From Dilemma to Decomposition" (21). In *Beyond Ethnicity*, Sollors states that "after an elaborate search for the origins of the word" (23), he tracked it down to volumes 1 and 2 of the *Yankee City* series, which he describes enthusiastically as "the Kunte Kinte of ethnicity scholarship!" (24). My own pursuit of the literature has found no earlier use of *ethnicity* in its modern sense but, more importantly, implicit in my argument is that it would not have been conceptually possible much before this time. That is, the word *ethnic* was only gradually emerging from the shadow of race, and the "inbetween people" had only begun to assimilate into the white race, the phenomenon the word was originally coined to name.

   9. Matthew Frye Jacobson's suggestive phrase "probationary whites" refers to the racial status of the European immigrants in the period before they are fully inducted into whiteness with all of its rights and privileges. It is an especially apt metaphor because it captures the doubtful nature of the new immigrants' whiteness while they waited for history to render its verdict, as well as the idea that they were being evaluated by native whites in terms of their compliance with white American racial protocol.

   10. A full assessment of the validity of Cox's representation of Indian caste is beyond the scope of the present discussion. However, Gerald D. Berreman argues that Cox's description of caste in India is one of "the erroneous, stereotyped [views]" ("Letter" 511) typical of detractors of the race-caste comparison. Cox and others, Berreman argues, get it wrong because they view Indian caste "as it is supposed to work rather than as it does work" ("Caste" 121), while "American race relations are seen as they do work rather than as they are supposed, by the privileged, to work" ("Caste" 121). Evidence from the study of caste in India does suggest that Cox misrepresents the caste system as stable and nonhierarchical and one in which caste members accept their status without resistance. I take the central point of Cox's refusal of the caste analogy for American race to be that Warner and others used it to suppress, behind the image of a static social structure in equilibrium, the issues of exploitation and oppression. Further disqualifying the analogy for Cox were his conclusions that racism is a feature specific to Western capitalism and that it would only be resolved through the assimilation of blacks, ideas incongruent with any model of caste. For a discussion on the history and suitability of using caste in the analysis of racial stratification, see van den Berghe, *Ethnic Phenomenon* (157–84).

   11. Despite the consensus that labels him a Marxist sociologist, Cox himself asserted that, while he used Marx's texts in his critiques of capitalism extensively, he was not a Marxist. Robert Miles, as well, makes a strong case that Cox's theoretical positions depart from Marx's on fundamental points, most significantly in the absence of a concept of mode of production (183). On the debate of Cox's Marxism, see also Hunter, *The Sociology of Oliver C. Cox* (xxxix–xlv).

   12. The *Oxford English Dictionary*'s first entry for *white ethnic* cites a text from 1964 in which the phrase is an appositive for "first the Irish, later the Jews, and still more recently the Italians" (Miller 297). It appears in a discussion on the expansion

of citizen rights and is used to differentiate the working class from other whites and from "Negroes." An online search of journals (JSTOR) locates a first appearance of the phrase from 1939 (where *ethnic* carries no special sense distinct from *race*). It is infrequently used until the late 1960s and 1970s when it becomes quite common. Prior to that time, as I have tried to show, *ethnic* and *white* were, as Roediger puts it, references to "distinct, . . . often counterposed, forms of consciousness" ("White Ethnics" 182). That is, roughly before the end of World War II, ethnic was not quite white. The temporary fusion of these words suggests a transitional period from the time after the new immigrants had become white but while the markers of their differences from native Anglos were still salient. While there is a sense that there might have been nonwhite ethnics, it is more likely that the phrase refers to the whites who differed from standard (Anglo) whites, such that the emphasis was always on the second word (*ethnic*) rather than the first (*white*). Though "white ethnic" still occasionally appears in print, the phrase seems antiquated because of the more or less completed assimilation of the population in question.

4

Black Ethnicity and the Transformation of a Concept, 1962–1972

The preceding chapters have focused on the argument that the creation of the ethnicity concept, as a category designating difference on the basis of culture, derives from the problem of racial division among European Americans created out of the nineteenth-century discourse of race science. Ethnicity emerges as a kind of ideological resolution to the problem of such division by drawing on the work of cultural anthropologists, the Boasians, and those sociologists who shared the conviction that biological race no longer held sufficient credibility to explain the nature of group differences between Europeans. Clearing a space by showing the limits of race science, cultural anthropologists proceeded to fill it with their own alternative explanations for differences between human groups that focused on histories and customs. In so doing, they moved the ground of human identity from the biological to the arena of social practices, a shift for which current "social construction" theories of identity are indebted. Yet the assumption of a fundamental difference between whites and Negroes proved remarkably tenacious in both popular and scholarly discourse, despite the attack on scientific race; even when the discourse dispensed with race science, the terms of inferiority often merely changed from biological to cultural. As we saw in the work of Lloyd Warner's group, even as cultural theories of identity coalesced in the concept of ethnicity, race remained the special burden of African Americans and the other "colored races." The new cultural mode of identity was reserved for European Americans and applied in the sociology of race relations to the problem of immigrant assimilation. That is to say, the structural mechanisms that began to provide European immigrants and their children access to socioeconomic mobility after World War I prompted sociology to take up the tools provided by cultural anthropology to reconceive an amalgamated "white race." By this they were merely reading the writing on the wall, albeit through the privileged lens of their favorite bias—the assimilation model. That European Americans seemed to be melting into a broader white race only confirmed the central tenet of the sociology of race relations: that modernity would sweep away all relics of preindustrial society, including associations based on region, religion, nationality, and race. Ethnicity, in other words, was everything that the melting pot of modernity would dissolve.

Yet, while the consolidation of the white race in North America confirmed the faith in assimilation, it seemed as well to underscore the fundamental divisions of color. The disappearing differences between the world's whites into the pseudoscientific category of Caucasoid served to etch the lines more deeply between them and the other segments of the great tripartite division of humanity—the so-called Negroid and Mongoloid races. In the sociology of race relations from its inception throughout the post–World War II period, African Americans remained in an ambiguous conceptual position. The single most influential figure in the constitution of the field, Robert Park, as we have seen, offered inconsistent ways of understanding the trajectory of black people within the process of his race-relations cycle. They were, at times, a hopelessly premodern people who lacked the adaptive capacity to survive modernity's relentless advance. At other times, however, Park observed that African Americans were developing a sense of collectivity analogous to that of the nationalist minorities in eastern Europe, though such insights were neglected in the subsequent development of the discipline. The only major school to depart from the assimilationist "ethnic model," the caste school lead by Warner, consigned blacks to a permanent inferior status in a static social structure held in place by the implacable predispositions of white prejudice. The virtue of the caste school was that, as Robert Blauner argues, it did not assume race to be an epiphenomenon of a more primary condition that would be dissolved by the expanding class and bureaucratic stratifications of modern industrial society. Instead, the caste hypothesis presented an alternative to the dominant tradition by "treating race and racial oppression as independent realities" (Blauner, *Racial* 7). Yet caste rationalized racial hierarchy as the inherent structuring principle of biracial social formations. After World War II, the liberal moralism of Gunnar Myrdal's *An American Dilemma* (1944) established the dominant framework for the discourse on race, confirming that assimilation and integration[1] of Negro Americans was the only conceivable trajectory for racial progress. Identifying white prejudice as the primary hurdle for such an eventuality, Myrdal's liberal race relations helped raise the study of white racial attitudes as the field's central focus for much of the 1950s (McKee 251–52).

Throughout almost the entirety of the tradition in the sociology of race relations, however, one element consistently omitted was a consideration of American blacks as developing a distinctive cultural tradition.[2] McKee notes that "from the 1930s until 1970, therefore, sociologists were blind to evidence about a black culture and black identity and assumed that blacks had no other objective than to be integrated into American society and to disappear as a racially distinct population" (McKee 343). Even Glazer and Moynihan's 1963 *Beyond the Melting Pot*, for example, exhibits this bias despite its reputation for being among the first to reject the assimilationist thesis of American ethnicity.[3] They argue that Negroes will not be assimilated but, unlike other groups, neither do they have a distinct culture from which to remain apart: "It is not possible for Negroes to view themselves as other ethnic groups viewed themselves because—and this is key to much in the Negro world—the Negro is only an American, and nothing else. He has no values and culture to guard and protect" (Glazer and Moynihan 53). Instead, white sociologists had predominantly assumed that the American Negro had imperfectly adopted general white American culture, and in a way that rendered it "pathological" (McKee 302–3).[4]

This fallacy formed the basis of other characteristic assumptions, such as the failure to consider black Americans as having the cultural resources to survive modern industrial progress or to mount an organized, collective effort against white prejudice on their own behalf. As McKee notes, "While much sociological work documented the unmistakably destructive consequences of oppression, there was no comparable work identifying cultural and institutional resources among blacks" (307). Most sociologists shared the assumption that blacks also wished nothing other than to integrate into American society and "to disappear as a racially distinct population" (McKee 343). As critics have argued, this series of theoretical missteps left the sociology of race relations completely unprepared to account for the black movement of the 1950s and 1960s. As Blauner notes, an examination of sociologists' central assumptions about race explains why they, like most white Americans, "were caught napping by the intensity and scale of the civil rights protests, the furor of ghetto revolt, and the rapidity with which black power, cultural nationalism, and other militant Third World perspectives emerged and spread" (*Racial* 6). The subtitle of McKee's book, *The Failure of a Perspective*, refers precisely to this lacuna in sociology's fundamental theoretical framework that left it incapable of predicting or explaining the black rebellion of the 1960s. In fact, "not only had they failed to foresee the coming of new forms of racial struggle, they had even denied such a possibility" (McKee 2).

The black movement of the 1960s also demonstrated conclusively the profound bankruptcy of the dominant framework of race relations sociology regarding black American cultural identity. Particularly at the historic point in the mid-1960s in which Black Power eclipsed the Civil Rights framework of racial integration, black cultural identity became a significant political force. This strategic shift threw into question fundamental assumptions not only about the nature of African American collective identity, and about the assimilation of minority groups into the American mainstream, but also about the nature of cultural identity itself. The emerging discourse of black cultural nationalism, and the analysis of American racial minorities in terms of "internal colonialism," provided a theoretical foundation from which significant interventions would be made in the sociology of race relations.

In particular, the work of Robert Blauner brought the colonial critique to bear on the sociological discourse of race, especially with respect to the concept of ethnicity and, in so doing, effectively transformed it. Though initially embedded in the caste model and assigned to the resolution of racial division among whites, as shorthand for cultural identity, the term *ethnicity* becomes available for other projects. Indeed, Blauner's work was to wrest it from its initial context and reconstruct the concept through the lens of black cultural nationalism such that, when devoted to the black experience, ethnicity is transformed in at least four significant ways. First, quite simply, he makes it black. Given the predispositions of mainstream sociology to bestow a culturally based subjectivity exclusively on whites, this feat carries important implications, particularly if we recall the political stakes involved in whether a group is regarded as racial or ethnic. Second, ethnicity thereafter becomes no longer exclusively white but is "publicly" available to other groups regardless of the color line. Third, black ethnicity in Blauner's revaluation is disarticulated from the assimilation paradigm. It becomes the opposite instead, a quality that distinguishes a group from the majority and resists absorption, an aspect that ethnicity still assumes. Last, whereas ethnicity initially accommodated its bearer to his or her place in the hierarchical social order, the language of black nationalism briefly radicalizes ethnicity with its revolutionary and liberatory agenda. While this aspect is largely neutralized in the later context of multicultural pluralism, ethnicity revised by the revolution in black consciousness of the 1960s transforms it in ways unimagined in its white inception.

THE ORIGINS OF BLACK ETHNICITY

Yet if black ethnicity is a surprisingly recent revelation to sociology, within the tradition of African American letters, the question of cultural identity has been one of the most considered and debated of issues, going back much further than the sociology of race itself. The question, however, has not been whether Americans of African descent possessed a distinct identity but rather in what that distinctness consists, the status of the African heritage, and the implications of that identity for the future of blacks in America. DuBois's famous pronouncement on "double-consciousness," in which he describes the unique nature of African American identity as composed of two incommensurate impulses, is perhaps the best-known statement on the question of black identity: "One ever feels his two-ness,—an American, a Negro; two souls, two thoughts, two unreconciled strivings; two warring ideals in one dark body, whose dogged strength alone keeps it from being torn asunder" (*Black Folk* 17). The history of the American Negro is, in fact, DuBois adds, the history of the struggle between these two parts to synthesize the antipathies into a higher self. But since both have a special mission in the world, he does not wish that either originary self be lost, either by "Africaniz[ing] America," nor by assimilating "his Negro soul in a flood of white Americanism" (*Black Folk* 17). Rather, he seeks the reconciliation of selves in such a form that simply allows "a man to be both a Negro and an American" without being despised by whites nor refused at "the doors of Opportunity" (*Black Folk* 17).

Indeed, as John H. Bracey Jr. suggests, the dilemma of double-consciousness encapsulates the history of black struggle in America as it oscillates between the poles of assimilationist and separatist campaigns. That is, while neither movement has been entirely without aspects of the other, the long history of black struggle against racial oppression has taken either a predominantly integrationist approach, which strove for equality, or a nationalist approach, which strove for racial solidarity and autonomy. In four periods, nationalist strategy has been predominant (from 1790 to 1820, from the late 1840s and 1850s, from the 1880s through the 1920s, and then from the mid-1960s to the early 1970s), each generally coinciding with times in which, as Bracey observes, "the Negroes' status has declined, or when they have experienced intense disillusionment following a period of heightened but unfulfilled expectations" (xxvi). Moreover, the tendencies for either assimilation or nationalism have been strongly influenced, though not determined, by class division within the black community such that, very generally, "the thrust toward integration and assimilation has been strongest among the black middle and upper classes, while separatist tendencies have probably been strongest among the lower class, whose members are most alienated from the larger society" (Bracey liv). And though periods of black nationalism have waxed and waned for more than two hundred years, its central feature, the distinctness of African American identity, has remained a guiding assumption among black writers, even while it has rarely been considered among white sociologists.

The power of the black movement of the 1960s, however, dramatically revealed the liabilities of such theoretical oversights. Having omitted consideration of the discourse and practice of the African American struggle, the majority of sociologists was unprepared for the strength of the Civil Rights Movement and lacked the conceptual apparatus to account for it. Despite sociological predispositions to the contrary, "throughout the 1960s the black-led civil rights movement provided convincing empirical evidence that blacks had the capacity to act effectively in their own interests and the sense of themselves as distinct people with their own agenda of change" (McKee 344). African Americans were also asserting a cultural distinctness in ways that became increasingly difficult to ignore (McKee 344).

L. Singer, in his 1962 essay "Ethnogenesis and Negro-Americans Today," provides us with an index of the degree to which his white colleagues disregarded these new realities. That is, he must make the argument, and he appears to be the first within sociology to explicitly do so, for the recognition of Negro-Americans as an ethnic group or, at the very least, as a group in the process of becoming an ethnic group who possess ethnic qualities comparable to other groups in America. He notes that previous sociological conceptions of Negro-Americans, either in terms of caste or race relations (as we have seen), relegated them to an objective social category without consciousness of identity or agency. Singer argues for a conception of ethnic group that not only recognizes the gradual, historical development of a social group but also attends to groups' internal organization, to defining features such as shared values and beliefs, and identifies "an awareness of their own distinctiveness, partially reflected in a 'we-feeling'" (Singer 423n).

Singer was here referring to the work of E. K. Francis, whose contribution to the development of ethnicity as a concept was his notion that it named a subjective as well as an objective reality. Francis related ethnicity in his 1947 article to Ferdinand Tönnies's concept of *Gemeinschaft*, a communal kind of association among people whose most salient experience of identity is a "we-feeling." Unlike *Gesellschaft*, in which individuals form an association as a means to a shared goal but which never becomes more than a collection of individuals, members of a *Gemeinschaft* organization share a collective sense of group identity. Francis also recommended that this character of group experience be identified in all communal sets, such as the dominant, native group as well as racialized minorities. Specifically citing Lloyd Warner, officially the first to use and define *ethnicity*, Francis notes that "undue distinction is made between minority and majority groups, although both seem to belong basically to the same type of plurality patterns" (Francis 395n).

Sociology did not, however, take up this expanded sense in the 1940s, although by Singer's time in the early 1960s, ethnicity was beginning to include the sense of a group's interior, their shared worldview. In fact, as Philip Gleason explains, after World War II ethnicity became increasingly a subjective matter in part because of its association with the near-simultaneous emergence of another concept—identity. Gleason explains that while the concept entered philosophical discourse in the seventeenth century through Locke, *identity* only became a significant term in American sociological discourse in the 1950s, after it had been put into circulation in the work of psychologist Erik Erikson. Gleason speculates that one of the reasons that *identity* resonated for sociologists at mid-century was that it responded to the problem of how to think about the relationship between the individual and his or her distinctive social circumstances. The terms *ethnicity* and *identity* are closely aligned conceptually or, as Gleason puts it, "there is in the nature of the case a close connection between the notion of identity and the awareness of belonging to a distinctive group set apart from others in American society by race, religion, national background, or some other cultural marker" (478). Gleason further argues that the black revolution and the so-called ethnic revival of the 1970s "forged an even more intimate bond between the concepts of ethnicity and identity" (479). Indeed, as we shall see below, the subjective sense of ethnicity would become increasingly significant in large measure because black cultural identity hinges on the idea of a transformation of ethnic consciousness.

Yet, by the early 1960s, Singer seems to have been in the minority among sociologists who recognized that African Americans might qualify for ethnicity in this subjective (or, in fact, any) sense. He agues that while blacks showed no recognizable signs of ethnicity in the antebellum period, through the successive stages of Emancipation, Reconstruction, Jim Crow, the Great Migration, the Garvey Movement, and the Negro Renaissance up through the present Civil Rights initiatives, Negro-Americans have developed and "[intensified] the consciousness of being a Negro" (Frazier qtd. in Singer 427). Thus Singer proposes that a more useful concept to replace the static categories of caste and race relations is "ethnogenesis," or "the process whereby a people, that is an ethnic group, comes into existence" (423). More precisely, ethnogenesis names the process that begins when a segment of the population becomes distinguished and is positioned through power relations in a particular role in the social structure. On this basis, the group develops its own internal structures and self-consciousness. In regards to this process, African Americans constitute an ethnic group not only distinct from other Negro groups in other countries but also distinct from other American groups. Whereas all other immigrant groups brought a native culture with them to America that required that "members of some ethnic groups become transformed into another ethnic group," slavery's elimination of the African cultural heritage required of Negroes "ethnogenesis starting *ab initio*," that is, from scratch (Singer 429).

However, black Americans are also distinct from other ethnic groups in that the group lacks two qualities necessary for, in Singer's view, "full-fledged" ethnic group status. That is, Negro-Americans have neither a "long tradition," since presumably it began only with Emancipation, nor a tendency for "self-perpetuation," usually expressed through endogamy. Because of the lack of these features, "while it is proper to regard the Negroes as an ethnic group, it is also proper to say that they are still in the *process of becoming* an ethnic group, that is, their ethnicity is still *developing*" (Singer 430). As their ethnicity continues to emerge, Singer predicts, their actions will be increasingly motivated by "their goal of full, individual participation in the larger society" rather than by their reactions to white aggression (431). Moreover, Singer suggests that the momentum of their success will generate a frustration over the difference between expectations and the pace of change, which "may prompt segments of the Negro group to manifest radical and separatist (anti-white) sentiments, such as the 'black Muslim' movement" (431). Such relative prescience and awareness, however, went largely unnoticed in the discipline. Further indication of sociologists' resistance to recognize African Americans as an ethnic group is the fact that, as McKee points out, almost none seem to have taken up Singer's observations. With few exceptions, Singer's paper "went unread and uncited by sociologists" (McKee 344).

While the black movement would in time give the lie to the fundamental assumptions of the mainstream sociological paradigm, as Robert Blauner points out, the early phase of the Civil Rights Movement seemed to confirm the universality of assimilation for all minorities: "The predominant goal of Southern blacks was integration and equality in institutional treatment" (*Racial* 8). The assertion of the ethnicity paradigm, however, was more than sufficient to challenge the logic of racist segregation (Omi and Winant 96). Yet, as the black movement unfolded, black ethnicity or the question of a distinct African American cultural identity increasingly came to play a central role, along the way revealing the theoretical paucity of the dominant sociology of race. Namely, it is the growing radical wing within the Civil Rights coalition that would eventually split from it and take over the initiative and momentum in the struggle for racial change. Within this radical segment of the black movement, the notion of African American cultural identity would become a central ideological instrument. Black nationalism and the discourse of a unique African destiny in America, as noted above, date from at least the late eighteenth century. And just as its fortunes have vacillated from one historical period to the next, by the early 1960s black nationalism included a small number of intellectuals and artists and a small but growing segment of the black population, most notably the Nation of Islam and the followers of Malcolm X. However, resistance and reaction at virtually every institutional level of the white social order, from local to federal government, especially the Justice Department and the FBI, exacerbated internal contradictions and divisions within the movement. Structural barriers to the Civil Rights agenda in the early 1960s and the resulting frustrations and outrage fueled a revival for the next cycle of black nationalism. The radical wing of the movement began to see the system as so thoroughly racist that reform through standard institutional channels, or even through the strategy of nonviolent civil disobedience, was not possible.[5] Even as the Civil Rights Movement achieved arguably its greatest victories in the Civil Rights Bill and the Voting Rights Act of 1964 and 1965 respectively, the coalition of which it was composed was coming apart. Legal remedies aimed at dismantling segregation in the South could not address the structural conditions of racial inequality in the urban North.

Historians point to Stokely Carmichael's call for "Black Power" on 17 June 1966 during the "March Against Fear" as the moment when the paradigms shifted from the integrationist politics of Civil Rights to the more radical separatism of black nationalism. Yet, the historical roots for such a shift were deep, and the multiple historical conditions that made it possible had been under way for some time. Besides the almost two-hundred-year tradition of black nationalism itself, the organic intellectuals of its reemergence in the 1960s drew inspiration from the postwar nationalist revolutions in the Third World. Moreover the post–World War II wave of the Great Migration had delivered the greatest proportion of the seven million African Americans that had moved from the rural South to the industrialized North since the end of the nineteenth century. These urban African American communities were a major factor in the development of black nationalist culture and consciousness, as were the rebellions that broke out in almost every major Northern city during the second half of the 1960s. Jack Bloom argues that "black riots would become the most widespread form of political expression" (177), and they would be the catalyst for an immense shift in the movement (200). Ironically, it is black Americans' exclusion in Northern cities during the twentieth century that contributes significantly to the development of a distinct black consciousness and culture on which the expressions of black nationalism would be based (Woodard 31–34). Black nationalism and the urban riots, as Bloom suggests, were both the expression and cause of the disintegration of the Civil Rights coalition. By the same token, Black Power not only isolated the black movement but was also symptomatic of the isolation that was already occurring as former allies of the Civil Rights coalition, such as the federal government, business, and the middle class, rejected the demands that went beyond desegregation legislation to redress more deeply rooted conditions of social and economic inequality.

REVOLUTIONARY VERSUS CULTURAL NATIONALISM

Black Power is an elusive concept, but it has direct bearing on the development of the concept of black ethnicity. As William L. Van Deburg has observed, the strength of the "Black Power" slogan lies in its polyvalence such that it could be embraced to articulate a variety of agendas (63). Kobena Mercer makes a similar point: "What made /Black Power/ such a volatile metaphor was its political indeterminacy: it meant different things to different people in different discourses" (302). The central figure of Black Power in the 1960s is Malcolm X. Even after his assassination, "he became a Black Power paradigm—the archetype, reference point, and spiritual adviser in absentia for a generation of Afro-American activists" (Van Deburg 2). While Malcolm X was claimed by many of the various stripes of Black Power, his strongest influence may be that which he exercised over black nationalism, a complex multiplicity of ideologies and organizational networks. Alphonso Pinkney claims that "more than any other individual, [Malcolm X] changed the direction of the black movement from an emphasis on assimilation through integration to black liberation through black nationalism" (74). Moreover, he was, as Komozoi Woodard argues, a kind of bridge between traditional black nationalism and a new, modernized black nationalism that was more secular, built on the organizational achievements of the Civil Rights Movement, and was astute about the importance of the mass media (59–60).

Eldridge Cleaver has argued that Malcolm X also held together two aspects of black nationalism whose relationship in his absence would become increasingly internecine (Flowers 24). After Malcolm X's assassination in 1965, these two tendencies grew into an opposition between revolutionary nationalists, who focused on armed struggle, and cultural nationalists, who focused on African and black culture and consciousness. Revolutionary nationalists, best represented in the Black Panther Party, generally took the position that black liberation was only possible through the overthrow of the existing political and economic system. A central goal of most black revolutionary nationalists was control of black community businesses and institutions. The question of armed revolt was generally central even though, as Sandra Flowers suggests, the language of revolutionary nationalists, as with Malcolm X on this point, tended to be evasive and euphemistic (54–55).

At the same time, emerging alongside revolutionary nationalism, and likewise inspired by Malcolm X and the connotations of Black Power, was black cultural nationalism. Such a formation is characterized by the belief that, prior to political revolution, a black cultural revolution and a transformation of black consciousness is necessary. Cultural nationalists took inspiration from Malcolm X's assertion that "we must recapture our heritage and our identity if we are ever to liberate ourselves from the bonds of white supremacy. . . . We must launch a cultural revolution to unbrainwash an entire people" (Van Deburg 5). Revolutionary nationalists attacked their cultural nationalist adversaries for their apolitical, regressive, and reactionary "pork chop nationalism" (Pinkney 123). In response, cultural nationalists such as, most notably, Ron Karenga and Amiri Baraka (LeRoi Jones) agreed that nationalism was necessary to black liberation but its precondition was nationalist awareness (Pinkney 143). They argued that revolutionary nationalists were, as Baraka put it, "violent integrationists" (130). Baraka argued that only a revolution by the people, rather than a revolutionary Marxist vanguard, would be able to sustain itself. In response to the revolutionary nationalist's call to "Pick Up The Gun," Baraka argues this imperative merely replicates what they are attempting to overthrow, and uses "the same sick value system of the degenerate slavemaster" (130). Ironically, cultural nationalism seems to accept to some degree the traditional sociological assumption that black culture in America had become merely a secondhand version of the dominant white culture. However, they argued that this condition was the most significant element of black oppression and thus the key to liberation would require first the development and dissemination of an autonomous black culture and value system distinct from that of the white American mainstream (Flowers 31).[6]

Furthermore, Baraka (during his cultural nationalist period) opposes what he calls the "right around the cornerism" of nationalist revolutionaries because, he argues, winning national liberation should not be "fantasized as the result of unprepared spontaneous outbursts of emotionalism" (139). Instead liberation will be a long, slow process whose basis is the transformation of black people's minds and values by means of black controlled cultural and political institutions. Baraka summarizes the agenda of black cultural nationalism:

> But you must have the cultural revolution, i.e. you must get the mind before you move another fuhtha [sic]. There is no revolution except as a result of the Black mind expanding, trying to take control of its own space. Our armies are not yet formed as armies. We cannot fight a war, as actual physical war with the forces of evil just because we are angry. We can begin to build. We must build Black institutions. In all the different aspects of culture. Political, Religious, Social, Economic, Ethical, Creative, Historical institutions, all based on a value system that is beneficial to Black people. (140–41)

In contrast to revolutionary nationalists, cultural nationalists emphasized race over class as the predominant axis of oppression and so eschewed "unnatural alliances" with whites, even radical whites (Baraka 139). Black nationalists "do not want what Marx wanted or what Abbie Hoffman wants" (Baraka 145). Moreover, such associations, so crucial to the Civil Rights coalition and its achievements, will undermine the liberatory agenda of black nationalism because "there is no future for the black nation addicted to the integrated political consciousness! That is just the newest order of white rule" (Baraka 153). Despite their claims, the young white radicals' conflict with the older generation represents not the promise of "regeneration but simply a change of generation in degeneration" (Baraka 127). That is, the "bush-smoking, wine-drinking, homo-superhetero sexual bellbottomed life of the hippy (a truly interracial tho [sic] white committed phenomenon) is just a phase of the death rattle for a culture and a people" (Baraka 140). Those allied to a dying people with a dying culture will suffer the same consequences. Thus at the heart of the struggle for black liberation is a "death struggle between two cultures, one that generates and signifies life and the other which is death" (Baraka 125).

THE BLACK ARTS MOVEMENT

Among the most significant achievements of black cultural nationalism in the 1960s is the Black Arts Movement. Amiri Baraka's founding of Harlem's short-lived Black Arts Repertory Theater/School in early 1965 is often regarded as the movement's inception (Pinkney 128). However, Van Deburg argues that the Black Arts Movement was more the result of the pervasive influence of the Black Power spirit of the time, which "moved creative talents of varying political persuasion to manifest the existence of a distinctive black world-view through cultural expression" (181). Thus, while Baraka's first attempt quickly folded, the idea of Black Arts centers nevertheless spread nationally and by the end of the 1960s Black Arts theaters, cultural centers, and journals were active throughout the country. Artists and theorists of the Black Arts Movement inspired by Black Power self-consciously assumed roles as its artistic, intellectual, and cultural ambassadors. As Van Deburg notes:

> Their major goal was to spur the growth of a dynamic, functional black aes-
> thetic that (1) emphasized the distinctiveness of African-American culture—
> along with its unique symbols, myths, and metaphors; (2) extolled the virtues
> of black life-styles and values, [sic] and (3) promoted race consciousness, pride,
> and unity. If successful in this quest, they would bring about the "destruction of
> the white thing," putting an end to the "alien sensibility" that long had tainted
> black creative expression. (181)

Often compared to the Harlem Renaissance, its differences are revealing. While both movements can be described as dynamic cultural explosions devoted to the expression of a new Negro/black aesthetic and identity, the Black Arts Movement differed significantly by being a conscious effort at nationalism and, as Black Arts practitioners themselves stressed, they were more independent of white audiences, critics, and patrons than their counterparts of the Harlem Renaissance had been (Woodard xii–xiii).

In addition to greater control, the Black Arts Movement involved increased mass participation and proponents considered themselves "the cultural van-guard of the imminent black revolution" (Flowers 15). Indeed, this connection between the intelligentsia and the black masses is a hallmark of 1960s black cultural nationalism in general. The Black Power movement influenced the proliferation of a folk-cultural style referred to as "Soul" (Van Deburg 194). Soul style expressed itself in the multiple elements of everyday lived culture such as music, hair style, fashion, speech, the soul handshake, and so on. Moreover, Woodard's history of black nationalism details the way that cultural nationalism is harnessed to a national grassroots political formation, the Modern Black Convention Movement. Begun in 1966 with the Black Arts Convention and headed by Baraka, the assemblies of the Convention Movement became a nation-wide network of black community, cultural, and political organizations devoted to black nationalism and control of urban political power. "Before the black assemblies," Woodard argues, "the politics of cultural nationalism was confined to small circles of students, artists, and intellectuals; in terms of the black nationality formation, it remained a head without a body" (255–56). But with the mid-1960s urban uprisings and the paradigmatic shift in the black movement from Civil Rights to Black Power, conditions were set "for the fusion between the nationalism of small circles of radical artists and intellectuals and the grassroots nationalism of the broad urban masses; out of that explosive mix came a new generation of militant Black Power organizations, demanding self-determination, self-respect, and self-defense" (Woodard 256). And indeed, the mobilized political network, fueled by the ideology of black nationalism, had demonstrable effects on the dynamics of social change. In March 1972, for example, Baraka organized the Gary (Indiana) Convention. Bringing together representatives of virtually every political tendency of the black movement with every significant black American elected politician, the event became "the largest black political convention in US history" (Marable, *Race* 137). In his comparison between the post–World War II black struggle and Reconstruction, Manning Marable rates the Gary Convention as, "in retrospect, the zenith not only of black nationalism, but the entire black movement during the Second Reconstruction" (*Race* 138). Indicative of the degree to which black nationalism had become a central political factor is the fact that "what was particularly important about Gary was the political tone of black nationalism which filled the convention hall, and affected the policies and even the rhetoric of all BEOs [Black Elected Officials] and diehard integrationists" (Marable, *Race* 138).

CULTURAL NATIONALISM IS BLACK ETHNICITY

It is in this context of a growing grassroots mobilization, guided by the ideology of black cultural nationalism, that Robert Blauner addresses the issue of black ethnicity in *Racial Oppression in America* (1972). Taking up and extending the argument L. Singer had begun ten years earlier, Blauner's work differs from his predecessor to a significant degree because black cultural identity had become by the late 1960s a significant historical force. Blauner had been trained in the late 1940s at the University of Chicago, perhaps the most prestigious school of sociology until that time and with which so many eminent sociologists had been associated, such as Robert Park, W. Lloyd Warner, and Oliver Cox (*Big News* viii). And yet, while he speaks within the discipline and discourse of sociology, Blauner reflects that "my own developing framework probably owes more to the social movements of the oppressed than to standard sociology" (*Racial* viii).

The powerful contributions of Blauner's work thus derive from this inter-section of the sociological tradition with the transformative discourse of pop-ular political struggle. From this vantage point, Blauner finds that the black movement exposes a gap between the theoretical framework of sociology and the reality it was attempting to explain. On the one hand, sociology had traditionally denied the existence of a distinct black culture able to form the basis of a black identity in America, much less an autonomous organiza-tional capacity that could mobilize a constituency on such a basis. Yet, as Blauner points out, "The depth and volatility of contemporary racial conflict challenge sociologists in particular to assess the adequacy of the theoretical models by which we have explained American race relations in the past" (*Racial* 2). In fact, the black movement reveals the inadequacy of sociology's primary assumptions and the limits of its European theoretical basis for the analysis of the American racial order. Blauner notes that the work of Ameri-can sociologists is founded on European theorists, chiefly Marx, Durkheim, Weber, Simmel, and Tönnies, who, despite significant differences, focused their analysis on the bourgeois industrial order in ways that downplayed its ethnic or racial dimensions. Concerned with the growth of modern bureau-cracies and stratification by class and the divisions of labor, sociology's predecessors neglected race and ethnic group formation as premodernist, preindustrial relics that would simply collapse as their foundations eroded in the newly emerging social order.

Marginalizing race in modern society thus left sociology ill equipped to account for significant historical developments that by the 1960s had become difficult to ignore. Blauner further isolates three other fundamental assumptions of the sociology of race relations that underscored the urgent need for the development of alternative theories. First, the "assimilationist bias," as we have seen, dominated almost all accounts of the trajectory of race relations (except the caste school). The corollary of this assumption is the denial that African Americans might embrace and preserve a distinct culture rather than assimilate into the dominant American mainstream. Sec-ond, especially since the 1950s and as a result of the influence of Myrdal's *An American Dilemma* (1944), social scientists increasingly focused on the origins and measurement of white prejudice, assuming that any change in race relations was dependent on the actions and attitudes of whites. While Blauner agrees that white dominance is a central issue in the understanding of race in America, and that racial stereotypes wield a significant influence, the primacy traditional sociology afforded white prejudice rested on a failure to consider the possibility of black agency in the transformation of race relations (*Racial* 9).

Finally, Blauner points to the prominence of the "immigrant analogy" in the sociology of race which, as discussed previously, takes the retrospective arc of European immigrant mobility in the twentieth century as the general pattern for the destiny of every minority group in America. It is, Blauner suggests, an "updated and perhaps sophisticated version" of the assimilationist bias that, in practice, minimizes the impact of racial discrimination by distancing it as a feature of the historical past (*Racial* 10). In imposing the template of the immigrant experience over minority groups in general, regardless of racial factors, the model emphasizes economic issues and, in so doing, reduces race to a matter of class. Thus the cultural and political particularities of racialized minority groups are read as functions of poverty and economic class status. Blauner points out that Marxists as well as liberals commit economic class reductionism, though they incorporate it in different ways. While Marxists typically assume that racial features will recede as lower-class groups identify their common economic class interests, liberal policy makers, such as Daniel Moynihan, rely on the assumption that groups will lose interest in racial concerns as individuals merge into the middle class. Each of these theoretical tendencies, Blauner argues, have been proven untenable by historical development and, especially, the black movement. They therefore testify to a general sociological framework that not only fails to illuminate the dynamics of social life but, moreover, is a hindrance to such analysis (Blauner, *Racial* 2).

THE COLONIAL MODEL

Indeed, every other sociological explanation thus far of "the Negro situation" (Blauner, "Internal" 394) has failed to come to terms with, rather than merely subsume under some other social or economic dynamic, the reality of race and racism. "Into this theory vacuum," announces Blauner, "steps the model of internal colonialism" ("Internal" 394).[7] This approach, which maps a qualified analogy of European colonialism onto domestic race relations, offers the possibility of recuperating the incomplete views glimpsed from previous perspectives into "a framework that can integrate the insights of caste and racism, ethnicity, culture, and economic exploitation into an overall conceptual scheme" (Blauner, "Internal" 394). Critics of the colonial model point to the differences between domestic race relations and international examples of European colonies. Typically, colonialism refers to the economic and political control of a geographically distinct political entity or people, usually of a differentiated race and culture than the dominant, colonizing country. The superordination of the colonizing "mother" country is formally acknowledged and maintained through a set of institutions and agencies in the colony. In the case of American racism, however, few of the characteristic colonial conditions seem to apply: there is no geographical separation between the dominant country and the putative "colony"; whites have not settled any area in North America that had previously been under black control; since the end of slavery, there has been no formal recognition of the power differentials between colonizer and colonized. And while colonialism usually involves domination of inhabitants by a minority of outsiders, African Americans are themselves both "outsiders," to the degree they are structurally marginalized, and in the minority (Blauner, "Internal" 395).

While aware that there are important distinctions between a Third World colony and the black ghetto in America, Blauner argues that these differences only serve to emphasize that there are multiple colonialisms that vary in historical circumstance, political structure, and appropriate liberation strategies (*Racial* 75). Despite these differences, multiple colonial situations nevertheless share a "common core element—which I shall call colonization—" that Blauner argues becomes especially relevant in the context of the racial crisis in the United States ("Internal" 395). That is, the colonial analogy for Blauner is justified by the fact that classical colonialism and American racism have common roots insofar as both developed from the same set of historical forces. The slave trade preceded the European imperial partition but prepared the way for its success through the resulting accumulation of capital and the weakening of African resistance to eventual imperialist penetration. Moreover, Blauner notes, both European imperialism and American slavery proceed from Western technological and military domination over peoples of color and from an ideology of European cultural superiority developed as justification for that domination. Blauner argues that "because classical colonialism and America's internal version developed out of a similar balance of technological, cultural, and power relations, a common *process* of social oppression characterized the racial patterns in the two contexts—despite the variation in political and social structure" ("Internal" 396).

Moreover, the two situations share the four fundamental features of the colonial dynamic that, at the same time, also distinguish the history of racial minorities in America from that of European immigrant groups. First, the circumstances by which the populations in question enter the colonial system, through force, have determinate, long-term effects. Those groups whose entry is involuntary must be subject to ongoing modes of control that are deliberately designed to maintain their subjugated status. Thus, a second feature of colonization designed for psychological control is the strategic deculturation of the colonized through the repression of traditional cultures. Along the same lines, a third feature of colonization is the regulation of the colonized population through the institutionalized administration by the colonizers. And fourth, colonization, whether domestic or international, is almost always accompanied by an ideology of racism that socially and psychologically subjugates the colonized on the basis of a hierarchy rooted in physical difference. Unlike Third World groups, the European immigrant's entry has been voluntary and therefore the cultural foundations they imported were spared systematic uprooting. Blauner glosses over the reality of administrative intervention immigrant communities experienced and, as we have seen, the European experience is not free of native racism, though of a very different kind than that of Third World populations of color. Yet, despite these qualifications, Blauner's point is valid that, unlike the involuntarily incorporated, such as the Indians, Mexican Americans, and African Americans, European immigrants have been far more able to assimilate into America "more or less at their own pace and on their own terms" (*Racial* 68). While Blauner may overstate the degree of immigrant autonomy in the process, he is correct that European groups had far greater latitude than communities of color in developing and adapting institutions to suit their own needs. And because their cultures and "group realities" have not been subject to so thorough and determined an attack, their acculturation has occurred on the basis of group and individual advantage, allowing them to give up "ethnic values and institutions when it was seen as a desirable exchange of improvements in social position" (Blauner, "Internal" 396). As a result, "the immigrants have become part of the white majority, partaking of the racial privilege in a colonizing society" (Blauner, *Racial* 69). Thus, in comparing the histories of each, it is fair to say that "the white ethnics who entered the class system at its lowest point were exploited, but not colonized" (Blauner, *Racial* 69).[8]

At the same time Blauner refutes the immigrant analogy as an explanatory model for the case of Third World groups, he develops the colonial analogy for comparing groups colonized inside and outside American national borders. If anything, Blauner argues, the comparison of the United States "with English, French, and Dutch overseas rule lets our nation off too easily!" (*Racial* 74). In many ways, the results of internal colonialism have been more devastating for Third World racial minorities than those colonies in Asia and Africa with the "relative 'advantage' of being colonized" in their own homeland (Blauner, *Racial* 74). Unlike their American domestic counterparts, colonized groups in the Third World are in the majority and, while it is the colonizer's culture that is dominant, the culture of the colonized is more pervasive. Moreover, while overseas colonies have had time to develop an economy and their own indigenous social institutions, internal colonies, lacking their own institutions, are dependent on "the larger society's structure of occupations, education, and mass communication" (Blauner, "Internal" 404). Thus, the colonial analogy has gained an audience because of its validity but also, in part, because rhetorically it allows for an emphatic and graphic denunciation of racism in America. Analytically, however, it may not go far enough to do justice to the levels of destruction and subjugation internally colonized groups have experienced nor does it adequately guide a strategy for national liberation: "In the United States, the more total cultural domination, the alienation of the Third World people from a land base, and the numerical minority factor have weakened the group integrity of the colonized and their possibilities for cultural and political self-determination" (Blauner, *Racial* 74).

Yet, while the colonial framework may fall short of a fully adequate account of the levels of difficulty that intranational colonialism poses compared to its international version, Blauner argues that the model can nevertheless illuminate the concurrent racial crisis better than any other available form of sociological analysis. Specifically, the colonization lens helps us to understand historical phenomena that are arguably the most significant aspects of racial conflict in the latter half of the 1960s: the ghetto revolts that exploded in virtually every northern, urban area in America, such as Watts, Detroit, and Newark between 1964 and 1969; the popular, grassroots movements for ghetto control organized by such groups as the Black Panther Party; and the emergence of cultural nationalism in such forms as the Black Arts Movement and Karenga's US organization. Each of these disparate developments, Blauner posits, "represent[s] a different strategy of attack on domestic colonialism in America" ("Internal" 398). For instance, the colonial model explains the ghetto rebellions better than the dominant liberal or assimilationist immigrant analogy, which surmised that rioters' rage stemmed from a desire for material and political inclusion. Rather, says Blauner, surveys of "ghetto rebels" suggest they were motivated by a desire to "decolonize" or stake out an area of control in their own neighborhoods by driving out the exploitative and alien white presence ("Internal" 402). Unlike a race riot, the targets were less white individuals than white businesses and the equivalent of "an army of occupation"—the police. However, the lasting significance of the urban riot period may be, notes Blauner, the degree to which it has led to the development of ghetto control organizations ("Internal" 399). Again, the colonial framework helps analysts make sense of this development and, indeed, community activists have themselves increasingly resorted to the language of anticolonialism "in pressing for local home rule" (Blauner, "Internal" 403). In particular, the institutions of business, social services, education, and law enforcement have become the sites of struggle through which African Americans mean to wrest local black control. The colonial rubric helps explain the black movement's strategic shift from school integration to local control of schools in every aspect from school board supervision, faculty and staff hiring, to curriculum development to suit the self-defined needs of the black community (Blauner, "Internal" 403). At the same time, the colonization perspective recasts the role of the police and police brutality in the ghetto as "police colonialism" and as "the most crucial institution maintaining the colonized status of Black Americans" (Blauner,

"Internal" 404). As such, decolonization requires the gradual replacement of individual officers and then whole departments with local personnel and community-based policing organizations (Blauner, "Internal" 406).

COLONIALISM AND CULTURAL NATIONALISM

Blauner's case for the colonization framework also extends to his analysis of the emergence of cultural nationalism in the 1960s. A crucial stratagem of colonization is the razing of indigenous cultural traditions and their replacement, especially among the middle, professional, and intellectual classes, with the colonizer's values and culture. The object of deculturation is to disrupt the colonized's social integrity and to shift their identification to the dominant nation. And again, Blauner points out that this process has been more destructive for a longer period to populations colonized in the core than in the periphery. As a result of "this more drastic uprooting and destruction of culture and social organization, much more powerful agencies of social, political, and psychological domination developed in the American case" (Blauner, "Internal" 400). In either location (core or periphery), however, the reconstruction of the oppressed cultures is an essential prerequisite for a solidarity that might lead to national resistance ("Internal" 402). Thus the various forms of black cultural nationalism that took shape in the 1960s can be understood as responses to the colonial relations between African Americans and the dominant social order of the United States and part of a larger cultural and political movement aimed at nation building and national liberation.

Racism and the imposition of racial identities have been fundamental to the Western colonial project. The utility of racial ideology in this context is the systematic undermining of indigenous cultures, replacing them with the colonizer's own racialized frameworks that rationalize the colonized inferior position. Western racial hierarchies also generally minimize and eliminate cultural differences among the colonized, imposing the same subordinate status and identity on various distinct groupings. For example, "one tradition of British colonials was to call all indigenous people of color 'niggers' despite the incredible diversity in history and culture among the Africans, Indians, Burmese, and Chinese who received this appellation" (Blauner, *Racial* 113). In other words, the colonial imposition of race on the colonized has been destructive of distinct ethnicities in the sense of individual and group cultural identities. In overseas colonialism, where "ethnic groups were rooted in the land and the natural clusterings of people," this process has been less complete (Blauner, *Racial* 116). In the case of internal colonialism, however, people uprooted from the land and systematically denied the capacity to carry on traditional cultural practices have been far more vulnerable to the suppression of their ethnic (i.e., culturally specific) identities. And with the suppression of ethnic differences in the New World among distinct African peoples as a result of slavery, the various peoples of African descent became Negro, that is, they "became a race in objective terms" (Blauner, *Racial* 115, 117). To put it another way, in slavery and postslavery societies, and in the United States specifically, "race replaced ethnicity" (Blauner, *Racial* 117). At the same time, African Americans became an ethnic group, too, or "one of the many cultural segments of the nation" (Blauner, *Racial* 117), though racialization overshadowed their ethnicity to the point of distorting and denying it. Yet, Blauner argues, subjugation based on the imposition of a racialized status would, paradoxically, become the single most important influence on the construction of black ethnicity (*Racial* 140):

> This merging of ethnicity with race, in the eyes of people of color as well as whites, made it inevitable that racial consciousness among blacks would play a central part in the historic project of culture building, and that their institutions, politics, and social characters would be misinterpreted in a restricted racial paradigm. (*Racial* 117)

Besides pervading every cultural and political form, racism's suppression in America of multiple African ethnicities also "ironically created the conditions for a more unified regrouping and a new sense of peoplehood unimpaired by ethnic division" (Blauner, *Racial* 118).

WHAT IS AFRICA TO BLACK ETHNICITY?

While the racism of colonization (and, implicitly, the concomitant struggle to resist it) constitutes the single most salient aspect of black American experience and cultural identity, Blauner argues that these are not the only elements to consider. Blauner's conception of black American ethnicity is interwoven with the complex historical narrative of Black America itself. Thus, while Blauner implies that his theorization of black ethnicity can be generalized to virtually all African Americans, it should be noted that his position cannot fairly be deemed essential. Rather, such a charge might more accurately be leveled against the conception of identity that emerges from the discourse of Afrocentrism. Indeed, a further clarification of Blauner's project may be obtained through a comparison with the claims characteristic of the Afrocentric approach to the question of black identity.

While rooted like Blauner's work in the cultural nationalist turn of the 1960s black movement (Howe 87), Afrocentrism generally reduces the original stream of black identity to one source, that of Africa or, more specifically, ancient Egypt. Taking the writing of Molefi Asante as representative of Afrocentrism's approach to black history, culture, and identity, Stephen

Howe suggests it is characterized by three underlying assumptions that he designates as unanism, diffusionism, and primordialism (232). That is, Afrocentrism proceeds on the basis of a belief in a cultural unanimity among all peoples and cultures of Africa, a common African worldview that forms the bedrock of all African and diasporic identity. Moreover, the African basis of identity and culture is isolated as the only significant feature of the African American personality. Second, Afrocentrism proposes that the common core of the unitary African social character derives from its origin in ancient Egyptian civilization, which simply spread, without alteration, to the rest of Africa and on to the diaspora. And third, Afrocentricity, as expounded by Asante, its most influential proponent (Howe 231), hypothesizes an unbroken continuity through time between the ancient, primordial genesis of black culture in Egypt and its subsequent and present manifestations in black culture throughout the world.

Little of this mythicized understanding of black culture and identity, however, can be substantiated by the available evidence and, as Stephen Howe observes, most scholars of African history reject the kinds of claims that typify Afrocentric writing (232). The historical literature on the complex process by which tribal identities have been constantly reconstructed through time would seem to belie the kind of cultural continuity central to Afrocentrism. The extensive work treating the question of African cultural survivals in the New World likewise discounts the kind of unanimity of African culture on which the Afrocentric claims are based. Such arguments require concrete connections between "particular Afro-American cultural traits and those of *particular* African peoples," rather than some kind of African culture in general (Howe 233). And whereas Afrocentrism's notion of black identity characteristically excludes all but the African aspect of black identity, the scholarly consensus, as well as the historical record, recognizes "*hybridity* and *syncretism*" in the multiple influences contributing to black cultural identity (Howe 233).

Unlike the mythicized identity of Afrocentrism, Blauner grounds his conception of black American ethnicity not in a primordial African essence but in the rich history of the black experience in America. Blauner largely seems to accept the sociological truism that slavery uprooted African cultural traditions though, in his view, as a consequence of internal colonization. That is:

> The manner in which North American slavery developed—in contrast to the Caribbean and South American slavery—eliminated the most central African traits, those elements of ethnicity that European and Asian immigrants brought to this country: language, dress, religion and other traditional institutions, and a conscious identification with an overseas homeland. (*Racial* 128)

However, Blauner rejects the conclusion of mainstream sociology that slavery's systematic deculturation rendered black Americans henceforth a people, unlike all other minority groups, without a distinct culture. Nor does Blauner quite agree that deculturation was necessarily as absolute as has been thought, or that Africa could not assert an influence on the development of African American culture. While specific cultural practices might have lost their explicitly African identity, it remains possible that the influence of African traditions has been "transmitted for the most part subliminally, rather than through conscious awareness and identification" (*Racial* 134).

> We can assume that the slaves and later the freedmen who created and sang new musical forms, expressed themselves in *nonstandard (Black) English*, moved about in distinct fashions, and worshipped in their own way did not know that they were behaving according to African linguistic, aesthetic, and theological precepts—as contemporary scholars are now discovering. (*Racial* 134)[9]

Moreover, Blauner suggests looking at the issue from a view of culture that takes into account the more subtle, "spiritual" aspects of identity (such as "orientations to the problems of existence, as ways of being in the world, as ethos or philosophy of life," those aspects that are proper rather to literature and art than the standard data of social science). From such a perspective on culture, we may find a very close congruence between African aesthetics and the black American cultural style known as "soul" (*Racial* 134).

Blauner's point here is to refute not only the idea that there is no African-ness to African American identity, but more broadly that there is no African American culture fundamentally distinct from that of American culture in general. Not only do African cultural influences continue to exert themselves, but Blauner argues that each of the phases of African American history have also lent their own particular contributions to its unique formation, including "the South, slavery, Emancipation and Northern migration, and, above all, racism" (*Racial* 133). The experience of slavery, for example, introduced the desire for freedom and a deep ambivalence about whiteness, among other qualities, while Emancipation involved "the betrayals, and frustrations" and, nevertheless, the "promise of the North" (*Racial* 137). The Great Migration contributed the Northern urban ghetto experience, which Blauner maintains must also be seen as lending a crucial aspect to the development of black ethnicity.

Blauner also denounces the tendency, of both liberals and Marxists, to negate black ethnicity on the grounds that it is merely an economically determined reflection of ghetto or class conditions. "The special target of my wrath," Blauner warns, "is the view that the ways of life of black people in America is [*sic*] primarily a class, namely, a lower-class, phenomenon" (*Racial* 133). Blauner is here countering the view that the study of lower-class black life needlessly romanticizes its object, making overmuch of what is no more than a culture of poverty. As such, so goes the argument, this way of thinking misdirects scholarly attention from the real problem of finding more promising bases for the integration of blacks into the American social and economic mainstream (*Racial* 127). What this criticism misses, however, rooted as it is in the assimilationist paradigm, is that the focal point of economic class exploitation is the sphere of production whereas the nature of racial oppression is "to dehumanize, to violate dignity and degrade personalities in a much more pervasive and all-inclusive way than class exploitation" (*Racial* 146). And while lower-class black styles may share certain features in common with other economically vulnerable populations, there remains a certain quality that distinguishes black style. Soul, for example, refers to that sense of "tough resiliency" in the face of hardship, and the experience not just of survival but of "making it" in the sense of "maintaining life, sanity, and dignity in a racist society" (*Racial* 145). Blauner notes that race is "the single most important split within the society, the body politic, and national psyche" in America in general and reiterates the paradox that "racial subjugation in the black experience has been the single most important source of the developing ethnic peoplehood" (*Racial* 140–41). The economic reductionism that denies these aspects minimizes the reality of racial oppression. But more than merely missing the point, this position, like traditional sociology, colludes in "neoracism" by perpetuating "past patterns of negating or appropriating the cultural possessions and productions of black people" (*Racial* 154).

BLACK ETHNICITY AND DOUBLE-CONSCIOUSNESS

Blauner theorizes a black American cultural identity based on a complex historical experience that includes the influences of both class and Africa without reducing that identity to a function of either one. In so doing, Blauner reworks the idea of ethnicity in ways that are significant with respect to the concept's broader history. In short, ethnicity refashioned for blackness transforms the concept. Rather than being tied to the process and paradigm of assimilation, ethnicity becomes radicalized as a revolutionary weapon. But the mere fact that it becomes black, or available to people of color, would in itself be sufficiently subversive. We have seen that ethnicity's initial conceptualization took place within the context of interwar whiteness and the confirmation of the assimilationist paradigm in the case of European immigrant groups. It should be recalled that ethnicity was explicitly and exclusively reserved as a special quality of "probationary whites" who were in the transitional state of gradual absorption into the white race. This conception of ethnicity by the Warner group occurred as well within the framework of the "caste model" of social stratification (Warner's more noted contribution to the sociology of race relations). As such, those Americans whose ancestors hailed from beyond the boundaries of Europe found themselves on the other side of the color line in ever-darkening gradations of racialized color.

Thus even Blauner's utterance of the phrase "black ethnicity" would constitute—as he was well aware—an audacious affront to the discursive tradition within which he speaks. Ethnicity before Blauner's time had been
a quality meant to distinguish cultural varieties of whiteness with almost
no consideration of its possible bearing on identities of color. Race, as we
have seen, is historically the ideological arm of colonial subjugation and,
to the degree that it denies the subjectivity of the racialized groups, charac-
terizes the projects of both Western imperialism and the tradition of mainstream sociology. As Alaine Locke had noted a half-century before, race
names nothing so much as a power relation in which the "inferior" racialized groups are merely those that have been subjugated (22–23). Because it
not only marked a change in the racial status of the "inbetween" European
American outcasts but also promised access to the privileges of social inclusion, the conferring of ethnicity signifies a considerable promotion in political status as well. For Blauner to claim ethnicity, which entails a recognition
of a group's historical sense of its own cultural heritage, for traditionally
racialized groups on the nonwhite side of the color line required one of the
most massive, progressive grassroots movements of the oppressed in American history. The reclassification of black American identity from a racial to
an ethnic group, as expressed in the name change from Negro to Black and
Afro-American,[10] relies upon and recognizes a promotion in political status
made possible by a powerful collective mobilization. With regard to sociological practice, "the great and historic gain of two decades of black protest"
is that "the white intellectual and social science communities are no longer
the primary interpreters of black people and their culture" (Blauner, *Racial*
152). At the level of disciplinary practice, the recognition of black subjectivity means hereafter that "we will learn what Afro-American culture is from
American blacks—when they are ready to tell us—rather than from our own
dogmas and fantasies" (*Racial* 155).

But because Blauner's theorization of black ethnicity took place within
the context of black cultural nationalism and the discourse of colonization,
his intervention transformed sociology's conception of ethnicity in another
significant way. Ethnicity is in Blauner's hands no longer an antechamber to
assimilation. It was one of Blauner's primary theoretical aims to conceptualize a black ethnic identity that, to refute long-standing sociological doctrine,
was not merely a "pathological" distortion of dominant American cultural
values. Black ethnicity instead exists distinctly and autonomously from other
American cultural formations. Blauner's theorization, as I have argued, was
only made possible with the black movement's historic shift away from the
Civil Rights ethos of integration. Though once conceived within the framework of assimilationist assumptions about the relation between majority and
minority groups, ethnicity now is premised on the refusal of assimilation
or, at the very least, a critical ambivalence toward such an eventuality that

further distinguishes white from black ethnicity. As we have seen, Blauner's black ethnicity is made up of the rich and complex material of the black American historical journey, with a continuous substratum provided by the ongoing political struggle with racial oppression.

But in addition to its centrality in the historical account, the effect of racism has also been to structure black ethnicity around a contradictory set of impulses. That is, the cultural decimation of slavery left blacks "particularly vulnerable to American values," which they have "assimilated [but] from a unique perspective, that of the outsider" (Blauner, *Racial* 146–47). Thus, the lure of American culture's dream of material reward exists alongside "a deep skepticism about the big myths of America" (*Racial* 147). Black ethnicity is thus distinguished by its experience of the contradiction between the compelling fantasies of American values and the reality of its social structure:

> In its racist dimension America excludes people of color and maintains the ghettoized communities that provide fertile ground for ethnicity, while in its inclusive, mass homogenizing dimension America beckons blacks and others to identify with its material and ideal symbols and participate in at least the middle levels of consumption and life styles. Out of these contradictions have emerged a distinctive ethnic consciousness of the social costs of American values and a sensitivity to the hypocrisy in public and private life and to the gap between the ideal and reality. (*Racial* 147)

Blauner notes that this contradiction may help to explain why many black Americans were rejecting dominant American values at precisely the moment that American social benefits were beginning to be made available to them. From the standpoint of the previous conception of ethnicity, this situation would seem paradoxical since European American ethnic groups typically shed their ethnicity as they gain social access. But if we understand this newer sense of ethnicity remade by the contradictory nature of the black experience of America, it becomes easier to reconcile the fact that "the period of integration and potential assimilation for blacks is coinciding with the upsurge of the group's sense of peoplehood and with the institutionalization of its culture, rather than with the decline of these phenomena" (Blauner, *Racial* 148). The result is that black Americans are becoming more "bicultural," that is, concurrently proficient in two modes of American cultural competency.

Although Blauner only alludes to it here, this formulation of the contradictory, bicultural quality of black ethnicity echoes the familiar thesis of the bipolar nature of black political history, mentioned above, as it oscillates its way between integration and nationalism, assimilation and independence, equality and liberation. Elsewhere, however, Blauner notes the relevance of DuBois's double consciousness for the complex character of Third World people's experience within colonialism (*Racial* 70n). On the one hand, in

the internal colony the colonized are dependent on the more fully developed economic and political apparati of the colonizer and, as such, "the vast
majority of third world people in America 'want in'" (*Racial* 69). At the same
time, however, the inherent racism of the colonial order renders individual assimilation difficult and undermines group solidarity and culture. The
dynamics of colonization, "embedded in a context of industrial capitalism,"
are thus the condition of possibility for the contradictory doubleness of the
black American experience (*Racial* 69). As Blauner notes, "Both integration
into the division of labor and class system of American capitalism as well as
the 'separatist' culture building and nationalist politics of third world groups
reflect the complex realities of a colonial capitalist society" (*Racial* 69).

Yet, in another instance, the situation for black Americans seems to point
beyond colonization, to point, in fact, to the limitation of the colonial model
for the analysis of black America. Again, it is precisely "the lack of fully developed indigenous institutions other than the church" in the black community that results in their dependence and integration into the socioeconomic
structure of the dominant social formation (*Racial* 97). Blauner describes
this state of affairs also in terms of the black American duality—but with
a significant difference. Instead of constituting the entire binary structure,
colonialism has moved to but one of its poles: "Thus the ethnic nationalist
orientation, which reflects the reality of colonization, exists alongside an
integrationist orientation, which reflects the reality that the institutions of the
larger society are much more developed than those of the incipient nation"
(*Racial* 97). In other words, in this formulation, colonization drives only the
nationalist half of the binary, not the binary structure as a whole. Its opposition is integration, a social and political goal reflecting not the colonialist
framework but rather the continuity of black involvement in the American
social structure. For this reason, Blauner admits, "the Afro-American community is not parallel in structure to the communities of colonized nations under
traditional colonialism" (*Racial* 97). Critics have since noted that the colonial
analogy in general, and Blauner's application of it in particular, fails because,
among other shortcomings, it underestimates the "extensive interpenetration
in the U.S. of minority and majority societies" (Omi and Winant 46). Blauner,
however, noted from the outset the weaknesses of the colonial model.[11] He
offers his provisional analysis in hopes that it would nevertheless shed light
on contemporary problems until he could find a theory that worked out the
"mutual interpenetration of the colonial-racial and the capitalist class realities" in a form that was more "integrated and convincing" (*Racial* 13–14).

Regardless of its theoretical limitations, it should not surprise us that the
internal colonial model, which privileges the nationalist side of the black
American duality, emerges at the high point of one of black nationalism's
most pronounced historical periods. Nor should it surprise us that its limitations are in part due precisely to such privileging of only one phase. For

the present discussion it is significant that the colonial analogy provides the framework within which Blauner articulates black ethnicity because it is this feature that supplies the third way that Blauner's reformulation of ethnicity differs from its original version. We have already seen that Blauner's reconstruction of ethnicity is subversive of the theoretical paradigm that produced its white debut insofar as it is both black and resists assimilation. But also unlike its traditional incarnation, which serves the racial status quo, black ethnicity, in empowering black people, is transformative of the social order. Blauner notes the direct relation between black empowerment and wider social change: "The stronger that Afro-American ethnicity becomes, the greater the possibility for black people to utilize both group power and individual mobility to take what they can from, and give what will be accepted to, this basically racist society—a process that in time will contribute to its transformation" (*Racial* 150).

Though his project is quite different from Blauner's, Harold Cruse also compared the American racial order to colonialism and regarded the black movement a rare historical opportunity for black Americans to develop a cultural identity. Cruse suggests, "The Negro rebellion comes at this time to give voice to the long suppressed ethnic consciousness of the American Negro as he rises to the task to throw off his semi-colonial yoke" (*Rebellion* 111). In fact, Cruse argues that the black movement's chances for success depend almost entirely on the development of a black American ethnic or cultural identity. He argues that "as long as the Negro's cultural identity is in question, or open to self-doubts, then there can be no positive identification with the real demands of his political and economic existence" (*Crisis* 12–13). In his view, the shift to Black Power signals not the radicalization of the movement but rather its exhaustion and defeat as a result of an inadequate historical understanding of its predecessors (*Crisis* 565). If, however, the movement is to become truly revolutionary, it will not do so in any familiar form such as that offered within the Marxist tradition (*Rebellion* 98). Nor, because of uniquely American circumstances, can the proper strategy of resistance take the same form as it does in classic colonial situations. Rather, the only path available for the movement to move forward and to become truly radical, "the only observable way in which the Negro rebellion can become revolutionary in terms of American conditions is for the Negro movement to project the concept of Cultural Revolution in America" (*Rebellion* 111). Cruse assigns this task to the "Negro creative intellectual" whose ultimate aim is to liberate black American ethnic identity: "The political task of the Negro artist, then is to fight for the over-all democratization of the American apparatus of cultural communication in order to make a place for the unrestricted expression of his [*sic*] own ethnic personality, his own innate creative originality" (*Rebellion* 124).

REFUNCTIONING THE SIGN OF ETHNICITY

Thus in Cruse and Blauner, black American ethnicity, in the sense of a unique, historically grounded conception of a cultural identity, is articulated to an overtly revolutionary agenda. Though they differ in other ways, Cruse and Blauner share a historical understanding of racialization as a legacy of colonization. Conversely, they argue, de-racialization by virtue of an ethnic reconception of identity constitutes an essential anticolonial, revolutionary practice. The political significance of this reclassification of identity, it bears repeating, is that race expressly diminishes the subjectivity and agency of the racialized party, foundations on which rights and citizenship are based. The approval of ethnic status, by contrast, means a recognition of subjectivity and all its ramifications. In Cruse and Blauner, regardless of whether their theoretical bases are ultimately sound, this transition is seen through the lens of black nationalism and cast in revolutionary terms.[12] Black ethnicity, then, differs from ethnicity as it was originally formulated not only insofar as it crossed the color line and refused the assimilation trajectory, but also because it was radicalized.

Ethnicity is thus, to use a term suggested by Laura Kipnis, "refunctioned" (Kipnis 13). That is, because signifiers gain their specific signifieds, or are "interpellated," as an effect of the way they are embedded or articulated in historically specific discourses, the recontextualization of a signifier from one discourse to another will change its signifieds. Signifiers are, in a sense, "raw materials" which "may be appropriated and transformed by opposition discourses—a process of *disarticulation* from a discourse of which the interpellations were formerly a part, and *rearticulation* to a competing or antagonistic discourse" (Kipnis 13). The signifier *ethnicity* is a crystallization of the emerging analysis of group identity as a function of culture, provided by cultural anthropology and the critique of race science. Within the discourse of sociology and, more specifically, the caste model of race relations, it is articulated to other concepts in its discursive circuit: whiteness, assimilation, and the hierarchy of dominant American capitalist race-class power relations. Yet, as a condensation into a signifier of the concept of cultural identity, it becomes a potential raw material available for extraction for other discursive purposes. It is only with the muscle of a powerful, insurgent social movement behind it that the signifier can be retrofitted to the designs of black cultural nationalism. Black subjectivity becomes a force to be reckoned with, a potent social entity that creates a credibility gap for sociology between the discourse and its object. Within this window of opportunity, black cultural nationalism seizes ethnicity and refunctions it for the purposes of decolonizing racialized black identity. As such, assimilation, having become highly problematic in the shift from Civil Rights to Black Power, is replaced with an avowal of independence and autonomy resting on the foundation of a hard-won, historically specific black American cultural identity. And insofar as it is articulated to the revolutionary thrust of black nationalism, ethnicity becomes not an accommodation to existing power relations but an element within the social order that threatens to transform it.

This conflicted recoding of ethnicity is analogous to what Kobena Mercer argues is the significance of the black movement for "the subjective reconstruction of black consciousness and black identity" (302). The conferring or seizing, as the case may be, of ethnicity involves the refusal of the racialized position and the demand for a recognition of group subjectivity and agency. In other words, "the process of 'coming to voice' which transformed the objects of racist ideology into subjects empowered by their own sense of agency was inscribed in the dialectical flux of slogans such as Black is Beautiful and Black Power" (Mercer 302). Mercer argues that the formal properties of this transformation in blackness allowed for an expansion of popular democratic struggles because it was metaphorically transferable to other social movements whose struggles were other than race. That is, "the radical reconstruction of black subjectivity inscribed in the transformation of the proper name from /Negro/ to /Black/, can be seen as an expression of widening forms of counter-hegemonic struggle in which the liberal goal of equality was displaced in favor of the radical democratic goal of freedom" (Mercer 302). Thus the expansion of the Civil Rights Movement's demands for integration and equality into the black liberation movement's "affirmation of negated subjectivity" offered a "strategic analogy" taken up, in their own terms, by the gay and women's liberation movements (Mercer 302–3). But Mercer points out in his analysis of England's right-wing Powellism, that the metaphors and slogans developed within one form of struggle can be reappropriated for a diversity of projects across the political spectrum.

Indeed, just as ethnicity is reappropriated from mainstream sociology and transformed within the discourse of black nationalism, we can chart a further reappropriation of the transformed concept back toward the purposes of white ethnicity. In writing about the "New Ethnicity" in 1975, Howard Stein notes that the short-lived movement of the early 1970s to "revitalize" the culture, community, and identity of the white ethnics modeled itself after the period's other militant movements. Stein also mentions the reaction of African Americans to the shift in the meaning of *ethnic* engendered by the New Ethnicity: "Many Blacks who had thought that they were ethnics have expressed surprise to me when I explain that in this classification system Blacks are not ethnic" (283). Thus having wrested the concept from whiteness in an effort to renegotiate the restrictions of their discursive position, some African Americans may well have felt chagrin that ethnic status had already been taken back by a new form of whiteness. And ironically, the means of appropriation was itself appropriated. As Stein further observes, "That Black-white relations and 'racism' are implicit in white ethnic revitalization is attested to by the simultaneous admiration, envy, and resentment of the 'Black is Beautiful' and 'Black Power' movements. . . . Blacks were to be modeled after, and outdone" (284).

Thus Black Power provided not only a kind of "metanymic leverage" (Mercer 303) to gay and women's liberation, but it also underwrote the short-lived currency that such slogans as "Irish Power" and "Italian Power" enjoyed as well. Hijacking the new sense of (black) ethnicity for the "New Ethnicity" had further implications. That is, the discourse of the white ethnic revival employed a sense of ethnicity that is new for whiteness but strikingly parallel to the concept we have been discerning around black identity. The new white ethnicity becomes, unlike its former self, resistant to assimilation; it is now defiantly "unmeltable."[13] And while it once fell quietly into place in the hierarchy of dominant power relations, in the hands of some of its most prominent intellectuals the new white ethnicity is articulated as part of new progressive coalition politics. Not quite so revolutionary as its black antecedent, some versions of the new white ethnicity in the 1970s nevertheless differ notably from its pre-1960s original in borrowing from black ethnicity's socially transformative intentions. The white ethnic becomes a contested figure as progressive intellectuals labored to win it back from the ominous hordes of Nixon's silent majority. The white ethnic, like its black counterparts, was defined by adherents of the new ethnicity as alienated from dominant WASP culture and exploited by capitalism. The prevailing charge that white ethnics were the racist shock troops of George Wallace became a sticking point for those writers who wished to articulate the new white ethnicity to democratic social movements.[14]

But the shift away from a liberation discourse to the language of progressive coalitions is significant because it contributes to a retreat from ethnicity's momentary "revolutionary" potential and a step toward its contemporary centrality in the formation of liberal cultural pluralism (i.e., multiculturalism). The project of the new white ethnicity could not be sustained under the growing realization that ethnicity for European Americans had largely become, as Herbert Gans puts it, merely symbolic (Gans, "Symbolic" 425). Indeed, some degree of the white ethnic revival's enthusiasm must be attributed to the fact that ethnic differences between European Americans had become, as Warner had predicted thirty years before, negligible and therefore safely celebrated. White ethnics proved more susceptible to interpellation as white than ethnic and, despite the hopes of their progressive advocates, supported the backlash on black political achievements in attacking such programs as affirmative action (Hill 37).

Yet despite the "blacklash" and the general rightward shift of American politics since the 1970s, ethnicity did not revert to its initial formulation but bears the battle scars of its discursive history. Its past as an objective socio-logical category has largely been eclipsed by its sense as a form of conscious-ness and identity, a result of black ethnicity's emphasis on a transformative subjectivity. Most significantly, it is no longer a transitional state within a nar-rative of Americanizing assimilation. Nor is it exclusively white and available only to the dominant European American groups of a biracial social forma-tion as it was in Warner's schema. Ethnicity, once "liberated" by the opposi-tional discourse of black nationalism, is now freely applicable to the analysis of virtually all national and tribal groups. At the same time, however, the social and political benefits of an ethnic ascription are, in practice, routinely withheld from groups of color. Ethnicity has become a "symbolic" option for European Americans, and thus one of the privileges of whiteness, while in socioeconomic terms, the racialization of groups of color continues to take precedence over their ethnicity and ascribes positionality without option.[15] The ideal with which the sociology of race relations began, that of a national unity through assimilation whose completion is constantly deferred, has more broadly been superseded by the image of the American body politic as a multicultural mosaic, a contradictory image of unity in fragmentation. Ethnic-ity now speaks to the notion of group cultural identity within the context of a cultural pluralism that defines itself in opposition to the melting pot. But this image often obscures the political difference between what Stuart Hall calls the old and new ethnicities ("Ethnicity" 20). Folded back into the domi-nant discourse, ethnicity takes the form of an ideological compromise com-posed of the unresolved contradictions from its history. It retains its resistance to absorption into some other cultural system, but its mission to transform an oppressive order and liberate its people has been suppressed. Perhaps, as Hall suggests, the term may yet be contested and disarticulated from the dominant discourse: "That appropriation will have to be contested, the term [*ethnicity*] dis-articulated from its position in the discourse of 'multi-culturalism' and transcoded, just as we previously had to recuperate the term 'black' from its place in a system of negative equivalences" ("New Ethnicities" 446). But, as Hall is well aware, theorists alone, without the power of a move-ment, can only propose but not accomplish the ambitious reconstruction of which he speaks. We can bring to light the unfulfilled promises of ethnicity, of dignity and self-determination, now shrouded by the shadow of the racial order, and help it struggle to recall its forgotten legacy of liberation.

NOTES

1. In arguing that the crisis of the Civil Rights Movement resulted from its lack of awareness of the history of black struggle, Harold Cruse notes that the word "*inte-gration*" only became axiomatic for racial issues and civil rights after World War II and derives from the context of race mixing in the military (*Rebellion* 131).

2. McKee is at pains to redeem the reputation of Robert Park by pointing out that in the 1920s he was one of the first and only sociologists to note a collective Negro culture emerging in the United States. However, neither Park nor his followers went on to develop the insight. The noted exception in the social sciences to this general dismissal of black culture is the work of Melville Herskovits, a student of Boas, who argued that Negro Americans had created a culture from the remnants of an African heritage that had been retained in America. By far the more predominant sociological assumption was that nothing of the African cultural experience had survived the institution of slavery, which had stripped its victims of all previous culture and heritage (McKee 234). The current status of this debate is much less polarized and is perhaps most influentially framed by Paul Gilroy, who argues for the idea of a "Black Atlantic" cultural hybrid created from multiple sources (Howe 101).

3. Richard Alba notes that what is often said about *Beyond the Melting Pot* is that it "heralded" a general trend in sociology of the 1960s and 1970s toward a rejection of assimilation and the melting-pot narrative (2). Though, at least since Jefferson, there has been a deep skepticism that the melting pot could accommodate blacks, what is new is the idea that European American groups might not all melt. The book is best known for the following observation: "The point about the melting pot is that it did not happen" because of "some central tendency in the national ethos which structures people, whether those coming afresh or the descendents of those who have been here for generations, into groups of different status and character" (Glazer and Moynihan 290–91). Upon closer examination, however, the book attests to the assimilation of European groups to a greater whiteness while confirming the intransigence of the color line. For example, while an Irish identity "persists," it is also in decline and requires "constant reinforcement" (Glazer and Moynihan 250, 251). The Germans "as a group are vanished" as a result of being "'assimilated' by the Anglo-Saxon center" (Glazer and Moynihan 311). Unlike these groups, however, the Negro and Puerto Rican communities are separated from the rest by economic conditions (Glazer and Moynihan 300). Wages are relatively high in the city but, "amidst such plenty, unbelievable squalor persists: the line of demarcation is a color line in the case of Negroes, a less definite but equally real ethnic line in the case of Puerto Ricans" (Glazer and Moynihan 299). And it is the whiteness of European Americans, rather than the nationality of their predecessors, that will become significant in the future: "Religion and race seem to define the major groups into which American society is evolving *as the specifically national aspect of ethnicity declines*" (Glazer and Moynihan 314, emphasis added). Thus, even this landmark treatise on the persistence of groups with distinct ethnic characteristics, especially as political units, attests to the benefits of assimilation and mobility that have come to some groups, depending on the color they could claim.

4. The idea of a distinct African American culture did not become unanimous among social scientists even after the 1970s. In his 1981 *The Ethnic Phenomenon*, van den Berghe simply dismisses the possibility, writing: "It has become fashionable in the 1970s to claim that blacks have a distinctive culture and language of their own, but that claim is largely ideological and romantic" (177).

5. My argument here relies upon accounts of the complex series of events that compelled what historians describe as the shift from Civil Rights to Black Power in the mid-1960s. For a brief overview, especially with emphasis on the compli-

cated relationship between Martin Luther King and Student Nonviolent Coordinating Committee (SNCC), see William H. Chafe, *The Unfinished Journey*. More complete accounts on which I am relying here are Manning Marable's *Race, Reform and Rebellion* and Jack M. Bloom's *Class, Race, and The Civil Rights Movement*.

6. Perhaps the most notable version of this value system was that developed by Karenga and promoted by Baraka. Called Kawaida, it included, most famously, the holiday ceremonies of Kwanzaa and the Nguzo Saba or Seven Principles of Umoja (unity), Kujichagulia (self-determination), Ujima (collective work and responsibility), Ujamaa (cooperative economics), Nia (purpose), Kuumba (creativity), and Imani (faith) (Van Deburg 172–73).

7. The idea of black nationalism, as we have seen, traces its roots to the beginnings of black political writings in America, but the related concept of "internal colonialism" is of much more recent origin. The prehistory of the idea emerged within the Comintern and the Communist Party USA in the 1920s and 1930s (Howe 88–90). It became a prominent feature of the discourse of Black Power in the 1960s. I do not, therefore, mean to imply that Blauner was the first to adopt the colonial model for the purposes of analyzing race relations in America. As he himself notes, several of his contemporaries, specifically Harold Cruse, Kenneth Clark, Stokely Carmichael, and Charles Hamilton, had previously or, in the case of Robert Allen, simultaneously developed the framework in their own respective works. Omi and Winant discuss Blauner's work more than that of other possible authors because his work is "probably the most familiar general discussion of race in the U.S. written from an internal colonialism perspective, and the one most tailored to U.S. conditions" (Omi and Winant 45). I am focusing on Blauner because, more than the other theoreticians of the internal colonialist model, he directly confronted the discourse of sociology, whose development we have been following, within its own terms. More importantly for my purposes, Blauner's analysis, more than any of the other writers before him, re-theorizes the concept of ethnicity. Since he does it within the context of the colonial model, it is crucial to understand that theoretical framework.

8. Blauner also shows how the differences between European immigrant and what he is calling "Third World" communities (specifically, black, Chicano, and Native Americans) are revealed in a comparison of their respective ghettos. For the former, the formation of the ghetto emanates more from voluntary (if often stark) choice, both to come to America and to cohabit with one's compatriots. For the latter, ghetto or reservation life has been imposed by law and housing policy. For European Americans, the ghetto has been a "way-station" like ethnicity itself, through which they passed in one or two generations (Blauner, "Internal" 397). Finally, and most revealing of the colonial difference, while European and Chinese American groups gained control of neighborhood businesses and institutions, African Americans "are distinct in the extent to which their segregated communities have remained controlled economically, politically, and administratively from the outside" (Blauner, "Internal" 397).

9. Indeed, the scholarly work on the question of African cultural survival has been arrested until fairly recently by the widespread conviction in the American social sciences that there was no work to do—that Africa had no history and African Americans had no distinct cultural identity (Blauner, *Racial* 135). Howe notes that the literature on the subject is now "vast" though, with the exception of Herskovits's

pioneering work, most of it dates subsequent to the time of Blauner's *Racial Oppression* (Howe 111n).

10. The more widely noted shift in self-designation from colored to Negro to Black and Afro-American (to African American) is parallel to and an expression of the shift I am noting from racial to ethnic identity among Americans of African descent, and both are conditioned by the historic shift from Civil Rights to Black Power. Van Deburg describes the attainment of the psychological dimension of Black Power, or "black consciousness," as the "Negro to Black conversion experience" (51–53). The designation "Negro" came to be read in the 1960s by the more radical, usually younger, black nationalist–oriented wing of the black movement as a white imposed label from slave times, and they associated it with the older, liberal, and integration-oriented wing of the Civil Rights Movement. A report from 1967 noted the view that the "adoption of [Afro-American] will force 'these prejudiced European-Americans' to reevaluate black people in terms of their history and culture" (Bennett 54). Interestingly, the first choice as a replacement for Negro has been black, while Afro-American and later African American have generally been second and third (T. Smith 503), though African American has been more popular with the "upwardly mobile" Americans of African descent (Philogène 183). As Blauner puts it, "African American" is "a conscious attempt to move the discourse from a language of race to a language of ethnicity" (*Still the Big News* 203). For a concise history of the name changes of Americans of African descent, see T. Smith.

11. Blauner has recently noted that even though he abandoned the "internal colonial" theory in the mid-1970s, he nevertheless became associated with it thereafter. After publishing *Racial Oppression*, he was increasingly concerned that while the classical analysis of colonialism included a solution—expelling the colonizer—the internal colonialism analysis dictated no analogous response. This "disconnect between theory and practice" suggested an inherent weakness of the theory. He also explained that he was becoming suspicious of all theory in general, to the degree that it seemed self-serving and distracting from the problems it meant to address (Blauner, *Still the Big News* 189). But it should be noted that Blauner recognized the inadequacies of the internal colonial model as early as the introduction to *Racial Oppression*. Among the available models of race relations, he concluded that only colonialism related racial oppression to the broader social structure. Marxism offers a theory of total structure but inadequately addresses the specific circumstances of racial conflict. And yet, Blauner admits, the colonial perspective does not fully accomplish such a task: "When the colonial model is transferred from the overseas situation to the United States without substantial alteration, it tends to miss the total structure, the context of advanced industrial capitalism in which our racial arrangements are embedded—a context that produces group politics and social movements that differ markedly from the traditional colonial society" (*Racial* 13). Blauner was the first to point out, then, that "this suggests a major defect of my study" (*Racial* 13).

12. Blauner's inconsistencies and self-criticism have already been noted. Robert Allen argues that Cruse's argument fails to adequately explain why the attack on American industrial capitalism should take the form of cultural revolution or why it would work. Allen notes other problems such as the contradiction between, on the one hand, Cruse's argument that the black intellectual must be the agent of social change and, on the other, his critique of this group as alienated from black culture

and inclined to the values of the black middle class (150–51). But my point here does not depend on either Blauner or Cruse articulating a viable revolutionary politics (a difficult standard), but rather that ethnicity in their writing is linked to the discourse of revolution, inflecting the concept in a way that differs significantly from its previous, liberal connotation.

13. Michael Novak's *The Rise of the Unmeltable Ethnics* (1972) is the most famous work on the "New Ethnicity" of European Americans that came out in the early 1970s. It is an anxious response to the transformation of black subjectivity. One of the most significant features of Novak's argument was his rejection of the assimilation paradigm in the case of eastern, central, and southern European Americans, a departure that indicates the changed meaning of ethnicity.

14. There is a sense from the spate of works on the subject published in the late 1960s and 1970s that the "white ethnic" (usually understood as the third-generation working-class descendants of the "new immigrants") was politically up for grabs and could be articulated to either the progressive or reactionary coalitions of the time. A good example besides Novak of the intellectuals who argued for the possibility of grounding a progressive populist movement on this segment was Richard Krickus in *Pursuing the American Dream: White Ethnics and the New Populism* (1976). However, in retrospect it was probably Kevin Phillips's *The Emerging Republican Majority* (1969) that got it right. He argued that appealing to the formerly Democratic white ethnic working class would be a key constituency of Nixon's victory and the ascendancy of the Republican right.

15. Mary C. Waters argues that ethnicity for European Americans in the 1990s is now a choice in two senses: first, they can choose to identify with a European nationality or be white; and, second, they can choose which of their (usually various) European ancestries they wish to constitute their ethnicity. She contrasts this situation with people whose ancestries have been racialized, for whom no corresponding choice exists: "African Americans, for example, have been highly socially constrained to identify as Blacks, without other options available to them, even when they know that their forebears included many people of American Indian or European background" (Waters 447).

Conclusion: Toward a Hybrid Discourse of Ethnicity

The black community was told time and again how other immigrants finally won acceptance: that is, by following the Protestant Ethic of Work and Achievement. They worked hard; therefore, they achieved. We were not told that it was by building Irish Power, Italian Power, Polish Power, or Jewish Power that these groups got themselves together and operated from positions of strength. We were not told that "the American dream" wasn't designed for black people. (Carmichael and Hamilton 51)

THE RISE AND FALL OF WHITE ETHNICITY

The problem that originally led me to the present study was that of sorting through the apparent inconsistencies in the application of *race* and *ethnicity* in American social science discourse. The need to get a better sense of their meanings prompted me to reconstruct a history of the ways the terms have been used and the conditions that called for them in the first place. What I found is that the history of race and ethnicity's conflicted affair can be periodized into four phases. First, before *race* is elevated to a philosopher's stone in the nineteenth century, the term had little application in America but carried the sense of family lineage. *Ethnick*, at the same time, prior to the nineteenth century, is governed by the Biblical interpretations of human difference and refers to those who fall outside the Judeo-Christian sphere of being. However, in the early part of the nineteenth century, both terms seem to converge or, rather, *ethnic* is gathered up under the expanding hegemonic umbrella of *race*, whose meaning is decisively interpreted in the way it popularly still is—the primordial basis of human divisions, rooted in an unalterable biological substratum that determines all the particularities of each group. *Ethnic* becomes a synonym of *race* though it retains, in its secondary meaning, its sense of a theologically based otherness. Until the mid-twentieth century, an ethnic group was a racial group because the two terms were used interchangeably. In other words, technically, ethnic groups did not exist in the sense that phrase carries today until well into the twentieth century.

However, in the twentieth century, with the rise of the social sciences, the resurrection of "environmental" explanations of human difference, or social constructionism, challenged the ideology of race and introduced the third phase of the relations between *ethnic* and *race*. But this challenge was devoted to the crisis of whiteness and racial divisions among Europeans. At the same time, the "immigrant analogy" of the "race relations cycle," based on evidence supplied by the European immigrants' experience, provided a single model for the assimilation of all minority groups. When it addressed the issue, the theory explained the exclusion of African Americans as either temporary or inevitable, depending on whether or not they were viewed as a primitive people who failed to adapt to the onward rush of modern progress. In Warner's caste model, the emerging theories of culturally defined identities, and the promised privilege of assimilation that went with them, remained limited to a pocket of European Americans within the larger framework of inherent, biological race divisions bounded by color. Included in this phase is the splitting of *race* from *ethnicity*, a kind of ideological compromise that allows a limited place for the social constructionist challenge within the enduring logic of racial divisions and the hierarchical racial structure it rationalizes.

The era of white ethnicity was surprisingly short-lived. The twentieth century's consolidation of the white race as a Pan-European formation had been largely completed in the period after World War II and so had outgrown a need for ethnicity. The exclusive suburbs that stretched across the postwar America white-washed over the significance of what remained of intra-European differences. As George Lipsitz observes,

> During the decades following World War II, urban renewal helped construct a new "white" identity in the suburbs by helping destroy ethnically specific European-American urban inner-city neighborhoods. . . . As increasing numbers of racial minorities moved into cities, increasing numbers of European-American ethnics moved out. Consequently, ethnic differences among whites became a less important dividing line in American culture, while race became more important. The suburbs helped turn European Americans into "whites" who could live near each other and intermarry with relatively little difficulty. (373–74)

In a sense, ethnicity had done the job it was constructed to do. Today, for most American whites, ethnicity is a quaint symbolic option that, like the good china, is rarely brought out except on special family occasions. The older ethnic enclaves have been broken up; ethnicity for many whites has

become less a group effort than a matter of voluntary individual identification with signs "'abstracted' from that culture and pulled out of its original
moorings, so to speak, to become stand-ins for it" (Gans, "Symbolic" 204).
With the dissipation of a lived ethnic group reality, white Americans' only reference points of identity are a vague (and so open to constant manipulation
by the purposes of statecraft) American nationalism and only the foreboding
sense that they are not black, nor Latino, nor Asian. Whiteness, as Roediger
points out, is an identity based on what one is not. And yet, paradoxically,
most American whites rarely even acknowledge they are white and often
avoid those uncomfortable situations in which they are likely to confront
such a realization. The reality of white privilege is that they can. When we
chart the gathering of ethnicity's ideological supports and the prerequisite
shift in the word *ethnic* in the 1930s, then the formal introduction of the term
in the 1940s, and the gradual disappearance of its object (European ethnic
experience) in the post–World War II period through the 1960s, we can mar-
vel at the rapidity of the process that ethnicity was invented to naturalize.

Ethnicity might have been destined for the ash heap of history if not for
the fact that it was resuscitated when Black Power burst on the historical
scene and breathed new life into the concept. In light of ethnicity's history
as an instrument of racial oppression and white supremacy, the project to
carry the concept across the color line in the late 1960s was, at its best, part
of an attempt to liberate the oppressed and destroy race once and for all.
For if groups of color could, like the eastern and southern European minorities before them, cast off the iron cage of race's permanent inferiority, there
would be no one left to racialize. All identities would differ on the basis of
culture and, for the first time since the Enlightenment, society might see once
again through an ideology of universal humanity. The difference would be
that such a view, unlike eighteenth-century environmentalism, would be
secular and, retaining the memory of the triumph over race science, distinctly
post-race and antiracist. Such efforts begin the fourth phase in the evolution of ethnicity's relation to race and the one in which we find ourselves.
Whiteness conceded the moral ground, legal segregation was abolished, and
all racial positions had been, if not destroyed, forced to find new terms.
Envious, perhaps, of the power of black ethnicity to energize a people and
revolutionize culture and consciousness, the white ethnic revival of the early
1970s might be seen as an effort by whites who wanted back what they had
discarded. Michael Novak, author of the white ethnic revival's most enduring manifesto, *The Rise of the Unmeltable Ethnics* (1971), observed that as a
result of the Black Movement, "the faces of blacks, as one watches them in
the streets, are purposive, resolute, often radiant"; but now, he hoped, "it is
the ethnics' turn" (Novak 22). Despite a remarkable propaganda campaign,
however, complete with buttons, books, slogans, and festivals, the white
ethnic movement could not withstand the rising tide of whiteness.

Today, ethnicity is surrounded by a multiplicity of references. *Ethnicity* is used as a synonym for *race* or its opposite; it is a subcategory of race or race is a special case of ethnicity. It was just this confusion that led me to attempt a historical untangling. Despite its polyvalency, perhaps ethnicity's most salient political function serves the "color-blind" nature of the current racial paradigm. Racial discourse is more covert, coded, and unstated, in contrast to the Jim Crow era, when racial subordination of blacks was open and enforced by dictatorial means. Today, whites avoid direct references to race unless claiming reverse discrimination. As Eduardo Bonilla-Silva has suggested, racial oppression and the evidence of white supremacy are naturalized by appeals to elements of liberalism such as free markets and individual choice. That is, white advantages in employment or finances are simply the blind operations of market forces while segregated neighborhoods and schools result from the free choices of individuals to live where they please. In such a context, especially as it replaces race, ethnicity's apparent generic multicultural neutrality, in which it is nonhierarchical and open equally to all, helps to hide the structural disparities that race continues to impose. From the perspective of color-blind liberalism, "whites become just one more 'ethnic group' like all the others" (Johnson, Rush, and Feagin 100). It is more than ironic that this condition may be the result of the Black Liberation Movement's effective disassociation of whiteness from ethnicity, rendering its conception of cultural identity universally available. Allowing that everyone has an ethnicity may be a nice way of avoiding the issues raised by the admission that everyone has a race.

Yet, by recovering the contested, racialized history of *ethnicity,* its curtain of racially innocent neutrality might be stripped away. Knowing that the term is loaded, we should remember to handle it more carefully. Remembering its resistant black recasting may help revitalize some of its potential for transformation. Still available within the welter of its multiple meanings is that part of *ethnicity's* history when it was held up in opposition to *race.* It arrived as an alternative to the confines of biological determinism and assigned the responsibility for human meaning and destiny to human agency. If we can envision a deracialized society, it is possible *ethnicity* will be part of the language that, like a life raft from a sinking ship, may help us navigate to more desirable futures.

ETHNICS VERSUS RACES

On the matter of the scholarly use of *ethnicity,* we can exercise some more specific cautions. Writing in response to Nathan Glazer's *Affirmative Discrimination* (1975), Alexander Saxton argues that the concept of ethnicity has become the property of what he calls the "cult of ethnicity," which uses ethnicity as the master trope for the experience of all American minority groups, whether "*racial* ethnics" or "*white* ethnics" (Saxton 147). The result is the leveling of all differences and the obscuring of power differentials inherent in a social order marked by racial stratification. As Saxton puts it, "It seems that the tendency to lose sight of white racism within the spectrum of ethnic diversity is characteristic of the cult of ethnicity which has been finding many advocates in recent times" (146). Saxton thus points to the importance of keeping the terminology straight in ways that have a central bearing on the present study: "Problems of inclusion and exclusion in United States history become hopelessly confused unless one can maintain some distinction between the meanings of ethnicity and race; or, more precisely, between the meaning of the modern term *ethnicity* and what nineteenth century and early twentieth century Americans thought they meant by *race*" (146). Yet Saxton seems to miss the implications of his own insight that *ethnicity* is a "modern term." The problem of the cult of ethnicity's reduction of all minority group patterns to the single model of the European immigrants is that it misses the fundamental difference the color line made in determining their fates: "Moderately tolerant of European *ethnic* diversity, the nation remained adamantly intolerant of *racial* diversity" (Saxton 146). Like Richard Williams (discussed in chapter 1), by reading back into the period to which he refers the sense of *ethnic* he knows came later, Saxton oversimplifies a historical process for which we need more careful specificity. He risks becoming an unwitting accomplice of the cult of ethnicity by investing it with ahistorical powers. During the period to which Saxton refers, as we have seen, America's racial intolerance was directed at those Europeans he calls ethnic, though in different ways than their "third world" counterparts. The color line that he correctly maintains is decisive had not yet been drawn definitively around Europe as a whole.

But if race was the only language in which to understand group differences, and southern and eastern European immigrants were widely seen as racially different from and inferior to native Anglo-Americans, a familiar question emerges, but in a slightly new way. That is, if both immigrants and African Americans faced social, political, and economic barriers to class mobility in America, and we cannot assume Europeans brought their ethnic status with them, why is it that the European groups have fared better? Neither of the usual answers to this question is quite satisfying. On the one hand is the response provided by the legacy of Robert Park and updated by authorities such as Nathan Glazer and Thomas Sowell. The latter argues that a group's mobility depends on the degree to which its "human capital" (Sowell 282), or its values, traditions, skills, and so on, correspond to those of the dominant society. The difference in black mobility when compared to that of European counterparts is, from this point of view, explained as a matter of inappropriate "human capital" and the relative lateness with which the Great Migration brought African Americans to industrial labor markets (Glazer, "Blacks" 453).

On the other hand, while the counterargument of the "black exceptionalism thesis" to the "immigrant analogy" is far more persuasive, it seems unsatisfactory in its own regard. That is, the evidence is convincing that the impediments to black opportunity differed in kind rather than degree from those placed before the new immigrant. That European Americans were never designated as a slave class would seem to end the matter and little more would need to be said; and yet, African Americans, and Americans of color generally, faced so many more barriers to the same rights and opportunities as their European counterparts that more must be said and remembered until the immigrant analogy is sufficiently chastened. For example, the Naturalization Act of 1790 that reserved the right of citizenship to "any alien, being a free white person," thus expressly identified American citizenship with whiteness while denying that right to persons of color. The history of federal court decisions ruling on the challenges made to the question of who was white consistently drew the line between Europe and the rest of the world (Barrett and Roediger 10; Jacobson 231; Haney-Lopez). Nor was there any equivalent of the Black Codes established for the new immigrants. Trade unions from the end of the nineteenth century onward admitted European immigrants, thus providing access to the means of assimilations and mobilization, while systematically excluding African Americans (Hill 7). More evidence could be mounted that would seem to put the issue to rest that, as Robert Blauner observed (the problems with the internal colonial model not withstanding), "the white ethnics who entered the class system at its lowest point were exploited, but not colonized" (Blauner, *Racial* 68).

Yet the "black exceptionalism" argument generally oversimplifies the issue by begging the question of the Europeans' whiteness. Witness the ease with which the concept of the "white ethnic" in Saxton's or Blauner's quotes above, for example, obscures the history of how the immigrants became either white or ethnic. Eugene J. Cornacchia and Dale C. Nelson, to take another example, make the case that "the Black experience at point of entry into politics was significantly different from that of *any* white ethnic group" (106), because "in contrast [to blacks], white ethnic groups were already on the 'inside' of the political system, fighting over the 'piece of the pie'" (121). Cornacchia and Nelson never question the whiteness (nor "ethnicity") of the groups they compare. It is interesting to note that in their comparison of various groups (the Irish, Jews, Italians, and blacks), the Italians repeatedly present exceptions to the "white ethnic" pattern established by the other groups they compare. They observe that "not only were Italian immigrants highly disadvantaged *vis-à-vis* the WASP mainstream, but the pattern of their resource deficiency was quite similar to that of Blacks" (Cornacchia and Nelson 119). Indeed, Robert Orsi has shown that the identity of Southern

Italians in America involved a strenuous effort to dissociate themselves from other groups of color with whom native Americans constantly identified them. Orsi demonstrates that "the immigrants' inbetweenness and the consequent effort to establish the border against the dark-skinned other required an intimate struggle, a contest against the initial uncertainty over which side of the racial dichotomy the swarthy immigrants were on" (318).

Thus historians' retroactive conferring of whiteness on European immigrants, while such status was often still in question, obscures the more complex historical process by which European Americans became white and enjoyed social and economic success withheld from their African American counterparts. Some credit must be given to the effect of competing racial schemas in the nineteenth and twentieth centuries, including the tradition from Crèvecoeur to Horace Kallen to Johnson-Reed and the invention of ethnicity that always kept alive the vision of American national identity in terms of a kind of European all-star team. Such a vision kept alive the chances of the swarthy European races to become Americans, even in the darkest days of Nordic scorn. Undoubtedly, it helped their case too that, by comparison, they were never so different nor so dark (nor suffered the stain of slavery) as their African American fellows. The answer to the question of how it is that they were able to become white is complicated, as critical white studies have shown, and it might have turned out otherwise. But this is a question that cannot be asked if the ethnic, and therefore safely white, status of groups is granted at the outset.

A HYBRID CONCEPT OF ETHNICITY

Thus, in the debate between the "immigrant analogy" and "black exceptionalism," both camps often agree and reinforce the identity of whiteness and ethnicity. Ironic, too, is that, despite the fact that ethnicity as an identity has largely disappeared from the lived experience of European Americans, it is habitually reconfirmed in academic discourse. The continued, implicit whiteness of ethnicity frequently allows for the discussion of immigrant history without relation to communities of color or the color line. For example, in Conzen et al.'s "The Invention of Ethnicity," discussed in the introduction to this book, the origins of ethnicity are located in the arrival of the Irish and other Europeans in the nineteenth century. Why such immigrants' differences would be designated as ethnic is never addressed, presumably because of the unexamined identification of whiteness and ethnicity. As a useful corrective, Dale Knobel's treatment of the stereotypical figure of "Paddy" (discussed in chapter 1) reveals in some detail the process by which the Irish are racialized in the early nineteenth century. *Race* seems the operative term because the changing descriptions of the Irish are consistent with the way race was defined and discussed during the time in question. Yet throughout, Knobel describes his project as a matter of ethnicity, an anachronism that hampers him from more fully reaping the implications of his illuminating study.

Even when the intention is to emphasize the historical reality of racial oppression against color, the unquestioned unity of whiteness and ethnicity often justifies discrete analyses. As Saxton, for example, argues, "in the United States—because of the importance of white racism as a causal factor—the two [race and ethnicity] have moved on separate tracks and demand separate treatment" (Saxton 146). Desmond King has recently pointed to the problematic effects of this separate treatment:

> Scholars of immigration have traditionally occupied a separate intellectual and historical terrain from those writing about race in the United States. This fragmentation has resulted in a partial and inadequate account—indeed, often no account—of the interaction between immigration and race in the construction of a national identity in the United States. (166)

The creation of the concept of ethnicity is not solely responsible for this scholarly segregation, but doubtless it has played an important part. The experience of "ethnicized" groups has been considered separate from the experience of racialized groups and the tendency for specialization in academia has encouraged a kind of scholarly parting of the ways. But recent scholarship has opened up historical vantage points from which we can see how profoundly the racial and the ethnic have been involved before and since their separation. Reconnecting the history of race to the concept of ethnicity requires some modification of the customary language. The application of the ethnic label in periods before the word was in use is one example where greater care is necessary. Some scholars have begun to develop a new language, a new set of terms, to discuss the revised terrain. Higham's "inbetween people," as it has been taken up by critical whiteness scholars, or Jacobson's "probationary whites," are inventive solutions to the problem of how we name those groups who, in the past, too easily assumed the ethnic mantle. Yet the danger of this language is the ever-present risk of the return of the repressed ethnic paradigm. The call to remember the immigrants' racial past can easily read like the same old arrogant chastisements to other groups who failed to use what bootstraps they had to rise above adversity.

The tradition of mainstream sociology is, in many ways, a casebook history of what goes wrong when white scholars ignore black writing. The fact that early social science did not need to limit the cultural critique of race to the situation of Europeans is revealed by the work of Alain Locke. His neglected lectures grasped the implications of the emerging critique of race, which led him to the startling insight, largely unimagined by his white contemporaries, that racial identity merely marks and masks the application of power. Likewise, Oliver Cox sustained and advanced this line of critique into the next generation. He was able to see further than his white contemporaries, like Warner, who could not think beyond the artificial limits of caste. But perhaps the more glaring lack that white blindness had inflicted was revealed by the rise of the Black Movement. As Blauner and McKee explain, sociology was simply theoretically underprepared, in part because the voices of black Americans had been excluded from their considerations. Sociology's failure to appreciate that black people had developed counter-dominant cultural and intellectual resources, when the evidence was so readily available, is now an oversight so glaring that it is difficult to explain. In retrospect, it seems obvious that, as Bonilla-Silva notes, "because the objective social, economic, and political conditions experienced by subordinated races are substantially different from those of the dominant race, they develop alternative frameworks to explain their position in society" (72). Thus I have tried in my use of the history of race-relations discourse to supply as a kind of countertradition the work of African American writers, who often anticipated later white "discoveries."

Predictably, the isolation from black writing in which white sociologists worked led to most inadequate conclusions about the people of whom they were making their assessments. Shelley Fisher Fishkin suggests a promising new direction that she identifies in a review of recent scholarship. What she describes running through the texts she mentions, from every field in the humanities, is a new hybrid mode of analysis that traces the interrelation and interpenetration of American identities and discourses from across the racial spectrum. In tracing the history of the concept of ethnicity, I have sought to gesture toward such a discourse to bring into conjunction what was severed in the bifurcation that ethnicity introduced between itself and race. We still exist in the long period of race and there is little to recommend the hope that any end is in sight. The great potential of ethnicity to place the responsibility for the formation of human identity into human hands was squandered when it was not shared. Instead, it bowed to the expediency of race and was limited to sustaining those fundamental differences that stunt the humanity of those on every side of its divisions. What we need are those languages that teach us how to see that who we are is what we have become in relation to each other, and that, in spanning those depthless divisions history has inscribed between us, we become ourselves.

Works Cited

Allen, Irving Lewis. *Unkind Words: Ethnic Labeling from Redskin to WASP*. New York: Bergin & Garvey, 1990.

Allen, Robert. *Black Awakening in Capitalist America*. Garden City, NY: Doubleday, 1969.

Allen, Theodore. *Invention of the White Race*. Vol. 1. London: Verso, 1994.

Althusser, Louis. *Lenin and Philosophy and Other Essays*. New York: Monthly Review, 1971.

Appiah, Anthony. "The Uncompleted Argument: DuBois and the Illusion of Race." *The Idea of Race*. Ed. Robert Bernasconi and Tommy L. Lott. Indianapolis: Hackett, 2000, 118–35.

Balibar, Étienne, and Pierre Macherey. "On Literature as an Ideological Form: Some Marxist Propositions." *Untying the Text: A Post-Structuralist Reader*. Ed. Robert Young. London: Routledge, 1981, 79–99.

Banks, William M. *Black Intellectuals: Race and Responsibility in American Life*. New York: Norton, 1996.

Banton, Michael. *The Idea of Race*. London: Tavistock, 1977.

———. *Racial and Ethnic Competition*. Cambridge, UK: Cambridge UP, 1983.

Baraka, Amiri. *Raise Race Rays Raze: Essays Since 1965*. New York: Random, 1969.

Barkan, Elazar. *The Retreat of Scientific Racism: Changing Concepts of Race in Britain and the United States between the World Wars*. Cambridge, UK: Cambridge UP, 1992.

Barnes, Tom. "'Hunky' Statue is Ethnic Slur, Flaherty Says." *Pittsburgh Post-Gazette*. 25 May 1990: 2.

———. "Sculptor Defends Statue as Dispute Rages." *Pittsburgh Post-Gazette*. 31 May 1990: 8.

Barrett, James R. "Americanization from the Bottom Up: Immigration and the Remaking of the Working Class in the United States, 1880–1930." *Journal of American History* 79 (1992): 996–1020.

Barrett, James R., and David Roediger. "Inbetween Peoples: Race, Nationality and the 'New Immigrant' Working Class." *Journal of American Ethnic History* 16 (1997): 3–44.

Bay, Mia. "'The World Was Thinking Wrong About Race': *The Philadelphia Negro* and Nineteenth-Century Science." *W.E.B. DuBois, Race, and the City:* The Philadelphia

Negro *and Its Legacy.* Ed. Michael B. Katz and Thomas J. Sugrue. Philadelphia: U of Pennsylvania P, 1998, 41–60.

Bennett, Lerone, Jr. "What's in a Name? Negro vs. Afro-American vs. Black." *Ebony* 23 (1967): 46–54.

Berreman, Gerald D. "Caste in India and the United States." *American Journal of Sociology* 66 (1960): 120–27. Rpt. in *Caste in India and the United States.* Gerald D. Berreman. Indianapolis: Bobbs, 196–.

———. Letter. *American Journal of Sociology* 66 (1961): 511–12. Rpt. in *Caste in India and the United States.* Gerald D. Berreman. Indianapolis: Bobbs, 196–.

Blakey, Michael L. "Skull Doctors Revisited: Intrinsic Social and Political Bias in the History of American Physical Anthropology. With Special Reference to the Works of Ales Hrdlicka." *Race and Other Misadventures: Essays in Honor of Ashley Montagu in His Ninetieth Year.* Ed. Larry T. Reynolds and Leonard Lieberman. New York: General Hall, 1996, 64–95.

Blauner, Robert. "Internal Colonialism and Ghetto Revolt." *Social Problems* 16 (1969): 393–408.

———. *Racial Oppression in America.* New York: Harper, 1972.

———. *Still the Big News: Racial Oppression in America.* Philadelphia: Temple, 2001.

Bloom, Jack M. *Class, Race, and the Civil Rights Movement.* Bloomington: Indiana UP, 1987.

Boas, Franz. *Changes in Bodily Form of Descendants of Immigrants.* Washington: GPO, 1911.

———. *The Mind of Primitive Man.* 1911. New York: MacMillan, 1938.

Bonilla-Silva, Eduardo. *White Supremacy and Racism in the Post-Civil Rights Era.* Boulder, CO: Lynne Rienner, 2001.

Bracey, John H., Jr., August Meier, and Elliott Rudwick, eds. Introduction. *Black Nationalism in America.* Indianapolis: Bobbs, 1970.

Carmichael, Stokely, and Charles V. Hamilton. *Black Power: The Politics of Liberation in America.* New York: Random, 1967.

Caspero, Ruth. Letter. *Pittsburgh Post-Gazette.* 2 June 1990: 8.

Cassidy, Frederic G., ed. *Dictionary of American Regional English.* Vol. II. Cambridge, MA: Belknap Press of Harvard UP, 1985.

Chafe, William H. *The Unfinished Journey: America since World War II.* New York: Oxford UP, 2003.

Conzen, Kathleen Neils, David A. Gerber, Ewa Morawska, George E. Pozzetta, and Rudolph J. Vecoli. "The Invention of Ethnicity: A Perspective from the USA." *Journal of American Ethnic History* 12 (1992): 3–41.

Coon, Carleton Stevens. *The Races of Europe.* New York: Macmillan, 1939.

Corcos, Alain F. *The Myth of Human Races.* East Lansing: Michigan State UP, 1997.

Cornacchia, Eugene J., and Dale C. Nelson. "Historical Differences in the Political Experiences of American Blacks and White Ethnics: Revisiting an Unresolved Controversy." *Ethnic and Racial Studies* 15 (1992): 102–24.

Cornell, Stephen, and Douglas Hartman. *Ethnicity and Race: Making Identities in a Changing World.* Thousand Oaks, CA: Pine Forge, 1998.

Cox, Oliver C. *Caste, Class, and Race: A Study in Social Dynamics.* New York: Monthly Review, 1948.

Cruse, Harold. *The Crisis of the Negro Intellectual*. New York: Morrow, 1967.

———. *Rebellion or Revolution?* New York: Morrow, 1968.

Dain, Bruce. *A Hideous Monster of the Mind: American Race Theory in the Early Republic*. Cambridge: Harvard UP, 2002.

Deegan, Mary Jo. "Oliver C. Cox and the Chicago School of Race Relations, 1892–1960." *The Sociology of Oliver C. Cox: New Perspectives*. Ed. Herbert M. Hunter. Stamford, CT: Jai, 2000, 271–88.

Deniker, Joseph. *The Races of Man: An Outline of Anthropology and Ethnography*. New York: Scribner's, 1901.

DuBois, W.E.B. *Black Reconstruction in America: An Essay Toward a History of the Part Which Black Folk Played in the Attempt to Reconstruct Democracy in America, 1860–1880*. Cleveland: World, 1935.

———. "Conservation of the Races." 1897. *The Oxford W.E.B. DuBois Reader*. Ed. Eric J. Sundquist. New York: Oxford UP, 1996.

———. *The Souls of Black Folk: Essays and Sketches*. 1903. Greenwich, NY: Fawcett, 1961.

———. "The Souls of White Folks." *Darkwater: Voices from within the Veil*. 1920. Intro. Herbert Aptheker. Millwood, NY: Kraus, 1975.

Feagin, Joe R. *Racist America: Roots, Current Realities, and Future Reparations*. New York: Routledge, 2000.

"A Festival of Censorship." Editorial. *Pittsburgh Post-Gazette*. 2 June 1990: 8.

"The Festival's 'Hunky' Statue." Editorial. *Pittsburgh Post-Gazette*. 29 May 1990: 6.

Fields, Barbara Jeanne. "Slavery, Race and Ideology in the United States of America." *New Left Review* 181 (1990): 95–118.

Fishkin, Shelley Fisher. "Interrogating 'Whiteness,' Complicating 'Blackness': Remapping American Culture." *American Quarterly* 47 (1995): 428–66.

Flowers, Sandra Hollin. *African American Nationalist Literature of the 1960s: Pens of Fire*. New York: Garland, 1996.

Foner, Philip S. *Organized Labor and the Black Worker, 1619–1981*. New York: International, 1982.

Francis, E. K. "The Nature of the Ethnic Group." *American Journal of Sociology* 52 (1947): 393–400.

Fredrickson, George M. *The Black Image in the White Mind: The Debate on Afro-American Character and Destiny, 1817–1914*. New York: Harper, 1971.

Gans, Herbert J. "Comment: Ethnic Invention and Acculturation, A Bumpy-Line Approach." *Journal of American Ethnic History* 12 (1992): 42–52.

———. "Symbolic Ethnicity: The Future of Ethnic Groups and Cultures in America." *On the Making of Americans: Essays in Honor of David Riesman*. Ed. Herbert Gans et al. Philadelphia: U of Pennsylvania P, 1979, 193–220. Rpt. in *Theories of Ethnicity: A Classical Reader*. Ed. Werner Sollors. Washington Square: New York UP, 1996, 425–59.

Gerstle, Gary. *American Crucible: Race and Nation in the Twentieth Century*. Princeton, NJ: Princeton UP, 2001.

Glazer, Nathan. "Blacks and Ethnic Groups: The Difference and the Political Difference It Makes." *Social Problems* 18 (1971): 444–61.

———. "The Emergence of an American Ethnic Pattern." *From Different Shores: Perspectives on Race and Ethnicity in America*. Ed. Ronald Takaki. New York: Oxford UP, 1994, 11–23.

————. Introduction. *Ethnicity: Theory and Experience*. Ed. Nathan Glazer and Daniel P. Moynihan. Cambridge: Harvard UP, 1975.

Glazer, Nathan, and Daniel P. Moynihan. *Beyond the Melting Pot: The Negroes, Puerto Ricans, Jews, Italians, and Irish of New York City*. Cambridge, MA: MIT Press, 1963.

Gleason, Philip. "Identifying Identity: A Semantic History." *The Journal of American History* 69 (1983): 910–31. Rpt. in *Theories of Ethnicity: A Classical Reader*. Ed. Werner Sollors. Washington Square: New York UP, 1996, 460–87.

Gossett, Thomas F. *Race: The History of an Idea in America*. New York: Schocken, 1963.

Grant, Madison. Introduction. *The Rising Tide of Color against White World-Supremacy*. New York: Scribner's, 1920, xi–xxxii.

————. *The Passing of the Great Race: Or, The Racial Basis of European History*. 1916. New York: C. Scribner's and Sons, 1924.

Hall, Stuart. "Ethnicity: Identity and Difference." *Radical America* 13 (1991): 9–20.

————. "New Ethnicities." *Stuart Hall: Critical Dialogues in Cultural Studies*. Ed. David Morely and Kuan-Hsing Chen. New York: Routledge, 1996, 441–49.

Haney-Lopez, Ian F. "The Evolution of the Legal Constructions of Race and 'Whiteness.'" *Major Problems in American Immigration and Ethnic History: Documents and Essays*. Ed. Jon Gjerde. Boston: Houghton Mifflin, 1998, 299–305.

Herskovits, Melville J. *The Myth of the Negro Past*. New York: Harper and Brothers, 1941.

Hesse, Barnor. "Im/Plausible Deniability: Racism's Conceptual Double Bind." *Social Identities* 10 (2004): 9–29.

Hier, Sean P. "Structures of Orthodoxy and the Sociological Exclusion of Oliver C. Cox." *The Sociology of Oliver C. Cox: New Perspectives*. Ed. Herbert M. Hunter. Stamford, CT: Jai, 2000, 289–309.

Higham, John. *Send These to Me: Immigrants in Urban America*. Rev. ed. Baltimore: Johns Hopkins UP, 1984.

————. *Strangers in the Land: Patterns of American Nativism, 1860–1925*. New York: Atheneum, 1977.

Hill, Herbert. "Race and Ethnicity in Organized Labor: The Historical Sources of Resistance to Affirmative Action." *The Journal of Intergroup Relations* 12 (1984): 5–49.

Hirschfeld, Magnus. *Racism*. Trans. and ed. Eden and Cedar Paul. Port Washington, NY: Kennikat Press, 1973.

Holt, Thomas C. "W.E.B. DuBois's Archaeology of Race: Re-Reading 'The Conservation of Races.'" *W.E.B. DuBois, Race, and the City: The Philadelphia Negro and Its Legacy*. Ed. Michael B. Katz and Thomas J. Sugrue. Philadelphia: U of Pennsylvania P, 1998, 61–76.

Horsman, Reginald. *Race and Manifest Destiny: The Origins of American Racial Anglo-Saxonism*. Boston: Harvard UP, 1981.

Howe, Stephen. *Afrocentrism: Mythical Pasts and Imagined Homes*. London: Verso, 1998.

Hunter, Herbert M. Introduction. "The Life and Career of Oliver C. Cox." *Race, Class, and the World System: The Sociology of Oliver C. Cox*. Ed. Herbert M. Hunter and Sameer Y. Abrahams. New York: Monthly Review, 1987, xvii–l.

———. ed. *The Sociology of Oliver C. Cox: New Perspectives*. Stamford, CT: Jai, 2000.

Huxley, Julian S., and A. C. Haddon. *We Europeans: A Survey of "Racial" Problems*. London, UK: Cape, 1935.

Ignatiev, Noel. *How the Irish Became White*. New York: Routledge, 1995.

Jacobson, Matthew Frye. "Malevolent Assimilation: Immigrants and the Question of American Empire." *Beyond Pluralism: The Conception of Groups and Group Identities in America*. Ed. Wendy F. Katkin, Ned Landsman, and Andrea Tyree. Urbana: U of Illinois P, 1998, 154–81.

———. *Whiteness of a Different Color: European Immigrants and the Alchemy of Race*. Cambridge, MA: Harvard UP, 1998.

Jefferson, Thomas. "Notes on the State of Virginia." William Wells Brown. *Clotel, or, The President's Daughter: a Narrative of Slave Life in the United States*. Ed. Robert S. Levine. Boston: Bedford/St. Martin's, 2000, 335–42.

Jennings, H. S. "'Pure Nordic'? It Doesn't Exist, Says Science—Nations Are Bound Together by Common Emotions Not by Race." *New York Herald Tribune Books,* 23 Feb. 1936: 1–2.

Johnson, Jacqueline, Sharon Rush, and Joe Feagin. "Reducing Inequalities: Doing Anti-Racism: Toward an Egalitarian American Society." *Contemporary Sociology* 29 (2000): 95–110.

Johnson, Ken. "The Vocabulary of Race." *Rappin' and Stylin' Out: Communication in Urban Black America*. Ed. Thomas Kochman. Urbana: U of Illinois P, 1972.

Jordan, Winthrop D. *White Over Black: American Attitudes Toward the Negro, 1550–1812*. New York: Norton, 1986.

Kaempffert, Waldemar. "The People of Modern Europe: A Scientific Survey Which Refutes the Old Conception of 'Race.'" *New York Times Book Review*. 23 Feb. 1936: 1+.

Kallen, Horace. "Democracy Versus the Melting-Pot: A Study of American Nationality." 1915. *Theories of Ethnicity: A Classical Reader*. Ed. Werner Sollors. Washington Square: New York UP, 1996, 67–92.

King, Desmond. "Making Americans: Immigration Meets Race." *E Pluribus Unum? Contemporary and Historical Perspectives on Immigrant and Political Incorporation*. Ed. Gary Gerstle and John Mollenkopf. New York: Russell Sage Foundation, 2001, 143–72.

Kipnis, Laura. "'Refunctioning' Reconsidered: Towards a Left Popular Culture." *High Theory/Low Culture: Analyzing Popular Television and Film*. Ed. Colin MacCabe. New York: St. Martin's, 1986, 11–36.

Knobel, Dale T. *Paddy and the Republic: Ethnicity and Nationality in Antebellum America*. Middletown, CT: Wesleyan UP, 1986.

Krickus, Richard. *Pursuing the American Dream: White Ethnics and the New Populism*. Bloomington: Indiana UP, 1976.

Laughlin, Harry Hamilton. *Analysis of the Metal and Dross in America's Modern Melting Pot*. Committee on Immigration and Naturalization of the House of Representatives. *Hearings*. 67th Congress, 4th session. H.R. 13269. 15, 16, 19 Dec. 1922, Serial I-C. Washington: GPO, 1923.

Lieberson, Stanley. *A Piece of the Pie: Blacks and White Immigrants since 1880*. Berkeley: U of California P, 1980.

Lindsay, Samuel McCune. Review of *The Races of Europe* by William Z. Ripley and *The Races of Man* by J. Deniker. *Annals of the American Academy of Political and Social Science* 17 (1901): 126–29.

Lindsey, Charlene. Letter. *Pittsburgh Post-Gazette.* 2 June 1990: 8

Lipsitz, George. "The Possessive Investment in Whiteness: Racialized Social Democracy and the 'White' Problem in American Studies." *American Quarterly* 47 (1995): 369–87.

Locke, Alain Leroy. *Race Contacts and Interracial Relations: Lectures on the Theory and Practice of Race.* c. 1915–1916. Ed. and intro. Jeffrey C. Stewart. Washington, DC: Howard UP, 1992.

Loewen, James W. *Lies My Teacher Told Me: Everything Your American History Textbook Got Wrong.* New York: New Press, 1995.

Lyons, Andrew P. "The Neotonic Career of M. F. Ashley Montagu." *Race and Other Misadventures: Essays in Honor of Ashley Montagu in His Ninetieth Year.* Ed. Larry T. Reynolds and Leonard Lieberman. New York: General Hall, 1996, 3–22.

MacDowell, E. C. "Races, Nations, and Fathers-in-Law." *Nation,* 18 March 1936: 354.

Major, Clarence, ed. *Juba to Jive: A Dictionary of African American Slang.* New York: Viking, 1994.

Marable, Manning. "The Problematics of Ethnic Studies." *Dispatches from the Ebony Tower: Intellectuals Confront the African American Experience.* Ed. Manning Marable. New York: Columbia UP, 2000, 243–64.

———. *Race, Reform and Rebellion: The Second Reconstruction of Black America, 1945–1982.* Jackson: UP of Mississippi, 1984.

McKee, James B. *Sociology and the Race Problem: The Failure of a Perspective.* Urbana: U of Illinois P, 1993.

Mercer, Kobena. *Welcome to the Jungle: New Positions in Black Cultural Studies.* New York: Routledge, 1994.

Miles, Robert. "Class, Race and Ethnicity: A Critique of Cox's Theory." *Ethnic and Racial Studies* 3 (1980): 169–87.

Miller, S. M. "Poverty, Race, and Politics." *The New Sociology: Essays in Social Science and Social Theory in Honor of C. Wright Mills.* Ed. F. L. Horowitz. New York: Oxford UP, 1964, 290–312.

Mitchell, Charles Dee. "A Baroque Populism—Luis Jimenez." *Art in America.* March 1999. www.findarticles.com/p/articles/mi_m1248/is_3_87/ai_54099527 (accessed 23 March 2005).

Myrdal, Gunnar. *An American Dilemma: The Negro Problem and Modern Democracy.* New York: Harper and Brothers, 1944.

The New Century Dictionary of the English Language. New York: Century, 1930.

Ngai, M. M. "The Architecture of Race in American Immigration Law: A Reexamination of the Immigration Act of 1924." *Journal of American History* 86 (1999): 67–92.

Novak, Michael. *The Rise of the Unmeltable Ethnics.* New York: MacMillan, 1972.

Omi, Michael, and Howard Winant. *Racial Formation in the United States: From the 1960s to the 1980s.* New York: Routledge & Kegan Paul, 1986.

Orsi, Robert. "The Religious Boundaries of an Inbetween People: Street Feste and the Problem of the Dark-Skinned Other in Italian Harlem, 1920–1990." *American Quarterly* 44 (1992): 313–47.

Park, Robert E. "The Nature of Race Relations." *Race Relations and the Race Problem: A Definition and an Analysis*. Ed. Edgar T. Thompson. Durham, NC: Duke UP, 1939, 3–45.

———. *Race and Culture*. Glencoe, IL: Free Press, 1950.

Park, Robert E., and Ernest W. Burgess. *Introduction to the Science of Sociology*. Chicago: U of Chicago P, 1921.

Persons, Stow. *Ethnic Studies at Chicago 1905–45*. Urbana: U of Illinois P, 1987.

Phillips, Kevin P. *The Emerging Republican Majority*. New Rochelle, NY: Arlington House, 1969.

Philogène, Gina. *From Black to African American: A New Social Representation*. Westport, CT: Praeger, 1999.

Pinkney, Alphonso. *Red, Black, and Green: Black Nationalism in the United States*. Cambridge, UK: Cambridge UP, 1976.

Ripley, William Z. *The Races of Europe: A Sociological Study*. 1899. New York: D. Appleton, 1915.

Roediger, David. *Towards the Abolition of Whiteness: Essays on Race, Politics, and Working Class History*. London: Verso, 1994.

———. *The Wages of Whiteness: Race and the Making of the American Working Class*. London: Verso, 1992.

———. "Whiteness and Ethnicity in the History of 'White Ethics' in the United States." *Towards the Abolition of Whiteness: Essays on Race, Politics, and Working Class History*. London: Verso, 1994.

Ross, Edward Alsworth. *The Old World in the New: The Significance of the Past and Present Immigration to the American People*. New York: Century, 1914.

Sacks, Karen Brodkin. "How Did Jews Become White Folks?" *Race*. Ed. Steven Gregory and Roger Sanjek. New Brunswick, NJ: Rutgers UP, 1994, 78–102.

Saxton, Alexander. "Nathan Glazer, Daniel Moynihan, and the Cult of Ethnicity." *Amerasia Journal* 4 (1977): 141–50.

Schlesinger, Arthur, Jr. "The American Creed: From Dilemma to Decomposition." *New Perspectives Quarterly* 8 (1991): 20–25.

Schur, Roberta. "'Hunky' Sanded Off 'Steelworker' Statue in Festival." *Pittsburgh Post-Gazette*. 2 June 1990: 1+.

Singer, L. "Ethnogenesis and Negro-Americans Today." *Social Research* 29 (1962): 419–32.

Smedley, Audrey. *Race in North America: Origin and Evolution of a Worldview*. Boulder, CO: Westview, 1993.

Smith, M. G. "Ethnicity and Ethnic Groups in America: The View from Harvard." *Ethnic and Racial Studies* 5 (1982): 1–22.

Smith, Samuel Stanhope. *An Essay on the Causes of the Variety of Complexion and Figure in the Human Species: To Which Are Added Strictures on Lord Kaim's Discourse, on The Original Diversity of Mankind*. Philadelphia: Robert Aitken, 1787.

Smith, Tom W. "Changing Racial Labels: From 'Colored' to 'Negro' to 'Black' to 'African American.'" *Public Opinion Quarterly* 56 (1992): 496–514.

Smitherman, Geneva. *Black Talk: Words and Phrases from the Hood to the Amen Corner*. Boston: Houghton Mifflin, 1994.

Snedeker, George. "Capitalism, Racism, and the Struggle for Democracy." *The Sociology of Oliver C. Cox: New Perspectives*. Ed. Herbert M. Hunter. Stamford, CT: Jai, 2000, 221–35.

Sollers, Werner. *Beyond Ethnicity: Consent and Descent in American Culture.* New York: Oxford UP, 1986.

———. "Ethnicity." *Critical Terms for Literary Study.* Ed. Frank Lentricchia and Thomas McLaughlin. 2d ed. Chicago: U of Chicago P, 1995.

———. Foreword. *Theories of Ethnicity: A Classical Reader.* Washington Square: New York UP, 1996.

Stanfield, John H. *Philanthropy and Jim Crow in American Social Science.* Westport, CT: Greenwood, 1985.

Stein, Howard F. "Ethnicity, Identity, and Ideology." *The School Review* 83 (1975): 273–300.

Steinberg, Stephen. "'Race Relations': The Problem with the Wrong Name." *New Politics* 8 (2001): 57–61.

Stepan, Nancy Leys, and Sander Gilman. "Appropriating the Idioms of Science: The Rejection of Scientific Racism." *The Bounds of Race: Perspectives on Hegemony and Resistance.* Ed. Dominick LaCapra. Ithaca: Cornell UP, 1991, 72–103.

Stewart, Jeffrey C. Introduction. *Race Contacts and Interracial Relations: Lectures on the Theory and Practice of Race. c. 1915–1916.* By Alain Leroy Locke. Ed. and intro. Jeffrey C. Stewart. Washington, DC: Howard UP, 1992, xix–lix.

Stoddard, Lothrop. *The Rising Tide of Color against White World-Supremacy.* Intro. Madison Grant. New York: Scribner's, 1920.

Takaki, Ronald. "Reflections on Racial Patterns in America." *From Different Shores: Perspectives on Race and Ethnicity in America.* Ed. Ronald Takaki. New York: Oxford UP, 1994, 24–40.

Thernstrom, Stephan, Ann Orlov, and Oscar Handlin, eds. *Harvard Encyclopedia of American Ethnic Groups.* Cambridge, MA: Harvard UP, 1980.

Thomas, William I. "The Scope and Method of Folk-Psychology." *American Journal of Sociology* 1 (1896): 434–45.

———. *Sex and Society: Studies in the Social Psychology of Sex.* Chicago: U of Chicago P, 1907.

Thomas, William I., and Florian Znaniecki. *The Polish Peasant in Europe and America.* 1918. Ed. and intro. Eli Zaretsky. Urbana: U of Illinois P, 1984.

Tönnies, Ferdinand. *Community and Society: Gemeinschaft and Gesellschaft.* Trans. and ed. Charles P. Loomis. East Lansing: Michigan State UP, 1957.

Van Deburg, William L. *New Day in Babylon: The Black Power Movement and American Culture, 1965–1975.* Chicago: U of Chicago P, 1992.

van den Berghe, Pierre L. *The Ethnic Phenomenon.* New York: Elsevier, 1981.

———. *Race and Ethnicity: Essays in Comparative Sociology.* New York: Basic Books, 1970.

———. *Race and Racism: A Comparative Perspective.* New York: Wiley, 1967.

Vezilich, Michael L. "'Hunky' Roots and Why the Term Offends." Letter. *Pittsburgh Post-Gazette.* 6 June 1990: 10.

Warner, W. Lloyd. "American Caste and Class." *American Journal of Sociology* 42 (1936): 234–37.

Warner, W. Lloyd, and Allison Davis. "A Comparative Study of American Caste." *Race Relations and the Race Problem: A Definition and an Analysis.* Ed. Edgar T. Thompson. Durham: Duke UP, 1939, 219–45.

Warner, W. Lloyd, and Leo Srole. *The Social Systems of American Ethnic Groups. Yankee City* Series. Vol. III. New Haven, CT: Yale UP, 1945.

Warner, W. Lloyd, and Paul S. Lunt. *The Social Life of a Modern Community. Yankee City* Series. Vol. I. New Haven, CT: Yale UP, 1941.

———. *The Status System of a Modern Community. Yankee City* Series. Vol II. New Haven, CT: Yale UP, 1942.

———. *System of a Modern Community*. New Haven, CT: Yale UP, 1942.

Waters, Mary C. "Optional Ethnicities: For Whites Only?" *Origins and Destinies: Immigration, Race, and Ethnicity in America*. Ed. Sylvia Pedraza and Rubén G. Rumbaut. Belmont, CA: Wadsworth, 1996, 444–54.

Webster, Noah. *An American Dictionary of the English Language*. New York: Harper, 1854.

Williams, Raymond. *Keywords: A Vocabulary of Culture and Society*. New York: Oxford UP, 1976.

Williams, Richard. *Hierarchical Structures and Social Values: The Creation of Black and Irish Identities in the United States*. Cambridge: Cambridge UP, 1990.

Williams, Vernon J. *Rethinking Race: Franz Boaz and His Contemporaries*. Lexington: UP of Kentucky, 1996.

Woodard, Komozi. *A Nation within a Nation: Amiri Baraka (LeRoi Jones) and Black Power Politics*. Chapel Hill: U of North Carolina P, 1999.

Woofter, T. J. *Race and Ethnic Groups in American Life*. New York: McGraw, 1933.

———. "The Status of Racial and Ethnic Groups." *Recent Social Trends in the United States; Report of the President's Research Committee on Social Trends*. President's Research Committee on Social Trends. New York: McGraw-Hill, 1933.

Young, Donald. *American Minority Peoples: A Study in Racial and Cultural Conflicts in the United States*. New York: Harper, 1932.

Zangwill, Israel. *The Melting Pot*. New York: Macmillan, 1914.

Zaretsky, Eli. Introduction. *The Polish Peasant in Europe and America*. 1918. William I. Thomas and Florian Znaniecki. Ed. Eli Zaretsky. Urbana: U of Illinois P, 1984, 1–53.

Index

About the Author

Richard W. Rees teaches literature, writing, and American Studies and has taught at Miami University, Antioch College, Coppin State University, and the University of Maryland at Baltimore County. His doctorate is from Carnegie Mellon University. This is his first book.